HISTORY OF THE DONNER PARTY

• THE BARNES & NOBLE LIBRARY OF ESSENTIAL READING •

HISTORY
OF THE
DONNER PARTY

A Tragedy of the Sierra

C. F. McGlashan

Introduction by John P. Langellier

BARNES & NOBLE BOOKS

NEW YORK

THE BARNES & NOBLE
LIBRARY OF ESSENTIAL READING

Introduction and Suggested Reading Copyright © 2004 by Barnes & Noble Books

Originally published 1880

This edition published by Barnes & Noble Publishing, Inc.

Cover Design by Pronto Design Inc.

2004 Barnes & Noble Publishing, Inc.

ISBN 0-7607-5242-7

Printed and bound in the United States of America

3 5 7 9 10 8 6 4 2

CONTENTS

To
Mrs. Elizabeth A. Keiser,
one of the Pioneer Mothers of California,
this book is Respectfully dedicated by the Author.

INTRODUCTION

WITHIN two weeks of its original printing, the entire press run of Charles Fayette McGlashan's *History of the Donner Party* (1880) had been purchased. The first book devoted to an accursed emigrant band who had been drawn to California in the antebellum era, McGlashan's volume continues to shed light on this dark saga more than a century after its debut. Since that time, this publication, which the author based on first-hand accounts and personal interviews with twenty-four survivors, has appeared in more than a dozen editions. The reason for these many reprints stems in large part from McGlashan's unprecedented access to those who lived through an unimaginable ordeal that reduced some to the unthinkable—cannibalism.

A native of Janesville, Wisconsin, McGlashan was born in 1847, a year after prominent sixty-two year old Springfield, Illinois, resident George Donner and his brother succumbed to California fever. The brothers and twenty-five other men, seventeen women, and forty-three children were caught up in the tide of Manifest Destiny, a powerful concept that swept the nation with an almost religious fervor. The lure of lush lands, verdant forests, adventure, and other compelling promises fueled the imaginations of thousands of Americans living east of the Mississippi River. The Donner family, as well as other families including the Breens, Eddys, Graves, Kesebergs, McCutchens, Murphys, Reeds, Wolfingers, and a few unmarried men who were hired on as teamsters, therefore, joined a steady stream of humanity willing to uproot from their relatively secure lives to brave the unknown.

Ahead of twenty-three oxen-pulled wagons full of families in quest of California lay 2,500 miles of prairies, mountains, and deserts. During this period some promoters, including Lansford Hastings, touted the future Golden State as "the garden of the world." An attorney turned would-be empire builder, Hastings wrote *The Emigrants Guide to Oregon and California* (1845) with the goal of triggering a mass exodus of American settlers bound for the West Coast.

George Donner numbered among those who responded to Hastings' persuasive prose. Armed with a copy of *The Emigrants Guide*, enthusiastic, self-confident, and successful businessman Donner evoked the aura of a patriarch. His demeanor instilled trust in many of his fellow travelers, and they elected him as their group's captain. Thus Donner's name became inextricably linked with the doomed pioneers.

This choice was but one of the ill-conceived decisions that would lead to catastrophe. Donner lacked the experience to conduct a band through unfamiliar, harsh territory. Unlike knowledgeable frontiersmen such as former U.S. dragoon officer and savvy mountain man James Clyman, who had traversed much of the Rocky Mountain region, Donner relied solely on second-hand information. In particular he followed Hastings' recommendations, as did many members of the party who failed to realize the flawed information found in this small, but influential pamphlet. Among Hastings' inaccurate pronouncements was his adamant assertion that a shortcut to California existed to the south of the more commonly trod road to the Pacific.

While Clyman argued against this route, the Donner Party ignored such sage advice. Rather they followed Hastings' advice, a move that all but sealed their destiny. They embarked into the arid wastes of Utah, a decision that almost claimed all their lives were it not for their timely rescue by a band of volunteers who brought them water.

This brush with death likewise cost the party valuable time. They arrived at the base of the mountains, which had to be scaled before snows made them impassable, with winter quickly approaching. To make matters worse, as they came upon the barrier of the Sierras, Piute Indians killed more than two dozen of the oxen required to haul the wagons over the steep passes before them. The loss of a substantial number of their livestock slowed the party's progress even further.

In late October 1846, despite the urgency to press on, the wagon train halted for nearly a week to rest after the grueling trial in the desert. They delayed in the Truckee basin at the very time the first storms set in, cutting them off and stranding them. The incredibly harsh weather, inadequate shelter, and a rapidly dwindling food supply ultimately spelled disaster.

By January 1847, in desperation some of the stranded survivors trudged over the 7,088 foot pass (now Donner Pass) through the mountains in hope of bringing aid. Ultimately, their grueling efforts, and other circumstances brought relief parties, whom themselves faced harrowing challenges before coming to the rescue of the forty-eight emaciated, forlorn survivors during the bitter cold of April.

Fortunately McGlashan, who in 1849 had come to California as a two-year old, did not share the unfortunate fate of the eighty-seven members of the Donner Party. Instead his journey to California and early years there for the most part proved calm. Growing up and reaching early manhood in his adopted state, he became a resident of Truckee, California, by 1871. McGlashan spent most of the next six decades in that community as a lawyer, local booster, politician, naturalist, inventor, and newspaperman. It was this latter pursuit that brought about his decision to run a serial related to the Donner episode for the Truckee *Republican,* the paper he edited in the mid-1870s. He hoped the advance announcement of this project would bolster declining readership for the paper because the subject of the Donners was widely known in the area. As such, McGlashan reasoned there would be built-in interest among his audience.

McGlashan barely had released publicity for the proposed stories when subscriptions jumped in anticipation of the series. In response, during 1879, McGlashan hurriedly printed a brief version of the project in a special edition of the paper. At the time he had little to draw on for his text except for a few previously published sources. These included Edwin Bryant's *What I Saw in California,* an account released in 1848 by a man who had been with the Donners on part of the journey through Kansas and Nebraska, and a chapter from J. Quinn Thornton's book *Oregon and California in 1848* that presented a grisly tabloid-like rendition printed in 1849.

His first foray into the topic provoked a backlash from at least one of the Donner family members. Benjamin Wilder, the late George Donner's son-in-law, questioned McGlashan's accuracy. He called for a meeting of survivors to review the matter. McGlashan responded in the May 20, 1879, issue of the *Republican* that he had taken great pains to publish "all the important facts of the history" in his paper "and as an error appears is corrected forthwith. . . ." Not content to let the matter rest, McGlashan continued his investigation. Besides reviewing letters, journals, and written materials, he sought out members of the Donner wagon train and others with direct knowledge of one of the most tragic events of the Westward movement. He succeeded in locating dozens of informants. In a number of instances he obtained extensive cooperation from those who remained alive or from their descendents. Among them, Judge James Breen, one of Patrick Breen's children, supposedly encouraged McGlashan to set the record straight. The result was an expanded and greatly altered version from his original writings. McGlashan's second effort also painted a more positive and detailed picture than previous publications and oral tradition had provided.

At first McGlashan received praise for the thoroughness of his revised work. In fact, Hubert Howe Bancroft, whose extensive late Victorian era encyclopedic studies of the American West set the standard for generations of historians, enthusiastically effused: "C.F. McGlashan published a volume on the subject [of the Donner Party] in 1879, treating it in a manner that has left little or nothing to be desired."

Despite this enthusiastic reception, McGlashan's literary endeavors would not rise to the importance of Bancroft's publications, nor the classic *Oregon and California Trail* by Francis Parkman. Later critics also charged McGlashan with extreme sentimentality. Moreover, he was accused of bias because he had befriended a few of those he interviewed, and in the process became sympathetic toward them and those who perished. The fact that he emphasized only the attributes of the people who suffered from madding thirst, starvation in the shadow of the bitter cold Sierras, and incredible grief of seeing loved ones die under the most abject conditions, brought his objectivity into question. Here again, Bancroft championed the book concluding: "I think McGlashan has done wisely in suppressing details and dwelling on the noble deeds of each member."

Of course, such a defense was in keeping with the Victorian sense of proprieties, but was not the view of later generations of researchers. George R. Stewart was a prominent student of the Donner episode who faulted McGlashan for being too close to his subject. Stewart set out to address the shortcomings of his predecessor in a 1936 volume titled *Ordeal by Hunger.* Although Stewart crafted a forceful narrative because of his academic background as an English professor, nonetheless his own presentation often reads more as a piece of fiction than an analytical history.

In more recent years other authors, including those who drew upon archaeological evidence, have attempted to avoid the shortfalls of Stewart and McGlashan. Additionally, Ken Burn's episode on the Donner Party for PBS' *American Experience* provided a major audience with a dramatic documentary based on some of the best research extant. Although lacking the accuracy of Burn's production, *One More Mountain,* a fictional feature by Disney, took its inspiration from the tragic tale first chronicled in *History of the Donner Party.* Consequently, the Donner Party would be remembered in the popular imagination along with George Custer's Seventh Cavalry at Little Bighorn and Big Foot's band at Wounded Knee. And generations after McClashan sought out the survivors of that horrible winter of 1846-1847 his volume still allows readers to relive and reflect on the nightmare and redemption of these tortured victims of the westward movement.

John P. Langellier has written dozens of books related to the American West and other historical topics as well as served as a media consultant on film and television productions since 1973. He received his B.A. and M.A. from the University of San Diego, and in 1982 he was awarded his Ph.D. in History from Kansas State University.

PREFACE

THE delirium preceding death by starvation, is full of strange phantasies. Visions of plenty, of comfort, of elegance, flit ever before the fast-dimming eyes. The final twilight of death is a brief semi-consciousness in which the dying one frequently repeats his weird dreams. Half rising from his snowy couch, pointing upward, one of the death-stricken at Donner Lake may have said, with tremulous voice: "Look! there, just above us, is a beautiful house. It is of costliest walnut, inlaid with laurel and ebony, and is resplendent with burnished silver. Magnificent in all its apartments, it is furnished like a palace. It is rich with costly cushions, elegant tapestries, dazzling mirrors; its floor is covered with Oriental carpets, its ceiling with artistic frescoings; downy cushions invite the weary to repose. It is filled with people who are chatting, laughing, and singing, joyous and care-free. There is an abundance of warmth, and rare viands, and sparkling wines. Suspended among the storm-clouds, it is flying along the face of the precipice at a marvelous speed. Flying? no! it has wheels and is gliding along on a smooth, steel pathway. It is sheltered from the wind and snow by large beams and huge posts, which are bolted to the cliffs with heavy, iron rods. The avalanches, with their burden of earth and rocks and crushed pines, sweep harmlessly above this beautiful house and its happy inmates. It is drawn by neither oxen nor horses, but by a fiery, hot-breathed monster, with iron limbs and thews of steel. The mountain trembles beneath his tread, and the rocks for miles re-echo his roar."

If such a vision was related, it but indicates, prophetically, the progress of a few years. California's history is replete with tragic, startling events. These events are the landmarks by which its advancement is traced. One of the most mournful of these is recorded in this work— a work intended as a contribution, not to the literature, but to the history of the State. More thrilling than romance, more terrible than fiction, the sufferings of the Donner Party form a bold contrast to the joys of pleasure-seekers who to-day look down upon the lake from the windows of silver palace cars.

The scenes of horror and despair which transpired in the snowy Sierra in the winter of 1846–7, need no exaggeration, no embellishment. From all the works heretofore published, from over one thousand letters received from the survivors, from ample manuscript, and from personal interviews with the most important actors in the tragedy, the facts have been carefully compiled. Neither time, pains, nor expense have been spared in ferreting out the truth. New and fragmentary versions of the sad story have appeared almost every year since the unfortunate occurrence. To forever supplant these distorted and fabulous reports— which have usually been sensational newspaper articles— the survivors have deemed it wise to contribute the truth. The truth is sufficiently terrible.

Where conflicting accounts of particular scenes or occurrences have been contributed, every effort has been made to render them harmonious and reconcilable. With justice, with impartiality, and with strict adherence to what appeared truthful and reliable, the book has been written. It is an honest effort toward the truth, and as such is given to the world.

C. F. McGLASHAN.

TRUCKEE, CAL., JUNE 30, 1879.

CHAPTER I

THREE miles from Truckee, Nevada County, California, lies one
of the fairest and most picturesque lakes in all the Sierra. Above,
and on either side, are lofty mountains, with castellated granite
crests, while below, at the mouth of the lake, a grassy, meadowy
valley widens out and extends almost to Truckee. The body of
water is three miles long, one and a half miles wide, and four
hundred and eighty-three feet in depth.

Tourists and picnic parties annually flock to its shores, and
Bierstadt has made it the subject of one of his finest, grandest
paintings. In summer, its willowy thickets, its groves of tamarack
and forests of pine, are the favorite haunts and nesting places of
the quail and grouse. Beautiful, speckled mountain trout plentifully abound in its crystalline waters. A rippling breeze usually
wimples and dimples its laughing surface, but in calmer moods it
reflects, as in a polished mirror, the lofty, overhanging mountains,

with every stately pine, bounding rivulet, blossoming shrub, waving fern, and—high above all, on the right—the clinging, thread-like line of the snow-sheds of the Central Pacific. When the railroad was being constructed, three thousand people dwelt on its shores; the surrounding forests resounded with the music of axes and saws, and the terrific blasts exploded in the lofty, o'ershadowing cliffs, filled the canyons with reverberating thunders, and hurled huge bowlders high in the air over the lake's quivering bosom.

In winter it is almost as popular a pleasure resort as during the summer. The jingling of sleighbells, and the shouts and laughter of skating parties, can be heard almost constantly. The lake forms the grandest skating park on the Pacific Coast.

Yet this same Donner Lake was the scene of one of the most thrilling, heart-rending tragedies ever recorded in California history. Interwoven with the very name of the lake are memories of a tale of destitution, loneliness, and despair, which borders on the incredible. It is a tale that has been repeated in many a miner's cabin, by many a hunter's campfire, and in many a frontiersman's home, and everywhere it has been listened to with bated breath.

The pioneers of a new country are deserving of a niche in the country's history. The pioneers who became martyrs to the cause of the development of an almost unknown land, deserve to have a place in the hearts of its inhabitants. The far-famed Donner Party were, in a peculiar sense, pioneer martyrs of California. Before the discovery of gold, before the highway across the continent was fairly marked out, while untold dangers lurked by the wayside, and unnumbered foes awaited the emigrants, the Donner Party started for California. None but the brave and venturesome, none but the energetic and courageous, could undertake such a journey. In 1846, comparatively few had dared attempt to cross the almost unexplored plains which lay between the Mississippi and the fair young land called California. Hence it is that a certain grandeur, a certain heroism seems to cling about the men and women composing this party, even from the day they began their perilous journey across the plains. California, with her golden harvests, her beautiful homes, her dazzling wealth, and her marvelous commercial facilities, may well enshrine the memory of these noble-hearted pioneers, pathfinders, martyrs.

The States along the Mississippi were but sparsely settled in 1846, yet the fame of the fruitfulness, the healthfulness, and the almost tropical beauty of the land bordering the Pacific, tempted the members of the Donner Party to leave their homes. These homes were situated in Illinois, Iowa, Tennessee, Missouri, and Ohio. Families from each of these States joined the train and participated in its terrible fate; yet the party proper was organized in Sangamon County, Illinois, by George and Jacob Donner and James F. Reed. Early in April, 1846, the party set out from Springfield, Illinois, and by the first week in May reached Independence, Missouri. Here the party was increased by additional members, and the train comprised about one hundred persons.

Independence was on the frontier in those days, and every care was taken to have ample provisions laid in and all necessary preparations made for the long journey. Ay, it was a long journey for many in the party! Great as was the enthusiasm and eagerness with which these noble-hearted pioneers caught up the cry of the times, "Ho! for California!" it is doubtful if presentiments of the fate to be encountered were not occasionally entertained. The road was difficult, and in places almost unbroken; warlike Indians guarded the way, and death, in a thousand forms, hovered about their march through the great wilderness.

In the party were aged fathers with their trusting families about them, mothers whose very lives were wrapped up in their children, men in the prime and vigor of manhood, maidens in all the sweetness and freshness of budding womanhood, children full of glee and mirthfulness, and babes nestling on maternal breasts. Lovers there were, to whom the journey was tinged with rainbow hues of joy and happiness, and strong, manly hearts whose constant support and encouragement was the memory of dear ones left behind in home-land. The cloud of gloom which finally settled down in a death-pall over their heads was not yet perceptible, though, as we shall soon see, its mists began to collect almost at the outset, in the delays which marked the journey.

The wonderment which all experience in viewing the scenery along the line of the old emigrant road was peculiarly vivid to these people. Few descriptions had been given of the route, and all was novel and unexpected. In later years the road was broadly and deeply marked, and good camping grounds were distinctly indicated. The bleaching bones of cattle that had perished, or the broken fragments of wagons or cast-away articles, were thickly strewn on either side of the highway. But in 1846 the way was through almost trackless valleys waving with grass, along rivers where few paths were visible, save those made by the feet of buffaloes and antelope, and over mountains and plains where little more than the westward course of the sun guided the travelers. Trading-posts were stationed at only a few widely distant points, and rarely did the party meet with any human beings, save wandering bands of Indians. Yet these first days are spoken of by all of the survivors as being crowned with peaceful enjoyment and pleasant anticipations. There were beautiful flowers by the roadside, an abundance of game in the meadows and mountains, and at night there were singing, dancing, and innocent plays. Several musical instruments, and many excellent voices, were in the party, and the kindliest feeling and good-fellowship prevailed among the members.

The formation of the company known as the Donner Party was purely accidental. The union of so many emigrants into one train was not occasioned by any preconcerted arrangement. Many composing the Donner Party were not aware, at the outset, that such a tide of emigration was sweeping to California. In many instances small parties would hear of the mammoth train just ahead of them or just behind them, and by hastening their pace, or halting for a few days, joined themselves to the party. Many were with the train during a portion of the journey, but from some cause or other became parted from the Donner company before reaching Donner Lake. Soon after the train left Independence it contained between two and three hundred wagons, and when in motion was two miles in length.

With much bitterness and severity it is alleged by some of the survivors of the dreadful tragedy that certain impostors and falsifiers claim to have been members of the Donner Party, and as such have written untruthful and exaggerated accounts of the sufferings of the party. While this is unquestionably true, it is barely possible that some who assert membership found their claim upon the fact that during a portion of the journey they were really in the Donner Party. Bearing this in mind, there is less difficulty in reconciling the conflicting statements of different narrators.

The members of the party proper numbered ninety, and were as follows:

George Donner, Tamsen Donner (his wife), Elitha C. Donner, Leanna C. Donner, Frances E. Donner, Georgia A. Donner and Eliza P. Donner. The last three were children of George and Tamsen Donner; Elitha and Leanna were children of George Donner by a former wife.

Jacob Donner, Elizabeth Donner (his wife), Solomon Hook, William Hook, George Donner, Jr., Mary M. Donner, Isaac Donner, Lewis Donner and Samuel Donner. Jacob Donner was a brother of George; Solomon and William Hook were sons of Elizabeth Donner by a former husband.

James Frazier Reed, Margaret W. Reed (his wife), Virginia E. Reed, Martha F. (Patty) Reed, James F. Reed, Jr., Thomas K. Reed, and Mrs. Sarah Keyes, the mother of Mrs. Reed.

The two Donner families and the Reeds were from Springfield, Illinois. From the same place were Baylis Williams and his half-sister Eliza Williams, John Denton, Milton Elliott, James Smith, Walter Herron and Noah James.

From Marshall County, Illinois, came Franklin Ward Graves, Elizabeth Graves (his wife), Mary A. Graves, William C. Graves, Eleanor Graves, Lovina Graves, Nancy Graves,

Jonathan B. Graves, F. W. Graves, Jr., Elizabeth Graves, Jr., Jay Fosdick and Mrs. Sarah Fosdick (*née* Graves). With this family came John Snyder.

From Keokuk, Lee County, Iowa, came Patrick Breen, Mrs. Margaret Breen, John Breen, Edward J. Breen, Patrick Breen, Jr., Simon P. Breen, James F. Breen, Peter Breen, and Isabella M. Breen. Patrick Dolan also came from Keokuk.

William H. Eddy, Mrs. Eleanor Eddy, James P. Eddy, and Margaret Eddy came from Belleville, Illinois.

From Tennessee came Mrs. Lavina Murphy, a widow, and her family, John Landrum Murphy, Mary M. Murphy, Lemuel B. Murphy, William G. Murphy, Simon P. Murphy, William M. Pike, Mrs. Harriet F. Pike (*née* Murphy), Naomi L. Pike, and Catherine Pike. Another son-in-law of Mrs. Murphy, William M. Foster, with his wife, Mrs. Sarah A. C. Foster, and infant boy George Foster, came from St. Louis, Missouri.

William McCutchen, Mrs. W. McCutchen, and Harriet McCutchen were from Jackson County, Missouri.

Lewis Keseberg, Mrs. Phillipine Keseberg, Ada Keseberg, and L. Keseberg, Jr., Mr. and Mrs. Wolfinger, Joseph Rhinehart, Augustus Spitzer, and Charles Burger, came from Germany.

Samuel Shoemaker came from Springfield, Ohio, Charles T. Stanton from Chicago, Illinois, Luke Halloran from St. Joseph, Missouri, Mr. Hardcoop from Antwerp, in Belgium, Antoine from New Mexico. John Baptiste was a Spaniard, who joined the train near the Santa Fé trail, and Lewis and Salvador were two Indians, who were sent out from California by Captain Sutter.

The Breens joined the company at Independence, Missouri, and the Graves family overtook the train one hundred miles west of Fort Bridger. Each family, prior to its consolidation with the train, had its individual incidents. William Trimble, who was traveling with the Graves family, was slain by the Pawnee Indians about fifty miles east of Scott's Bluff. Trimble left a wife and two or three children. The wife and some of her relatives were so disheartened by this sad bereavement, and by the fact that many of their cattle were stolen by the Indians, that they gave up the journey to California, and turned back to the homes whence they had started.

An amusing incident is related in the Healdsburg (Cal.) Flag, by Mr. W. C. Graves, of Calistoga, which occurred soon after his party left St. Joseph, Missouri. It was on the fourth night out, and Mr. Graves and four or five others were detailed to stand guard. The constant terror of the emigrants in those days was Indians. Both the Pawnees, the Sioux, and the Snakes were warlike and powerful, and were jealous, revengeful, and merciless toward the whites. That night a fire somehow started in the prairie grass about half a mile from camp. The west wind, blowing fierce and strong, carried the flames in great surging gusts through the tall prairie grass. A resin weed grows in bunches in this part of the country, generally attaining the height of four or five feet. The night being very dark, these weeds could be seen standing between the fire and the guards. As the flames swayed past the weeds, the impression was very naturally produced upon the mind of a timid beholder that the weeds were moving in the opposite direction. This optical illusion caused some of the guards to believe that the Indians had set fire to the grass, and were moving in immense numbers between them and the fire with intent to surround them, stampede the cattle, and massacre the entire party. The watcher next to Mr. Graves discovered the enemy, and rushed breathlessly to his comrade to impart the intelligence. Scarcely had Mr. Graves quieted him before it was evident that a general alarm had been spread in the camp. Two other guards had seen the Indians, and the aroused camp, armed to the teeth, marched out to give battle to the imaginary foe. It was a rich joke, and it was some time before those who were scared heard the last of the resin Indians.

Only once, before reaching Salt Lake, did death invade the joyous Donner company. It was near the present site of Manhattan, Kansas, and Mrs. Sarah Keyes was the victim. This estimable lady was the mother of Mrs. J. F. Reed, and had reached her four score and ten years. Her aged frame and feeble health were not equal to the fatigues and exposure of the trip, and on the thirtieth of May they laid her tenderly to rest. She was buried in a coffin carefully fashioned from the trunk of a cottonwood tree, and on the brow of a beautiful knoll overlooking the valley. A grand old oak, still standing, guards the lonely grave of the dear old mother who was spared the sight of the misery in store for her loved ones. Could those who performed the last sad rites have caught a vision of the horrors awaiting the party, they would have known how good was the God who in mercy took her to Himself.

CHAPTER II

PRESENTING, as they do, an interesting glimpse of the first portion of the journey, the following letters are here introduced. They were written by Mrs. Tamsen Donner, and were published in the Springfield (Illinois) Journal. Thanks for copies of these letters are due to Mrs. Eliza P. Houghton of San Jose, Mrs. Donner's youngest daughter. Allusions are made in these letters to botanical researches. Mrs. Donner, C. T. Stanton, and perhaps one or two others who were prominent actors in the later history, were particularly fond of botany. Mrs. Donner made valuable collections of rare flowers and plants. Her journal, and a full description of the contents of her botanical portfolios, were to have been published upon her arrival in California.

Though bearing the same date, the letters here presented were written at different times. The following appeared in the Springfield Journal, July 23, 1846:

Near the Junction of the North }
and South Platte, June 16, 1846. }

My Old Friend: We are now on the Platte, two hundred miles from Fort Laramie. Our journey so far has been pleasant, the roads have been good, and food plentiful. The water for part of the way has been indifferent, but at no time have our cattle suffered for it. Wood is now very scarce, but "buffalo chips" are excellent; they kindle quickly and retain heat surprisingly. We had this morning buffalo steaks broiled upon them that had the same flavor they would have had upon hickory coals.

We feel no fear of Indians, our cattle graze quietly around our encampment unmolested.

Two or three men will go hunting twenty miles from camp; and last night two of our men lay out in the wilderness rather than ride their horses after a hard chase.

Indeed, if I do not experience something far worse than I have yet done, I shall say the trouble is all in getting started. Our wagons have not needed much repair, and I can not yet tell in what respects they could be improved. Certain it is, they can not be too strong. Our preparations for the journey might have been in some respects bettered.

Bread has been the principal article of food in our camp. We laid in 150 pounds of flour and 75 pounds of meat for each individual, and I fear bread will be scarce. Meat is abundant. Rice and beans are good articles on the road; cornmeal, too, is acceptable. Linsey dresses are the most suitable for children. Indeed, if I had one, it would be acceptable. There is so cool a breeze at all times on the plains that the sun does not feel so hot as one would suppose.

We are now four hundred and fifty miles from Independence. Our route at first was rough, and through a timbered country, which appeared to be fertile. After striking the prairie, we found a first-rate road, and the only difficulty we have had, has been in crossing the creeks. In that, however, there has been no danger.

I never could have believed we could have traveled so far with so little difficulty. The prairie between the Blue and the Platte rivers is beautiful beyond description. Never have I seen so varied a country, so suitable for cultivation. Everything was new and pleasing; the Indians frequently come to see us, and the chiefs of a tribe breakfasted at our tent this morning. All are so friendly that I can not help feeling sympathy and friendship for them. But on one sheet what can I say?

Since we have been on the Platte, we have had the river on one side and the ever varying mounds on the other, and have traveled through the bottom lands from one to two miles wide, with little or no timber. The soil is sandy, and last year, on account of the dry season, the emigrants found grass here scarce. Our cattle are in good order, and when proper care has been taken, none have been lost. Our milch cows have been of great service, indeed. They have been of more advantage than our meat. We have plenty of butter and milk.

We are commanded by Captain Russell, an amiable man. George Donner is himself yet. He crows in the morning and shouts out, "Chain up, boys—chain up," with as much authority as though he was "something in particular." John Denton is still with us. We find him useful in the camp. Hiram Miller and Noah James are in good health and doing well. We have of the best people in our company, and some, too, that are not so good.

Buffaloes show themselves frequently.

We have found the wild tulip, the primrose, the lupine, the eardrop, the larkspur, and creeping hollyhock, and a beautiful flower resembling the bloom of the beech tree, but in bunches as large as a small sugar-loaf, and of every variety of shade, to red and green.

I botanize, and read some, but cook "heaps" more. There are four hundred and twenty wagons, as far as we have heard, on the road between here and Oregon and California.

Give our love to all inquiring friends. God bless them.

Yours truly,

Mrs. George Donner.

The following letter was published in the Journal of July 30, 1846:

> South Fork of the Nebraska, }
> Ten miles from the Crossing, }
> Tuesday, June 16, 1846. }

DEAR FRIEND: To-day, at nooning, there passed, going to the States, seven men from Oregon, who went out last year. One of them was well acquainted with Messrs. Ide and Cadden Keyes, the latter of whom, he says, went to California. They met the advance Oregon caravan about 150 miles west of Fort Laramie, and counted in all, for Oregon and California (excepting ours), 478 wagons. There are in our company over 40 wagons, making 518 in all, and there are said to be yet 20 behind. To-morrow we cross the river, and, by reckoning, will be over 200 miles from Fort Laramie, where we intend to stop and repair our wagon wheels. They are nearly all loose, and I am afraid we will have to stop sooner, if there can be found wood suitable to heat the tires. There is no wood here, and our women and children are out now gathering "buffalo chips" to burn, in order to do the cooking. These chips burn well.

MRS. GEORGE DONNER.

At Fort Laramie a portion of the Donner Party celebrated the Fourth of July, 1846. Arriving there on the evening of the third, they pitched camp somewhat earlier than usual, and prepared a grand dinner for the Fourth. At the Fort were a large party of Sioux who were on the war-path against the Snakes or Pawnees. The Sioux were, perhaps, the most warlike Indian nation on the great prairies, and when dressed in their war paint and mounted on their fleet ponies, presented a truly imposing appearance. The utmost friendliness prevailed, and there was a mutual interchange of gifts and genial courtesies. When the Donner Party pursued their march, and had journeyed half a day from the Fort, they were overtaken and convoyed quite a distance by about three hundred young warriors. The escort rode in pairs alongside the train in true military fashion. Finally halting, they opened ranks, and as the wagons passed, each warrior held in his mouth a green twig or leaf, which was said to be emblematic of peacefulness and good feeling.

The train was never seriously molested by the Sioux. On one occasion, about fifty warriors on horseback surrounded a portion of the train, in which was the Graves family. While generally friendly, a few of the baser sort persisted in attempting to steal, or take by force, trivial articles which struck their fancy. The main body of Indians were encamped about half a mile away, and when the annoyances became too exasperating, W. C. Graves mounted a horse, rode to the encampment, and notified the Chief of the action of his followers. Seizing an old-fashioned single-barreled shotgun, the Chief sprang upon his horse and fairly flew over the plain toward the emigrant wagons. When within about a hundred yards of the train he attracted attention by giving an Indian whoop, which was so full of rage and imprecation that the startled warriors forthwith desisted from their petty persecutions and scattered in every direction like frightened quail. One of the would-be marauders was a little tardy in mounting his pony, and as soon as the Chief got within range, the shotgun was leveled and discharged full at the unruly subject. Three of the buckshot entered the pony's side and one grazed the warrior's leg. As if satisfied that his orders to treat the emigrants in a friendly manner would not be again disregarded, the Chief wheeled his horse about, and in the most grave and stately manner rode back to his encampment.

On another occasion, Mary Graves, who was a very beautiful young lady, was riding on horseback accompanied by her brother. They were a little in the rear of the train, and a band of Sioux Indians, becoming enamored with the maiden, offered to purchase her. They made very handsome offers, but the brother not being disposed to accept, one of the Indians seized the bridle of the girl's horse and attempted to carry her away captive. Perhaps the attempt was made in half jest. At all events the bridle was promptly dropped when the brother leveled his rifle at the savage.

On the twentieth of July, 1846, George Donner was elected Captain of the train at the Little Sandy River. From that time forward it was known as the Donner Party.

One incident, not at all unusual to a trip across the plains, is pointedly described in a letter written by C. T. Stanton to his brother, Sidney Stanton, now of Cazenovia, New York. The incident alluded to is the unfriendliness and want of harmony so liable to exist between different companies, and between members of the same company. From one of Mr. Stanton's letters the following extract is made:

"At noon we passed Boggs' company on the Sweetwater; a mile further up the river, Dunlavy's; a mile further, West's; and about two miles beyond that, was Dunbar's. We encamped about half way between the two latter. Thus, within five miles were encamped five companies. At Indian Creek, twenty miles from Independence, these five companies all constituted one, but owing to dissensions and quarreling they became broken into fragments. Now, by accident, we all again once more meet and grasp the cordial hand; old enmities are forgot, and nothing but good feeling prevails. * * * * * The next morning we got rather a late start, owing to a difference of opinion arising in our company as to whether we should lie by or go ahead. Those wishing to lie by were principally young men who wished to have a day's hunting among the buffaloes, and there were also a few families out of meat who wished to lay in a supply before they left the buffalo country. A further reason was urged that the cattle were nearly fagged out by hard travel, and that they would not stand the journey unless we stopped and gave them rest. On the other side it was contended that if we stopped here the other companies would all get ahead, the grass would all be eaten off by their thousand head of cattle, and that consequently, when we came along, our cattle would starve. The go-ahead party finally ruled and we rolled out."

As will presently be seen, the dissension existing in the company, and the petty differences of opinion and interest, were the fundamental causes of the calamities which befell the Donner Party.

When the company was near Fort Bridger, Edward Breen's leg was broken by a fall from a horse. His mother refused to permit amputation, or rather left the question to Edward's decision, and of course, boy-like, he refused to have the operation performed. Contrary to expectation, the bone knitted, and in a month he walked without a crutch.

At Fort Bridger, which was at this time a mere camp or trading post, the party heard much commendation bestowed upon a new route via Salt Lake. This route passed along the southern shore of the Lake, and rejoined the old Fort Hall emigrant road on the Humboldt. It was said to shorten the distance three hundred miles. The new route was known as the Hastings Cut-off, and was named after the famous Lansford W. Hastings, who was even then piloting a small company over the cut-off. The large trains delayed for three or four days at Fort Bridger, debating as to the best course to pursue. It is claimed that but for the earnest advice and solicitation of Bridger and Vasquez, who had charge of the fort, the entire party would have continued by the accustomed route. These men had a direct interest in the Hastings Cut-off, as they furnished the emigrants with supplies, and had employed Hastings to pilot the first company over the road to Salt Lake.

After mature deliberation, the party divided, the greater portion going by Fort Hall and reaching California in safety. With the large train, which journeyed the old road, this narrative is no longer interested. Eighty-seven persons, however, took the Hastings Cut-off. Their names are included in the ninety mentioned in the preceding chapter, it being remembered that Mrs. Sarah Keyes had died, and that Lewis and Salvador where not yet members of the party. For several days the party traveled without much difficulty. They reached Weber River near the head of the well-known Weber Canyon. At the first crossing of this river, on the third of August, they found a letter from Hastings stuck in the split of a stick, informing them that the road down the Weber Canyon was in a terrible condition, and that it was doubtful if the sixty-six wagons which L. W. Hastings was then piloting through the canyon would ever succeed in reaching the plain. In the letter, Hastings advised all emigrants to avoid the canyon road, and pursue over the mountains a course which he faintly outlined. In order to obtain further information, and, if possible, to induce Hastings to return and act as guide, Messrs. Reed, Stanton, and Pike were sent forward to overtake the advance company. This was accomplished after a fatiguing trip, which so exhausted the horses of Stanton and Pike that these gentlemen were unable to return to the Donner Party. Hastings was overtaken at a point near the southern end of Great Salt Lake, and came back with Reed to the foot of the bluffs overlooking the present city of Salt Lake. Here he declared that he must return to the company he was piloting, and despite the urgent entreaties of Reed, decided that it was his duty to start back the next morning. He finally consented, however, to ascend to the summit of the Wahsatch Mountains, from which he endeavored, as best he could, to point out the direction in which the wagons must travel from the head of Weber Canyon. Reed proceeded alone on the route indicated, taking notes of the country and occasionally blazing trees to assist him in retracing the course.

Wm. G. Murphy (now of Marysville, Cal.) says that the wagons remained in the meadows at the head of Weber Canyon until Reed's return. They then learned that the train which preceded them had been compelled to travel very slowly down the Weber River, filling in many irregular places with brush and dirt; that at last they had reached a place where vast perpendicular pillars of rock approached so closely on either side that the river had barely space to flow between, and just here the water plunged over a precipice. To lower the wagons down this precipice had been a dreadful task.

The Donner Party unanimously decided to travel across the mountains in a more direct line toward Salt Lake. They soon found rolling highlands and small summit valleys on the divide between Weber River and Salt Lake. Following down one of the small streams, they found a varying, irregular canyon, down which they passed, filling its small stream with brush and rocks, crossing and recrossing it, making roads, breaking and mending wagons, until three weeks' time had expired. The entire country was heavily covered with timber and underbrush. When the party arrived at the outlet of this stream into Salt Lake Valley, they found it utterly impassable. It was exceedingly narrow, and was filled with huge rocks from the cliffs on either side. Almost all the oxen in the train were necessary in drawing each wagon out of the canyon and up the steep overhanging mountain. While in this canyon, Stanton and Pike came up to the company. These gentlemen encountered great hardships after their horses gave out, and were almost starved to death when they reached the train.

Instead of reaching Salt Lake in a week, as had been promised, the party were over thirty days in making the trip. No words can describe what they endured on this Hastings Cut-off. The terrible delay was rendering imminent the dangers which awaited them on the Sierra Nevada. At last, upon ascending the steep rugged mountain before mentioned, the vision of Great Salt Lake, and the extensive plains surrounding it, burst upon their enraptured gaze. All were wild with joy and gratitude for their deliverance from the terrible struggle through which they had just passed, and all hoped for a prosperous, peaceful journey over pleasant roads throughout the remainder of the trip to California. Alas! there were trials in the way compared with which their recent struggles were insignificant. But for the fatal delay caused by the Hastings Cut-off, all would have been well, but now the summer was passed, their teams and themselves were well-nigh exhausted, and their slender stock of provisions nearly consumed.

CHAPTER III

A GRAVE OF SALT — MEMBERS OF THE MYSTIC TIE — TWENTY
WELLS — A DESOLATE ALKALINE WASTE — ABANDONED ON
THE DESERT — A NIGHT OF HORROR — A STEER MADDENED
BY THIRST — THE MIRAGE — YOKING AN OX AND A COW —
"CACHEING" GOODS — THE EMIGRANT'S SILENT LOGIC — A
CRY FOR RELIEF — TWO HEROIC VOLUNTEERS — A PERILOUS
JOURNEY — LETTERS TO CAPT. SUTTER.

NEAR the southern shore of great Salt Lake the Donner Party
encamped on the third or fourth of September, 1846. The summer
had vanished, and autumn had commenced tinting, with crimson
and gold, the foliage on the Wahsatch Mountains. While
encamped here, the party buried the second victim claimed by
death. This time it was a poor consumptive named Luke Halloran.
Without friend or kinsman, Halloran had joined the train, and was
traveling to California in hopes that a change of climate might
effect a cure. Alas! for the poor Irishman, when the leaves began to
fall from the trees his spirit winged its flight to the better land. He
died in the wagon of Captain George Donner, his head resting in
Mrs. Tamsen Donner's lap. It was at sundown. The wagons had just
halted for the night. The train had driven up slowly, out of respect
to the dying emigrant. Looking up into Mrs. Donner's face, he
said: "I die happy." Almost while speaking, he died. In return for
the many kindnesses he had received during the journey, he left
Mr. Donner such property as he possessed, including about fifteen
hundred dollars in coin. Hon. Jas. F. Breen, of South San Juan,

writes: "Halloran's body was buried in a bed of almost pure salt, beside the grave of one who had perished in the preceding train. It was said at the time that bodies thus deposited would not decompose, on account of the preservative properties of the salt. Soon after his burial, his trunk was opened, and Masonic papers and regalia bore witness to the fact that Mr. Halloran was a member of the Masonic Order. James F. Reed, Milton Elliott, and perhaps one or two others in the train, also belonged to the mystic tie."

On the sixth day of September they reached a meadow in a valley called "Twenty Wells," as there were that number of wells of various sizes, from six inches to several feet in diameter. The water in these wells rose even with the surface of the ground, and when it was drawn out the wells soon refilled. The water was cold and pure, and peculiarly welcome after the saline plains and alkaline pools they had just passed. Wells similar to these were found during the entire journey of the following day, and the country through which they were passing abounded in luxuriant grass. Reaching the confines of the Salt Lake Desert, which lies southwest of the lake, they laid in, as they supposed, an ample supply of water and grass. This desert had been represented by Bridger and Vasquez as being only about fifty miles wide. Instead, for a distance of seventy-five miles there was neither water nor grass, but everywhere a dreary, desolate, alkaline waste. Verily, it was

> "A region of drought, where no river glides,
> Nor rippling brook with osiered sides;
> Where sedgy pool, nor bubbling fount,
> Nor tree, nor cloud, nor misty mount
> Appears to refresh the aching eye,
> But the barren earth and the burning sky,
> And the blank horizon round and round
> Spread, void of living sight or sound."

When the company had been on the desert two nights and one day, Mr. Reed volunteered to go forward, and, if possible, to discover water. His hired teamsters were attending to his teams and wagons during his absence. At a distance of perhaps twenty miles he found the desired water, and hastened to return to the train. Meantime there was intense suffering in the party. Cattle were giving out and lying down helplessly on the burning sand, or frenzied with thirst were straying away into the desert. Having made preparations for only fifty miles of desert, several persons came near perishing of thirst, and cattle were utterly powerless to draw the heavy wagons. Reed was gone some twenty hours. During this time his teamsters had done the wisest thing possible, unhitched the oxen and started to drive them ahead until water was reached. It was their intention, of course, to return and get the three wagons and the family, which they had necessarily abandoned on the desert. Reed passed his teamsters during the night, and hastened to the relief of his deserted family. One of his teamster's horses gave out before morning and lay down, and while the man's companions were attempting to raise him, the oxen, rendered unmanageable by their great thirst, disappeared in the desert. There were eighteen of these oxen. It is probable they scented water, and with the instincts of their nature started out to search for it. They never were found, and Reed and his family, consisting of nine persons, were left destitute in the midst of the desert, eight hundred miles from California. Near morning, entirely ignorant of the calamity which had befallen him in the loss of his cattle, he reached his family. All day long they looked and waited in vain for the returning teamsters. All the rest of the company had driven ahead, and the majority had reached water. Toward night the situation grew desperate. The scanty supply of water left with the family was almost gone, and another day on the desert would mean death to all he held dear. Their only way left was to set out on foot. He took his youngest child in his arms, and the family started to walk the twenty miles. During this dreadful night some of the younger children became so exhausted that, regardless of scoldings or encouragements, they lay down on the bleak sands. Even rest, however, seemed denied the little sufferers, for a chilling wind began sweeping over the desert, and despite their weariness and anguish, they were forced to move forward. At one time during the night the horror of the situation was changed to intense fright. Through the darkness came a swift-rushing animal, which Reed soon recognized as one of his young steers. It was crazed and frenzied with thirst, and for some moments seemed bent upon dashing into the frightened group. Finally, however, it plunged madly away into the night, and was seen no more. Reed suspected the calamity which had prevented the return of the teamsters, but at the moment, the imminent peril surrounding his wife and children banished all thought of worrying about anything but their present situation. God knows what would have become of them had they not, soon after daylight, discovered the wagon of Jacob Donner. They were received kindly by his family, and conveyed to where the other members of the party were camped. For six or eight days the entire company remained at this spot. Every effort was made to find Reed's lost cattle. Almost every man in the train was out in the desert, searching in all directions. This task was attended with both difficulty and danger; for when the sun shone, the atmosphere appeared to distort and magnify objects so that at the distance of a mile every stone or bush would appear the size of an ox. Several of the men came near dying for want of water during this search. The desert mirage disclosed against the horizon, clear, distinct, and perfectly outlined rocks, mountain peaks, and tempting lakelets. Each jagged cliff, or pointed rock, or sharply-curved hill-top, hung suspended in air as perfect and complete as if photographed on the sky. Deceived, deluded by these mirages, in spite of their better judgment, several members of the company were led far out into the pathless depths of the desert.

The outlook for Reed was gloomy enough. One cow and one ox were the only stock he had remaining. The company were getting exceedingly impatient over the long delay, yet be it said to their honor, they encamped on the western verge of the desert until every hope of finding Reed's cattle was abandoned. Finally, F. W. Graves and Patrick Breen each lent an ox to Mr. Reed, and by yoking up his remaining cow and ox, he had two yoke of cattle.

"Cacheing," or concealing such of his property on the desert, as could not be placed in one wagon, he hitched the two yoke of cattle to this wagon and proceeded on the journey. The word cache occurs so frequently in this history that a brief definition of the interesting process of cacheing might not be amiss. The cache of goods or valuables was generally made in a wagon bed, if one, as in the present instance, was to be abandoned. A square hole, say six feet in depth, was dug in the earth, and in the bottom of this the box or wagon bed containing the articles was placed. Sand, soil, or clay of the proper stratum was filled in upon this, so as to just cover the box from sight. The ground was then tightly packed or trampled, to make it resemble, as much as possible, the earth in its natural state. Into the remaining hole would be placed such useless articles as could be spared, such as old tins, cast-off clothing, broken furniture, etc., and upon these the earth was thrown until the surface of the ground was again level. These precautions were taken to prevent the Indians from discovering and appropriating the articles cached. It was argued that the Indians, when digging down, would come to the useless articles, and not thinking there was treasure further down would abandon the task. "But," says Hon. James F. Breen, in speaking on this subject, "I have been told by parties who have crossed the plains, that in no case has the Indian been deceived by the emigrant's silent logic." The Indians would leave nothing underground, not even the dead bodies buried from time to time. One of the trains in advance of the Donner Party buried two men in one grave, and succeeding parties found each of the bodies unearthed, and were compelled to repeat the last sad rites of burial.

Before the Donner Party started from the Desert camp, an inventory of the provisions on hand was accurately taken, and an estimate was made of the quantity required for each family, and it was found that there was not enough to carry the emigrants through to California. As if to render more emphatic the terrible situation of the party, a storm came during their last night at the camp, and in the morning the hill-tops were white with snow. It was a dreadful reminder of the lateness of the season, and the bravest hearts quailed before the horrors they knew must await them. A solemn council was held. It was decided that some one must leave the train, press eagerly forward to California, and obtaining a supply of provisions, return and meet the party as far back on the route as possible. It was a difficult undertaking, and perilous in the extreme. A call was made for volunteers, and after a little reflection two men offered their services. One was Wm. McCutchen, who had joined the train from Missouri, and the other was C. T. Stanton, of Chicago, a man who afterwards proved himself possessed of the sublimest heroism. Taking each a horse, they received the tearful, prayerful farewells of the doomed company, and set out upon their solitary journey.

Would they return? If they reached the peaceful, golden valleys of California, would they turn back to meet danger, and storms, and death, in order to bring succor to those on the dreary desert? McCutchen might come, because he left dear ones with the train, but would Stanton return? Stanton was young and unmarried. There were no ties or obligations to prompt his return, save his plighted word and the dictates of honor and humanity.

They bore letters from the Donner Party to Captain Sutter, who was in charge at Sutter's Fort. These letters were prayers for relief, and it was believed would secure assistance from the generous old Captain. Every eye followed Stanton and McCutchen until they disappeared in the west. Soon afterward the train resumed its toilsome march.

CHAPTER IV

GRAVELLY FORD — THE CHARACTER OF JAMES F. REED — CAUSES WHICH LED TO THE REED-SNYDER TRAGEDY — JOHN SNYDER'S POPULARITY — THE FATAL ALTERCATION — CONFLICTING STATEMENTS OF SURVIVORS — SNYDER'S DEATH — A BRAVE GIRL — A PRIMITIVE TRIAL — A COURT OF FINAL RESORT — VERDICT OF BANISHMENT — A SAD SEPARATION — GEORGE AND JACOB DONNER AHEAD AT THE TIME — FINDING LETTERS IN SPLIT STICKS — DANGER OF STARVATION.

GRAVELLY Ford, on the Humboldt River, witnessed a tragedy which greatly agitated the company. Its results, as will be seen, materially affected the lives not only of the participants, but of several members of the party during the days of horror on the mountains, by bringing relief which would otherwise have been lacking. The parties to the tragedy were James F. Reed and John Snyder. Reed was a man who was tender, generous, heroic, and whose qualities of true nobility shone brilliantly throughout a long life of usefulness. His name is intimately interwoven with the history of the Donner Party, from first to last. Indeed, in the Illinois papers of 1846–7 the company was always termed the "Reed and Donner Party." This title was justly conferred at the time, because he was one of the leading spirits in the organization of the enterprise. In order to understand the tragedy which produced the death of John Snyder, and the circumstances resulting therefrom, the reader must become better acquainted with the character of Mr. Reed.

The following brief extract is from "Powers' Early Settlers of Sangamon County:" "James Frazier Reed was born November 14, 1800, in County Armagh, Ireland. His ancestors were of noble Polish birth, who chose exile rather than submission to the Russian power, and settled in the north of Ireland. The family name was originally Reednoski, but in process of time the Polish termination of the name was dropped, and the family was called Reed. James F. Reed's mother's name was Frazier, whose ancestors belonged to Clan Frazier, of Scottish history. Mrs. Reed and her son, James F., came to America when he was a youth, and settled in Virginia. He remained there until he was twenty, when he left for the lead mines of Illinois, and was engaged in mining until 1831, when he came to Springfield, Sangamon County, Illinois."

Among the papers of Mr. Reed is a copy of the muster roll of a company which enlisted in the Blackhawk war, and in this roll are the names of Abraham Lincoln, Stephen A. Douglas, and James F. Reed. At the termination of this war, Mr. Reed returned to Springfield, engaged in the manufacture of cabinet furniture, and amassed a considerable fortune. He was married in 1835 to Mrs. Margaret Backenstoe, whose maiden name was Keyes. The death of his wife's mother, Mrs. Sarah Keyes, has already been mentioned as occurring on the Big Blue River, near Manhattan, Kansas.

During the progress of the train, Mr. Reed was always a prominent, active member. Full of life and enthusiasm, fearless of danger, he was ready at all times to risk his life for the company's welfare. On the desert, we have seen that his lonely expedition in search of water cost him his valuable oxen, and left him and his family almost destitute.

The deplorable affair about to be narrated was only the natural outgrowth of the trying circumstances in which the company were placed. The reader must bear in mind that many petty causes combined to produce discord and dissension among the members of the Donner Party. Coming from so many different States, being of different nationalities and modes of thought, delayed on the road much longer than was expected, rendered irritable by the difficulties encountered on the journey, annoyed by losses of stock, fearful of unknown disasters on the Sierra, and already placed on short allowances of provisions, the emigrants were decidedly inharmonious.

The action of the company, moreover, was doubtless influenced in a greater or less degree by Snyder's popularity. A young man, not over twenty-three years old, he was tall, straight, and of erect, manly carriage, and his habits of life as a frontiersman had developed him into a muscular, athletic being. He excelled and led in all the out-door sports most in favor with Western men, such as jumping, running, and wrestling. His manner was gentle, retired, and timid to a degree verging on bashfulness, until roused by the influence of passion. The lion in the man was dormant until evoked by the fiercer emotions. His complexion was dark, but as you studied his face you could not repress the suspicion that Nature had marked him for a blonde, and that constant exposure to the wind and sun and rain of the great plains of the West had wrought the color change, and the conviction was strong that the change was an improvement on Nature. His features were cast in a mold of great beauty—such beauty as we seldom look for in a man. He was never moody, despondent, or cast down, and at all times, and under all circumstances, possessed the faculty of amusing himself and entertaining others. In the evening camp, when other amusements failed, or when anticipated troubles depressed the spirits of the travelers, it was his custom to remove the "hindgate" of his wagon, lay it on the ground, and thereon perform the "clog dance," "Irish jigs," the "pigeon wing," and other fantastic steps. Many an evening the Donner Party were prevented from brooding over their troubles by the boyish antics of the light-hearted youth.

As stated above, the train had reached Gravelly Ford. Already the members of the company were beginning to scan eagerly the western plain in hopes of discovering the relief which it was believed Stanton and McCutchen would bring from Sutter's Fort. Of course there were the usual accidents and incidents peculiar to a journey across the plains. Occasionally a wagon would need repairing. Occasionally there would be a brief halt to rest and recruit the jaded cattle. The Indians had stolen two of Mr. Graves' oxen, and a couple of days later had stolen one of the horses.

In traveling, the Donner Party observed this rule: If a wagon drove in the lead one day, it should pass back to the rear on the succeeding day. This system of alternating allowed each his turn in leading the train. On this fifth of October, 1846, F. W. Graves was ahead, Jay Fosdick second, John Snyder third, and the team of J. F. Reed fourth. Milton Elliott was driving Reed's team. Arriving at the foot of a steep, sandy hill, the party was obliged to "double teams," that is, to hitch five or six yoke of oxen to one wagon. Elliott and Snyder interchanged hot words over some difficulty about the oxen. Fosdick had attached his team to Graves' and had drawn Graves' wagon up the hill. Snyder, being nettled at something Elliott had said, declared that his team could pull up alone. During the excitement Snyder made use of very bad language, and was beating his cattle over the head with his whip-stock. One account says that Reed's team and Snyder's became tangled. At all events, Snyder was very much enraged. Reed had been off hunting on horseback, and arriving at this moment, remonstrated with Snyder for beating the cattle, and at the same time offered him the assistance of his team. Snyder refused the proffered aid, and used abusive language toward both Reed and Elliott. Reed attempted to calm the enraged man. Both men were of fiery, passionate dispositions, and words began to multiply rapidly. When Reed saw that trouble was likely to occur, he said something about waiting until they got up the hill and settling this matter afterwards. Snyder evidently construed this to be a threat, and with an oath replied, "We will settle it now." As Snyder uttered these words, he struck Reed a blow on the head with the butt-end of his heavy whip-stock. This blow was followed in rapid succession by a second, and a third. As the third stroke descended, Mrs. Reed ran between her husband and the furious man, hoping to prevent the blow. Each time the whip-stock descended on Reed's head it cut deep gashes. He was blinded with the blood which streamed from his wounds, and dazed and stunned by the terrific force of the blows. He saw the cruel whip-stock uplifted, and knew that his wife was in danger, but had only time to cry "John! John!" when down came the stroke full upon Mrs. Reed's head and shoulders. The next instant John Snyder was staggering, speechless and death-stricken. Reed's hunting-knife had pierced his left breast, severing the first and second ribs and entering the left lung.

No other portion of the History of the Donner Party, as con-tributed by the survivors, has been so variously stated as this Reed-Snyder affair. Five members of the party, now living, claim to have been eye-witnesses. The version of two of these, Mrs. J. M. Murphy and Mrs. Frank Lewis, is the one here published. In the theory of self-defense they are corroborated by all the early published accounts. This theory was first advanced in Judge J. Quinn Thornton's work in 1849, and has never been disputed publicly until within the last two or three years. Due deference to the valu-able assistance rendered by Wm. G. Murphy, of Marysville, and W. C. Graves, of Calistoga, demands mention of the fact that their accounts differ in important respects from the one given above. This is not surprising in view of the thirty-three years which have elapsed since the occurrence. The history of criminal jurispru-dence justifies the assertion that eye-witnesses of any fatal difficulty differ materially in regard to important particulars, even when their testimony is taken immediately after the difficulty. It is not strange, therefore, that after the lapse of an ordinary life-time a dozen different versions should have been contributed by the sur-vivors concerning this unfortunate tragedy. James F. Reed, after nearly a quarter of a century of active public life in California, died honored and respected. During his life-time this incident appeared several times in print, and was always substantially as given in this chapter. With the single exception of a series of arti-cles contributed to the Healdsburg Flag by W. C. Graves, two or three years ago, no different account has ever been published.

This explanatory digression from the narrative is deemed necessary out of respect to the two gentlemen who conscientiously disagree with Mrs. Murphy and Mrs. Lewis. On all other important subjects the survivors are harmonious or reconcilable.

W. C. Graves, now of Calistoga, caught the dying man in his arms, and in a few minutes he was carried a little way up the hill and laid upon the ground. Reed immediately regretted the act and threw the knife from him. His wife and daughters gathered about him and began to stanch the blood that flowed from the gashes on his head. He gently pushed them aside and went to the assistance of the dying man. He and Snyder had always been firm friends, and Snyder had been most active in securing a team for Reed after the latter had lost his cattle in the desert. Snyder expired in about fifteen minutes, and Reed remained by his side until the last. Patrick Breen came up, and Snyder said, "Uncle Patrick, I am dead." It is not certain that he spoke again, though Reed's friends claim that he said to Reed, "I am to blame."

Snyder's death fell like a thunderbolt upon the Donner Party. Camp was immediately pitched, the Reed family being a little removed down the hill from the main body of emigrants. Reed felt that he had only acted in defense of his own life and in defense of the wife he adored. Nevertheless, it was evident that trouble was brewing in the main camp where Snyder's body was lying.

The Reed family were in a sad situation. They commenced the journey with a more costly and complete outfit than the other emigrants, and thereby had incurred the envy of some of their less fortunate companions. They had a fine race horse and good stock, and Virginia had a beautiful pony of her own, and was fond of accompanying her father on his horseback excursions. From these and other circumstances the Reeds had acquired the name of being "aristocratic." Ordinarily, this is a term which would excite a smile, but on this dreadful day it had its weight in inflaming the minds of the excited emigrants. On the desert Reed had cached many valuable articles, but all his provisions had been distributed among his companions. This, however, was forgotten in the turbulent camp, and the destitute, desolate family could plainly catch the sound of voices clamoring for Reed's death.

Meantime, Virginia Reed was dressing the wounds on her father's head. Mrs. Reed was overwhelmed with grief and apprehension, and the father came to Virginia for assistance. This brave little woman was only twelve years old, yet in this and all other acts of which there is a record she displayed a nerve and skillfulness which would have done credit to a mature woman. The cuts in Reed's scalp were wide and deep. Indeed, the scars remained to his dying day. In San Jose, long years afterwards, as James F. Reed lay dead, the gentle breeze from an open window softly lifted and caressed his gray hair, disclosing plainly the scars left by these ugly wounds.

Reed entertained none but the friendliest sentiments toward Snyder. Anxious to do what he could for the dead, he offered the boards of his wagon-bed from which to make a coffin for Snyder. This offer, made with the kindliest, most delicate feeling, was rejected by the emigrants. At the funeral, Reed stood sorrowfully by the grave until the last clod was placed above the man who had been one of his best friends. A council was held by the members of the company. A council to decide upon Reed's fate. It was in the nature of a court, all-powerful, from whose decision there was no appeal. Breathlessly the fond wife and affectionate children awaited the verdict. The father was idolized by the mother and the little ones, and was their only stay and support.

The friendship of the Donner Party for John Snyder, the conflicting and distorted accounts of the tragedy, and the personal enmity of certain members of the company toward Reed, resulted in a decree that he should be banished from the train. The feeling ran so high that at one time the end of a wagon-tongue was propped up with an ox-yoke by some of the emigrants with the intention of hanging Reed thereon, but calmer counsel prevailed.

When the announcement was communicated to Reed that he was to be banished, he refused to comply with the decree. Conscious that he had only obeyed the sacred law of self-defense, he refused to accede to an unjust punishment. Then came the wife's pleadings! Long and earnestly Mrs. Reed reasoned and begged and prayed with her husband. All was of no avail until she urged him to remember the want and destitution in which they and the entire company were already participants. If he remained and escaped violence at the hands of his enemies, he might nevertheless see his children starve before his eyes, and be helpless to aid them. But it he would go forward, if he would reach California, he could return with provisions, and meet them on the mountains at that point on the route where they would be in greatest need. It was a fearful struggle, but finally the mother's counsels prevailed. Prior to setting out upon his gloomy journey, Mr. Reed made the company promise to care for his family.

At the time of the Snyder tragedy, George and Jacob Donner, with their wagons and families, were two days in advance of the main train. Walter Herron was with them, and, when Reed came up, Herron concluded to accompany him to California.

It was contemplated that Reed should go out into the wilderness alone, and with neither food nor ammunition. Happily this part of the programme was thwarted. The faithful Virginia, in company with Milton Elliott, followed Mr. Reed after he had started, and carried him his gun and ammunition. The affectionate girl also managed to carry some crackers to him, although she and all the company were even then on short allowance.

The sad parting between Reed and his family, and the second parting with the devoted Virginia, we pass over in silence. James F. Reed, Jr., only five years old, declared that he would go with his father, and assist him in obtaining food during the long journey. Even the baby, only two and a half years old, would fret and worry every time the family sat down to their meals, lest father should find nothing to eat on his difficult way. Every day the mother and daughters would eagerly search for the letter Mr. Reed was sure to leave in the top of some bush, or in a split stick by the wayside. When he succeeded in killing geese or ducks, as he frequently did along the Humboldt and Truckee, he would scatter the feathers about his camping-ground, that his family might see that he was supplied with food. It is hardly necessary to mention that Mrs. Reed and the children regarded the father's camping-places as hallowed ground, and as often as possible kindled their evening fires in the same spot where his had been kindled.

But a day came when they found no more letters, no further traces of the father. Was he dead? Had the Indians killed him? Had he starved by the way? No one could answer, and the mother's cheek grew paler and her dear eyes grew sadder and more hopeless, until Virginia and Patty both feared that she, too, was going to leave them. Anxious, grief-stricken, filled with the belief that her husband was dead, poor Mrs. Reed was fast dying of a broken heart. But suddenly all her life, and energy, and determination were again aroused into being by a danger that would have crushed a nature less noble. A danger that is the most terrible, horrible, that ever tortured human breast; a danger— that her children, her babes, must starve to death!

CHAPTER V

GREAT HARDSHIPS — THE SINK OF THE HUMBOLDT — INDI-
ANS STEALING CATTLE — AN ENTIRE COMPANY COMPELLED
TO WALK — ABANDONED TO DIE — WOLFINGER MURDERED —
RHINEHART'S CONFESSION — ARRIVAL OF C. T. STANTON —
A TEMPORARY RELIEF — A FATAL ACCIDENT — THE SIERRA
NEVADA MOUNTAINS — IMPRISONED IN SNOW — STRUGGLES
FOR FREEDOM — A HOPELESS SITUATION — DIGGING FOR
CATTLE IN SNOW — HOW THE BREEN CABIN HAPENED TO BE
BUILT — A THRILLING SKETCH OF A SOLITARY WINTER —
PUTTING UP SHELTERS — THE DONNERS HAVE NOTHING BUT
TENTS — FISHING FOR TROUT.

STARVATION now stared the emigrants in the face. The shortest allowance capable of supporting life was all that was portioned to any member of the company. At times, some were forced to do without food for a day or more, until game was procured. The poor cattle were also in a pitiable condition. Owing to the lateness of the season, the grass was exceedingly scanty and of a poor quality. Frequently the water was bad, and filled with alkali and other poisonous deposits. George Donner, Jacob Donner, Wolfinger, and others, lost cattle at various points along the Humboldt. Mr. Breen lost a fine mare. The Indians were constantly hovering around the doomed train, ready to steal cattle, but too cowardly to make any open hostile attack. Arrows were shot into several of the oxen by Indians who slipped up near them during the night-time. At midnight, on the twelfth of October, the party reached the sink of the Humboldt. The cattle, closely guarded, were turned out to graze and recruit their wasted strength. About dawn on the morning of the thirteenth the guard came into camp to breakfast. During the night nothing had occurred to cause the least apprehension, and no indications of Indians had been observed. Imagine the consternation in camp when it was discovered that during the temporary absence of the guard twenty-one head of cattle had been stolen by the redskins. This left the company in terribly destitute circumstances. All had to walk who were able. Men, women, and children were forced to travel on foot all day long, and in many cases were compelled to carry heavy burdens in order to lessen the loads drawn by the weary cattle. Wm. G. Murphy remembers distinctly seeing his brother carrying a copper camp-kettle upon his head. The Graves family, the Breens, the Donners, the Murphys, the Reeds, all walked beside the wagons until overpowered with fatigue. The men became exhausted much sooner, as a rule, than the women. Only the sick, the little children, and the utterly exhausted, were ever allowed to ride. Eddy and his wife had lost all their cattle, and each carried one of their children and such personal effects as they were able. Many in the train were without shoes, and had to travel barefooted over the weary sands, and flinty, sharp-edged stones.

On the ninth of October a death had resulted from this necessity of having to walk. It was a case of desertion, which, under other circumstances, would have been unpardonably heartless. An old man named Hardcoop was traveling with Keseberg. He was a cutler by trade, and had a son and daughter in the city of Antwerp, in Belgium. It is said he owned a farm near Cincinnati, Ohio, and intended, after visiting California to dispose of this farm, and with the proceeds return to Antwerp, for the purpose of spending his declining years with his children. He was a man of nearly three-score years, and the hardships of the journey had weakened his trembling limbs and broken down his health. Sick, feeble, helpless as he was, this old man was compelled to walk with the others. At last, when his strength gave way, he was forced to lie down by the roadside to perish of cold and hunger. Who can picture the agony, the horror, the dreary desolation of such a death? The poor old man walked until his feet actually burst! — walked until he sank utterly exhausted by the roadside! It was a terrible death! To see the train disappear in the distance; to know he was abandoned to die of exposure and starvation; to think that the wolves would devour his flesh and gnaw his bones; to lie down on the great desert, hungry, famished, and completely prostrated by fatigue — to meet death thus is too dreadful to contemplate.

No one made any attempt to return and find the poor old fellow. This, however, is partially excused by the overwhelming dangers which now threatened the entire company. Each hour's delay rendered death in the Sierra Nevada Mountains more imminent.

About the fourteenth of October, beyond the present site of Wadsworth, another tragedy occurred. Wolfinger, who was supposed to be quite wealthy, was in the rear of the train, traveling with Keseberg. At nightfall, neither of the Germans made his appearance. It happened that both their wives had walked ahead, and were with the emigrants. Considering it suspicious that the men did not arrive, and fearing some evil had befallen them, a party returned to ascertain the cause of the delay. Before proceeding far, however, Keseberg was met traveling leisurely along. He assured them that Wolfinger was only a little way behind, and would be along in a few moments. Reassured by this information, the party returned with Keseberg to camp and awaited the arrival of Wolfinger. The night passed, and the missing man had not appeared. Mrs. Wolfinger was nearly frantic. She was a tall, queenly-looking lady, of good birth and much refinement. She was recently from Germany, and understood but little English, yet she was evidently a well-bred lady. Nearly all the survivors remember the elegant dresses and costly jewelry she wore during the first part of the journey. Her grief at her husband's disappearance was so heart-rending that three young men at last consented to start back in the morning and endeavor to find Wolfinger. W. C.

Graves, from whom this information is obtained, was one of the three who returned. Five miles back the wagon was found standing in the road. The oxen had been unhitched, but were still chained together, and were quietly grazing at a little distance. There were no signs of Indians, but Wolfinger was not to be found. At the time it was strongly conjectured that Keseberg had murdered Wolfinger for his money, and had concealed the body. This was doubtless unjust, for when Joseph Rhinehart was dying, some weeks later, in George Donner's tent, he confessed that he (Rhinehart) had something to do with the murder of Wolfinger. The men hitched the oxen to the wagon, and drove on until they overtook the emigrants, who, owing to the dangers by which they were encompassed, felt compelled to pursue their onward journey. The team was given to Mrs. Wolfinger, and she employed a German by the name of Charles Burger to drive it thereafter. Little was said about the affair at the time. Mrs. Wolfinger supposed the Indians had killed her husband.

On the nineteenth of October, C. T. Stanton was met returning with provisions. The company was near the present town of Wadsworth, Nevada. A great rejoicing was held over the brave man's return. McCutchen had been severely ill, and was unable to return with Stanton. But the latter, true to his word, recrossed the Sierra, and met the emigrants at a time when they were on the verge of starvation. He had brought seven mules, five of which were loaded with flour and dried beef. Captain Sutter had furnished these mules and the provisions, together with two Indian vaqueros, without the slightest compensation or security. The Indians, Lewis and Salvador, would assist in caring for the pack-animals, and would also be efficient guides. Without Stanton's aid the entire party would have been lost; not a single soul would have escaped. The provisions, though scant, were sufficient to entirely alter the situation of affairs. Had the party pressed immediately forward, they could have passed the summits before the storms began. For some cause, however, it was concluded to rest the cattle for a few days near the present site of Reno, preparatory to attempting to ascend the difficult Sierra. Three or four days' time was lost. This loss was fatal. The storms on the mountains generally set in about Thanksgiving, or during the latter days of November. The emigrants trusted that the storm season of 1846 would not begin earlier than usual. Alas! the terrible consequences of this mistaken trust!

After the arrival of Stanton, it was still deemed necessary to take further steps for the relief of the train. The generosity of Captain Sutter, as shown to Stanton, warranted them in believing that he would send still further supplies to the needy emigrants. Accordingly, two brothers-in-law, William Foster and William Pike, both brave and daring spirits, volunteered to go on ahead, cross the summits, and return with provisions as Stanton had done. Both men had families and both were highly esteemed in the company. At the encampment near Reno, Nevada, while they were busily preparing to start, the two men were cleaning or loading a pistol. It was an old-fashioned "pepper-box." It happened, while they were examining it, that wood was called for to replenish the fire. One of the men offered to procure it, and in order to do so, handed the pistol to the other. Everybody knows that the "pepper-box" is a very uncertain weapon. Somehow, in the transfer, the pistol was discharged. William Pike was fatally wounded, and died in about twenty minutes. Mrs. Pike was left a widow, with two small children. The youngest, Catherine, was a babe of only a few months old, and Naomi was only three years of age. The sadness and distress occasioned by this mournful accident, cast a gloom over the entire company, and seemed an omen of the terrible fate which overshadowed the Donner Party.

Generally, the ascent of the Sierra brought joy and gladness to weary overland emigrants. To the Donner Party it brought terror and dismay. The company had hardly obtained a glimpse of the mountains, ere the winter storm clouds began to assemble their hosts around the loftier crests. Every day the weather appeared more ominous and threatening. The delay at the Truckee

Meadows had been brief, but every day ultimately cost a dozen lives. On the twenty-third of October, they became thoroughly alarmed at the angry heralds of the gathering storm, and with all haste resumed the journey. It was too late! At Prosser Creek, three miles below Truckee, they found themselves encompassed with six inches of snow. On the summits, the snow was from two to five feet in depth. This was October 28, 1846. Almost a month earlier than usual, the Sierra had donned its mantle of ice and snow. The party were prisoners. All was consternation. The wildest confusion prevailed. In their eagerness, many went far in advance of the main train. There was little concert of action or harmony of plan. All did not arrive at Donner Lake the same day. Some wagons and families did not reach the lake until the thirty-first day of October, some never went further than Prosser Creek, while others, on the evening of the twenty-ninth, struggled through the snow, and reached the foot of the precipitous cliffs between the summit and the upper end of the lake. Here, baffled, wearied, disheartened, they turned back to the foot of the lake.

Several times during the days which succeeded, parties attempted to cross the mountain barrier. W. C. Graves says the old emigrant road followed up Cold Stream, and so crossed the dividing ridge. Some wagons were drawn up this old road, almost to the top of the pass, others were taken along the north side of Donner Lake, and far up toward the summit. Some of these wagons never were returned to the lake, but were left imbedded in the snow. These efforts to cross the Sierra were quite desultory and irregular, and there was great lack of harmony and system. Each family or each little group of emigrants acted independently.

At last, one day, a determined and systematic attempt was made to cross the summit. Nearly the entire train was engaged in the work. The road, of course, was entirely obliterated by the snow. Guided only by the general contour of the country, all hands pressed resolutely forward. Here, large bowlders and irregular jutting cliffs would intercept the way; there, dizzy precipices, yawning chasms, and deep, irregular canyons would interpose, and anon a bold, impassable mountain of rock would rear its menacing front directly across their path. All day long the men and animals floundered through the snow, and attempted to break and trample a road. Just before nightfall they reached the abrupt precipice where the present wagon-road intercepts the snow-sheds of the Central Pacific. Here the poor mules and oxen had been utterly unable to find a foothold on the slippery, snow-covered rocks. All that day it had been raining slightly—a dismal, drizzling, discouraging rain. Most of the wagons had been left at the lake, and the mules and oxen had been packed with provisions and necessary articles. Even at this day some of the survivors are unable to repress a ripple of merriment as they recall the manner in which the oxen bucked and bellowed when the unaccustomed packs were strapped upon their backs. Stanton had stoutly insisted upon taking the mules over the mountains. Perhaps he did not wish to return to Capt. Sutter without the property which he had borrowed. Many in the train dissented from this proposition, and endeavored to induce the Indians, Lewis and Salvador, to leave Stanton, and guide them over the summits. The Indians realized the imminent danger of each hour's delay, and would probably have yielded to the solicitations of these disaffected parties, had not Stanton made them believe that Capt. Sutter would hang them if they returned to the Fort without the mules. This incident is mentioned to illustrate the great differences of opinion and interest which prevailed. Never, from the moment the party encountered the first difficulties on the Hastings Cut-off until this fatal night in November, did the members of the company ever agree upon any important proposition. This night all decided upon a plan for the morrow. The great and overwhelming danger made them forget their petty animosities, and united them in one harmonious resolve. On the morrow the mules and cattle were all to be slain, and the meat was to be stored away for future emergency. The wagons, with their contents, were to be left at the lake, and the entire party were to cross the summits on foot. Stanton had become perfectly satisfied that the mules could not reach the mountain-top, and readily consented to the proposed plan.

Returning to the lake they sought their weary couches, comforted with the thought that to-morrow should see all the Donner Party safely over the summit. That night a heavy snow fell at the lake. It was a night of untold terror! The emigrants suffered a thousand deaths. The pitiless snow came down in large, steady masses. All understood that the storm meant death. One of the Indians silently wrapped his blanket about him and in deepest dejection seated himself beside a tall pine. In this position he passed the entire night, only moving occasionally to keep from being covered with snow. Mrs. Reed spread down a shawl, placed her four children, Virginia, Patty, James, and Thomas, thereon, and putting another shawl over them, sat by the side of her babies during all the long hours of darkness. Every little while she was compelled to lift the upper shawl and shake off the rapidly accumulating snow.

With slight interruptions, the storm continued several days. The mules and oxen that had always hovered about camp were blinded and bewildered by the storm, and straying away were literally buried alive in the drifts. What pen can describe the horror of the position in which the emigrants found themselves! It was impossible to move through the deep, soft snow without the greatest effort. The mules were gone, and were never found. Most of the cattle had perished, and were wholly hidden from sight. The few oxen which were found were slaughtered for beef. All were not killed during any one day, but the emigrants gave this business their immediate attention, because aside from the beef and a few slight provisions, the entire party were completely destitute. Mrs. Breen was compelled to attend personally to the slaughtering of their cattle, because her husband was an invalid. This family had by far the largest stock of meat. Too great praise can not be ascribed to

Mrs. Breen for the care and forethought with which she stored up this food for her children. The meat was simply laid away in piles, like cordwood, and by the action of the frost was kept fresh until consumed. Mrs. Reed had no cattle to kill. She succeeded, however, in purchasing two beeves from Mr. Graves, and two from Mr. Breen, pledging herself to pay when the journey was ended. Mr. Eddy also purchased one ox of Mr. Graves.

The flesh of many of the cattle which strayed away, and were buried several feet under the snow, was nevertheless recovered by their owners. It was soon ascertained that the cattle had endeavored to seek shelter from the fury of the storm by getting under the branches of the bushiest trees. Going to these trees, the emigrants would thrust down long poles with sharpened nails in the ends of them. By thus probing about in the snow, the whereabouts of a number of cattle was discovered, and the bodies were speedily dug out of the drifts.

Realizing that the winter must be passed in the mountains, the emigrants made such preparations as they could for shelter. One cabin was already constructed. It was located about a quarter of a mile below the foot of the lake. It had been built in November, 1844, by Moses Schallenberger, Joseph Foster, and Allen Montgomery. Moses Schallenberger now resides three and a half miles from San Jose, and when recently interviewed by Mrs. S. O. Houghton, *née* Eliza P. Donner, gave a very complete and interesting account of the building of this cabin, and the sufferings endured by his party. This cabin, known as the Breen cabin, is so intimately connected and interwoven with future chapters in the History of the Donner Party, that the following items, taken from Mr Schallenberger's narration, can not prove uninteresting:

"Mr. Schallenberger's party reached Donner Lake about the middle of November, 1844, having with them a large quantity of goods for California. Their cattle being very poor, and much fatigued by the journey, the party decided to remain here long enough to build a cabin in which to store their goods until spring. They also decided to leave some one to look after their stores, while the main portion of the party would push on to the settlement. Foster, Montgomery, and Schallenberger built the cabin. Two days were spent in its construction. It was built of pine saplings, and roofed with pine brush and rawhides. It was twelve by fourteen feet, and seven or eight feet high, with a chimney in one end, built "western style." One opening, through which light, air, and the occupants passed, served as a window and door. A heavy fall of snow began the day after the cabin was completed and continued for a number of days. Schallenberger, who was only seventeen years old, volunteered to remain with Foster and Montgomery. The party passed on, leaving very little provisions for the encamped. The flesh of one miserably poor cow was their main dependence, yet the young men were not discouraged. They were accustomed to frontier life, and felt sure they could provide for themselves. Bear and deer seemed abundant in the surrounding mountains. Time passed; the snow continued falling, until it was from ten to fifteen feet deep. The cow was more than half consumed, and the game had been driven out of the mountains by the storms.

"The sojourners in that lonely camp became alarmed at the prospect of the terrible fate which seemed to threaten them, and they determined to find their way across the mountains. They started and reached the summit the first night after leaving their camp. Here, young Schallenberger was taken ill with severe cramps. The following day he was unable to proceed more than a few feet without falling to the ground. It was evident to his companions that he could go no farther. They did not like to leave him, nor did they wish to remain where death seemed to await them. Finally Schallenberger told them if they would take him back to the cabin he would remain there and they could go on. This they did, and after making him as comfortable as possible, they bade him good-by, and he was left alone in that mountain wild. A strong will and an unflinching determination to live through all the threatening dangers, soon raised him from his bed and nerved him to action. He found some steel traps among the goods stored, and with them caught foxes, which constituted his chief or only article of food, until rescued by the returning party, March 1, 1845."

The Breen family moved into the Schallenberger cabin. Against the west side of this cabin, Keseberg built a sort of half shed, into which he and his family entered. The Murphys erected a cabin nearer the lake. The site of this cabin is plainly marked by a large stone about ten or twelve feet high, one side of which rises almost perpendicularly from the ground. Against this perpendicular side the Murphys erected the building which was to shelter them during the winter. It was about three hundred yards from the shore of Donner Lake, and near the wide marshy outlet. The Breen and Murphy cabins were distant from each other about one hundred and fifty yards. The Graves family built a house close by Donner Creek, and half or three quarters of a mile further down the stream. Adjoining this, forming a double cabin, the Reeds built. The Donner brothers, Jacob and George, together with their families, camped in Alder Creek Valley, six or seven miles from Donner Lake. They were, if possible, in a worse condition than the others, for they had only brush sheds and their tents to shield them from the wintry weather. Mrs. John App (Leanna C. Donner), of Jamestown, Tuolumne County, writes: "We had no time to build a cabin. The snow came on so suddenly that we had barely time to pitch our tent, and put up a brush shed, as it were, one side of which was open. This brush shed was covered with pine boughs, and then covered with rubber coats, quilts, etc. My uncle, Jacob Donner, and family, also had a tent, and camped near us."

Crowded in their ill-prepared dwellings, the emigrants could not feel otherwise than gloomy and despondent. The small quantity of provisions became so nearly exhausted that it is correct to say they were compelled to live on meat alone, without so much as salt to give it a relish. There was an abundance of beautiful trout in the lake, but no one could catch them. W. C. Graves tells how he went fishing two or three different times, but without success. The lake was not frozen over at first, and fish were frequently seen; but they were too coy and wary to approach such bait as was offered. Soon thick ice covered the water, and after that no one attempted to fish. In fact, the entire party seemed dazed by the terrible calamity which had overtaken them.

CHAPTER VI

ALL knew that death speedily awaited the entire company unless
some could cross over the mountain barrier and hasten back
relief parties. Out of the list of ninety persons mentioned in the
first chapter, only Mrs. Sarah Keyes, Halloran, Snyder, Hardcoop,
Wolfinger, and Pike had perished, and only three, Messrs. Reed,
Herron, and McCutchen, had reached California. This left
eighty-one persons at the mountain camps. It was resolved that at
the earliest possible moment the strongest and ablest of the party
should endeavor to cross the summits and reach the settlements.
Accordingly, on the twelfth of November, a party of twelve or fifteen persons set out from the cabins. It was found impossible,
however, to make any considerable headway in the soft, deep
snow, and at midnight they returned to the cabins. They had not
succeeded in getting more than a mile above the head of the
lake. In this party were Mr. F. W. Graves and his two daughters,
Mary A. Graves, and Mrs. Sarah Fosdick. The rest, with the exception of Jay Fosdick and Wm. H. Eddy, were young, unmarried

men, as, for instance, Stanton, Smith, Spitzer, Elliott, Antoine, John Baptiste, and the two Indians. It was comparatively a trifling effort, but it seemed to have the effect of utterly depressing the hopes of several of these men. With no one in the camps dependent upon them, without any ties of relationship, or bonds of affection, these young men were the first to attempt to escape from their prison walls of snow. Failing in this, many of them never again rallied or made a struggle for existence. Not so, however, with those who were heads of families. A gun was owned by William Foster, and with it, on the fourteenth of November, three miles north of Truckee, near the present Alder Creek Mill, Mr. Eddy succeeded in killing a bear. This event inspired many hearts with courage; but, alas! it was short-lived. No other game could be found except two or three wild ducks. What were these among eighty-one people! Mr. F. W. Graves was a native of Vermont, and his boyhood days had been spent in sight of the Green Mountains. Somewhat accustomed to snow, and to pioneer customs, Mr. Graves was the only member of the party who understood how to construct snow-shoes. The unsuccessful attempt made by the first party proved that no human being could walk upon the loose snow without some artificial assistance. By carefully sawing the ox-bows into strips, so as to preserve their curved form, Mr. Graves, by means of rawhide thongs, prepared very serviceable snow-shoes. Fourteen pair of shoes were made in this manner. It was certain death for all to remain in camp, and yet the first attempt had shown that it was almost equally certain death to attempt to reach the settlements. There was not food for all, and yet the ones who undertook to cross the mountains were undoubtedly sacrificing their lives for those who remained in camp. If some should go, those who were left behind might be able to preserve life until spring, or until relief came. The stoutest hearts quailed before the thought of battling with the deep drifts, the storms, and the unknown dangers which lurked on the summits. The bravest shuddered at the idea of leaving the cabins and venturing out into the drear and dismal wilderness of snow. Yet they could count upon their fingers the days that would elapse before the provisions would be exhausted, and starvation would ensue, if none left the camps.

Day after day, with aching hearts and throbbing brows, the poor imprisoned wretches gazed into each other's faces in blank despair. Who should be sacrificed? Who would go out and seek a grave 'neath the crashing avalanche, the treacherous drifts, or in the dreary famished wilderness, that those left behind might live? Who would be the forlorn hope of the perishing emigrants?

Once, Messrs. Patrick Breen, Patrick Dolan, Lewis Keseberg, and W. H. Eddy, are said to have attempted to reach the summit. On another occasion these same parties, with Mrs. Reed and family, Mr. Stanton and the two Indians, made an unsuccessful attempt. Still another time, a large party, among whom were Mrs. Murphy and the older members of her family, made the effort, and even succeeded in crossing the topmost ridge and reaching Summit Valley, one and a half miles west of the summit. But all these parties were forced to return to the cabins, and each failure confirmed the belief that no living being could cross the mountains. In this manner time dragged wearily along until the tenth, or, as some say, the sixteenth of December. The mere matter of the date is of trifling importance. At all events a forlorn hope was organized. Seventeen names were enrolled as volunteers. Of these, Charles Burger went only a short distance, turning back weary and exhausted. Wm. G. Murphy, who is described as a most brave and resolute boy of eleven years of age, accompanied the party as far as the head of Donner Lake. He and his brother Lemuel were without snow-shoes. It was expected they would step in the beaten tracks of those who had shoes, but this was soon proven to be utterly impracticable. The party made snow-shoes for Lemuel on the first night, out of the *aparajos* which had been brought by Stanton from Sutter's Fort. Wm. G. Murphy saved his life by returning to the cabins. No human being could have endured the trip without snow-shoes. Fifteen remained in the party, and these pressed forward without so much as daring to look back to the dear ones whose lives depended upon this terrible venture. Without forgetting William G. Murphy and Charles Burger, who started with this little band, the first party who crossed the Sierra will in future be termed the fifteen. Who composed this party? Mothers, whose babes would starve unless the mothers went; fathers, whose wives and children would perish if the fathers did not go; children, whose aged parents could not survive unless the children, by leaving, increased the parents' share of food. Each were included in the forlorn hope.

It was time for some one to leave the cabins. During the days that had elapsed, no word had been received from the Donner brothers at Alder Creek, nor from the emigrants who camped with them. Alder Creek is a branch of Prosser Creek, and the Donners encamped on the former stream about a mile and a half above the junction.

On the ninth of December, Milton Elliott and Noah James started back to learn some tidings of these people. Soon after they left the camps at the lake, a terrific storm came down from the mountains, and as nothing had been heard from them, it was considered certain they had perished.

About this time, starvation and exposure had so preyed upon one of the company, Augustus Spitzer, that one day he came reeling and staggering into the Breen cabin and fell prostrate and helpless upon the floor. Poor fellow, he never rallied, although by careful nursing and kindest attentions he lingered along for some weeks. The emigrants were no longer on short allowance, they were actually starving! Oh! the horror! the dread alarm which prevailed among the company! C. T. Stanton, ever brave, courageous, lion-hearted, said, "I will bring help to these famishing people or lay down my life." F. W. Graves, who was one of the noblest men who ever breathed the breath of life, was next to volunteer. Mr. and Mrs. Graves had nine children, the youngest being only nine months old. Generously had they parted with the cattle which they brought to the lake, dividing equally with those families who had no food. Mary A. Graves and her elder sister, Mrs. Sarah Fosdick, determined to accompany their father, and as will presently be seen, their hearts failed not during trials which crushed strong men. Mary Graves was about nineteen years old. She was a very beautiful girl, of tall and slender build, and exceptionally graceful carriage. Her features, in their regularity, were of classic Grecian mold. Her eyes were dark, bright, and expressive. A fine mouth and perfect set of teeth, added to a luxuriant growth of dark, rebelliously wavy hair, completed an almost perfect picture of lovely girlhood. Jay Fosdick resolved to share with his wife the perils of the way. Mrs. Murphy offered to take care of the infant children of her married daughters, Mrs. Foster and Mrs. Pike, if they would join the party. The dear, good mother argued that what the daughters would eat would keep her and the little ones from starving. It was nobly said, yet who can doubt but that, with clearer vision, the mother saw that only by urging them to go, could she save her daughters' lives. With what anguish did Mrs. Harriet F. Pike enroll her name among those of the "Forlorn Hope," and bid good-by to her little two-year-old Naomi and her nursing babe, Catherine! What bitter tears were shed by Mr. and Mrs. Foster when they kissed their beautiful baby boy farewell! Alas! though they knew it not, it was a long, long farewell. Mrs. Eddy was too feeble to attempt the journey, and the family were so poorly provided with food that Mr. Eddy was compelled to leave her and the two little children in the cabins, and go with the party. Mrs. McCutchen also had an infant babe, and Mrs. Graves employed the same reasoning with her that Mrs. Murphy had so effectively used with Mrs. Pike and Mrs. Foster. That these three young mothers left their infant children, their nursing babes, with others, and started to find relief, is proof stronger than words, of the desperate condition of the starving emigrants. The Mexican Antoine, the two Indians Lewis and Salvador, and an Irishman named Patrick Dolan, completed the fifteen. This Patrick Dolan deserves more than a passing word. He had owned a farm in Keokuk, Iowa, and selling it, had taken as the price, a wagon, four oxen, and two cows. With these he joined the Donner Party, and on reaching the lake had killed his cattle and stored them away with those killed by the Breens. Dolan was a bachelor, and about forty years of age. He was possessed of two or three hundred dollars in coin, but instead of being miserly or selfish, was characterized by generous open-heartedness. "When it became apparent that there was to be suffering and starvation" (this quotation is from the manuscript of Hon. James F. Breen), "Dolan determined to lighten the burden at the camps, and leave with the party that was to attempt the passage of the summit, so that there should be less to consume the scant supply of provisions. Previous to his departure, he asked my father (Patrick Breen) to attend to the wants of Reed's family, and to give of his (Dolan's) meat to Reed's family as long as possible." Accordingly, Mrs. Reed and her children were taken into Breen's cabin, where, as mentioned above, Dolan's meat was stored. Was ever a more generous act recorded? Patrick Dolan had no relative in the Donner Party, and no friends, save those whose friendship had been formed upon the plains. With the cattle which belonged to him he could have selfishly subsisted until relief came, but, whole-souled Irishman that he was, he gave food to the mothers and the children and went out into the waste of snow to perish of starvation! How many who live to-day owe their existence to Patrick Dolan's self-sacrifice! This blue-eyed, brown-haired Irishman is described as being of a jovial disposition, and inclined to look upon the bright side of things. Remembering how he gave his life for strangers, how readily can we appreciate Mr. Breen's tender tribute: "He was a favorite with children, and would romp and play with a child." As a token of appreciation for his kindness, Mrs. Reed gave Patrick Dolan a gold watch and a Masonic emblem belonging to her husband, bidding him to keep them until he was rewarded for his generosity. The good mother's word had a significance she wot not of. When Mrs. Reed reached Sutter's Fort she found these valuables awaiting her. They had been brought in by Indians. Patrick Dolan had kept them until his death—until the angels came and bore him away to his reward.

This party of fifteen had taken provisions to last only six days. At the end of this time they hoped to reach Bear Valley, so they said, but it is more than probable they dared not take more food from their dear ones at the cabins. Six days' rations! This means enough of the poor, shriveled beef to allow each person, three times a day, a piece the size of one's two fingers. With a little coffee and a little loaf sugar, this was all. They had matches, Foster's gun, a hatchet, and each a thin blanket. With this outfit they started to cross the Sierra. No person, unaccustomed to snowshoes, can form an idea of the difficulty which is experienced during one's first attempt to walk with them. Their shoes would sink deep into the loose, light snow, and it was with great effort they made any progress. They had been at Donner Lake from forty-two to forty-six days, and on this first night of their journey had left it four miles behind them. After a dreadful day's work they encamped, in full sight of the lake and of the cabins. This was harder for the aching hearts of the mothers than even the terrible parting from their little ones. To see the smoke of the cabins, to awake from their troubled dreams, thinking they heard the cry of their starving babes, to stifle the maternal yearnings which prompted them to turn back and perish with their darlings clasped to their breasts, were trials almost unbearable. The next day they traveled six miles. They crossed the summit, and the camps were no longer visible. They were in the solemn fastnesses of the snow-mantled Sierra. Lonely, desolate, forsaken apparently by God and man, their situation was painfully, distressingly terrible. The snow was wrapped about cliff and forest and gorge. It varied in depth from twelve to sixty feet.

Mrs. M. A. Clarke (Mary Graves), now of White River, Tulare County, speaking of this second day, says: "We had a very slavish day's travel, climbing the divide. Nothing of interest occurred until reaching the summit. The scenery was too grand for me to pass without notice, the changes being so great; walking now on loose snow, and now stepping on a hard, slick rock a number of hundred yards in length. Being a little in the rear of the party, I had a chance to observe the company ahead, trudging along with packs on their backs. It reminded me of some Norwegian fur company among the icebergs. My shoes were ox-bows, split in two, and rawhide strings woven in, something in form of the old-fashioned, split-bottomed chairs. Our clothes were of the bloomer costume, and generally were made of flannel. Well do I remember a remark one of the company made here, that we were about as near heaven as we could get. We camped a little on the west side of the summit the second night."

Here they gathered a few boughs, kindled a fire upon the surface of the snow, boiled their coffee, and ate their pitiful allowance of beef; then wrapping their toil-worn blankets, lay down upon the snow. As W. C. Graves remarks, it was a bed that was soft, and white, and beautiful, and yet it was a terrible bed—a bed of death. The third day they walked five miles. Starting almost at dawn, they struggled wearily through the deep drifts, and when the night shadows crept over crag and pine and mountain vale, they were but five miles on their journey. They did not speak during the day, except when speech was absolutely necessary. All traveled silently, and with downcast eyes. The task was beginning to tell upon the frames of even the strongest and most resolute. The hunger that continually gnawed at their vitals, the excessive labor of moving the heavy, clumsy snow-shoes through the soft, yielding snow, was too much for human endurance. They could no longer keep together and aid each other with words of hope. They struggled along, sometimes at great distances apart. The fatigue and dazzling sunlight rendered some of them snow-blind. One of these was the noble-hearted Stanton. On this third day he was too blind and weak to keep up with the rest, and staggered into the camp long after the others had finished their pitiful supper. Poor, brave, generous Stanton! He said little, but in his inner heart he knew that the end of his journey was almost at hand.

Who was this heroic being who left the beautiful valleys of the Sacramento to die for strangers? See him wearily toiling onward during the long hours of the fourth day. The agony and blindness of his eyes wring no cry from his lips, no murmur, no word of complaint. With patient courage and heroic fortitude he strives to keep pace with his companions, but finds it impossible. Early in the morning he drops to the rear, and is soon lost to sight. At night he drags his weary limbs into camp long after his comrades are sleeping 'neath the silent stars. It must be remembered that they had been accustomed to short allowance of food for months, while he had been used to having an abundance. Their bodies had been schooled to endure famine, privations, and long, weary walks. For many days before reaching the mountains, they had been used to walking every day, in order to lighten the burdens of the perishing oxen. Fatigues which exhausted them crushed Stanton. The weather was clear and pleasant, but the glare of the sun during the day had been like molten fire to their aching eyes.

On the morning of the fifth day Stanton was sitting smoking by the smoldering fire when the company resumed its journey. Mary Graves, who had a tender heart for the suffering of others, went kindly up to him, and asked him if he were coming. "Yes," he replied, "I am coming soon." Was he answering her, or the unseen spirits that even then were beckoning him to the unknown world? "Yes, I am coming soon!" These were his last words. His companions were too near death's door to return when they found he came not, and so he perished. He had begged them piteously to lead him, during the first days of his blindness, but seeming to realize that they were unable to render assistance, he ceased to importune, and heroically met his fate. He did not blame his comrades. They were weak, exhausted, and ready to die of starvation. With food nearly gone, strength failing, hope lost, and nothing left but the last, blind, clinging instinct of life, it was impossible that the perishing company should have aided the perishing Stanton. He was a hero of the highest, noblest, grandest stamp. No words can ever express a fitting tribute to his memory. He gave his life for strangers who had not the slightest claim to the sacrifice. He left the valleys where friends, happiness, and abundance prevailed, to perish amidst chilling snow-drifts—famished and abandoned. The act of returning to save the starving emigrants is as full of heroic grandeur as his death is replete with mournful desolation.

In May, 1847, W. C. Graves, in company with a relief party, found the remains of C. T. Stanton near the spot where he had been left by his companions. The wild animals had partially devoured his body, but the remains were easily identified by means of his clothing and pistols.

The following sketch of this hero is kindly furnished by his brother, Sidney Stanton, of Cazenovia, New York:

"Charles Tyler Stanton was born at Pompey, Onondaga County, New York, March 11, 1811. He was five feet five inches in height. He had brown eyes and brown hair. He possessed a robust constitution, and although rather slender during his youth, at the age of fifteen he became strong and hearty, and could endure as great hardships as any of his brothers. He had five brothers and four sisters, and was the seventh child. His grandparents, on his father's side, were well off at the close of the revolutionary war, but sold their large farms, and took Continental money in payment. Soon afterward this money became worthless, and they lost all. They were at the time living in Berkshire, Massachusetts, but soon after removed west to the county where C. T. Stanton was born. There were in his father's family fourteen children—seven sons and seven daughters."

In his younger days Stanton was engaged as a clerk in a store. He was honest, industrious, and greatly beloved by those with whom he came in contact. His early education was limited, but during his employment as clerk he used every possible endeavor to improve his mind. During his journey across the plains, he was regarded as somewhat of a savant, on account of his knowledge of botany, geology, and other branches of natural science. His disposition was generous to a fault. He never was happier than when bestowing assistance upon needy friends. His widowed mother, for whom he entertained the most devoted affection, was kindly cared for by him until her death in 1835. After this sad event he removed to Chicago. At Chicago he made money rapidly for a time, and his hand was ever ready to give aid to those about him. Charity and heroic self-sacrifice appear to have been his predominant characteristics. They stand out in bold relief, not only in his early history, but during his connection with the Donner Party. While in the mountains he had no money to give, but instead he gave his strength, his energy, his love, his all, his very life, for his companions.

That he had a premonition of the gloomy fate which overtook him in the Sierra, or at least that he fully realized the perils to which he was exposing his life, is indicated by the following incident: When he set out from Sutter's Fort to return to the Donner train with provisions, he left a vest with Captain Sutter. In one of the pockets of this vest was subsequently found a package directed to the Captain with the following memorandum: "Captain Sutter will send the within, in the event of my death, to Sidney Stanton, Syracuse, New York." The package contained a diamond breast-pin. Mr. Sidney Stanton writes as follows concerning this keepsake:

"I will give you a short history or account of the pin which was left for me at Sutter's Fort, which Mr. McKinstry forwarded to me. This was an event so peculiar at the time. He visited me here at Syracuse, while he was prospering in Chicago. He was on his way to New York, and wanted a sum of money, which I advanced. Before leaving he fastened this pin on the dress of my wife, remarking that she must consider it as a present from him. Nothing more was thought of this event until he again wanted money. Misfortune had overtaken him, and this event gave him much pain, not so much on his own account as because he could not relieve the distress of dear friends when asked for aid. I sent him a little more money; I had not much to spare, and in talking the matter over with my wife, she asked, 'Why not send him the pin? It is valuable, and in time of need he might dispose of it for his comfort.' In saying this she took the ground that it was left with her as a pledge, not as a gift. I therefore handed it to my sister to send to him for this purpose. But it appears by his keeping it and sending it back in the way he did, that he did consider it a gift, and hence he would not and did not dispose of it for necessary things for his own comfort. This pin was the only thing of value which he had at the time of his death."

Stanton was an excellent writer. His descriptions of his travels from Chicago to the South would make a good-sized and a very interesting book. His last composition is given below. It is an appropriate ending to this brief outline of the history of one who should be regarded as one of the noblest of California's pioneer heroes:

"TO MY MOTHER IN HEAVEN.

"Oh, how that word my soul inspires
With holy, fond, and pure desires!
    Maternal love, how bright the flame!
    For wealth of worlds I'd not profane
    Nor idly breathe thy sacred name,
        My mother.

"Thy sainted spirit dwells on high.
How oft I weep, how oft I sigh
    Whene'er I think of bygone time,
    Thy smile of love, which once was mine,
    That look so heavenly and divine,
        My mother.

"Thy warning voice in prayers of love,
Ascending to the throne above
    With tones of eloquence so rife,
    Hath turned my thoughts from wordly strife,
    And cheered me through my wayward life,
        My mother.

"When death shall close my sad career,
And I before my God appear—
     There to receive His last decree—
     My only prayer there will be
     Forever to remain with thee,
          My mother."

CHAPTER VII

A WIFE'S DEVOTION — THE SMOKY GORGE — CAUGHT IN A
STORM — CASTING LOTS TO SEE WHO SHOULD DIE — A HIDDEN
RIVER — THE DELIRIUM OF STARVATION — FRANKLIN WARD
GRAVES — HIS DYING ADVICE — A FRONTIERSMAN'S PLAN —
THE CAMP OF DEATH — A DREAD RESORT — A SISTER'S AGONY —
THE INDIANS REFUSE TO EAT — LEWIS AND SALVADOR FLEE
FOR THEIR LIVES — KILLING A DEER — TRACKS MARKED BY
BLOOD — NINE DAYS WITHOUT FOOD.

LET no one censure Stanton's companions for abandoning their
brave comrade. In less than twenty-four hours all were without food,
unless, indeed, it was Mr. Eddy, who, in his narration published by
Judge Thornton, states that on the day of Stanton's death he found
half a pound of bear's meat which had been secreted in a little bag by
his wife. Attached to this meat was a paper, upon which his wife had
written in pencil a note signed, "Your own dear Eleanor." Mr. Eddy
had not discovered this meat until the sorest hour of need, and the
hope expressed in Mrs. Eddy's note, that it would be the means of
saving his life, was literally fulfilled. There is something extremely
touching in the thought that this devoted wife, who, as will presently
be seen, was starving to death in the cabins, saved her husband's life
by clandestinely concealing about his person a portion of the food
which should have sustained herself and her infant children.

In the account given by Mary Graves, is mentioned the following incident in the fourth day's travel: "Observing by the way a
deep gorge at the right, having the appearance of being full of

smoke, I wanted very much to go to it, but the Indians said no, that was not the way. I prevailed on the men to fire the gun, but there was no answer. Every time we neared the gorge I would halloo at the top of my voice, but we received no answer."

On this day the horror of the situation was increased by the commencement of a snow-storm. As the flakes fell thick and fast, the party sat down in the snow utterly discouraged and heartsick.

Mary Graves says: "What to do we did not know. We held a consultation, whether to go ahead without provisions, or go back to the cabins, where we must undoubtedly starve. Some of those who had children and families wished to go back, but the two Indians said they would go on to Captain Sutter's. I told them I would go too, for to go back and hear the cries of hunger from my little brothers and sisters was more than I could stand. I would go as far as I could, let the consequences be what they might."

There, in the deep, pitiless storm, surrounded on all sides by desolate wastes of snow, the idea was first advanced that life might be sustained if some one were to perish. Since leaving the cabins, they had at no time allowed themselves more than one ounce of meat per meal, and for two entire days they had not tasted food. The terrible pangs of hunger must be speedily allayed or death was inevitable. Some one proposed that lots be cast to see who should die. The terrible proposition met with opposition from Foster and others, but slips of paper were actually prepared by some of the men, and he who drew the longest— the fatal slip—was Patrick Dolan. Who should take Dolan's life? Who was to be the executioner of the man who had so generously given up the food which might have sustained his life, and joined the forlorn hope that others might live? With one accord they rose to their feet and staggered forward. As if to banish from their minds the horrid thought of taking Dolan's life, they attempted to pursue their journey.

With the greatest exertion and suffering they managed to crawl, and stagger, and flounder along until they attained a distance of two or three miles. Here they camped, and passed a most wretched, desolate night. The morning dawned; it was dreary, rainy, and discouraging. The little party set out as usual, but were too weak and lifeless to travel. The soft snow clung to their feet in heavy lumps like snow-balls. Instead of making a fire in a new place, Mary Graves says they crawled back to the camp-fire of the night previous. Here they remained until night came on — a night full of horrors. The wind howled through the shrieking forests like troops of demons. The rain had continued all day, but finally changed to snow and sleet, which cut their pinched faces, and made them shiver with cold. All the forces of nature seemed to combine for their destruction. At one time during the night, in attempting to kindle a fire, the ax or hatchet which they had carried was lost in the loose snow.

A huge fire was kindled at last, with the greatest difficulty, and in order to obtain more warmth, all assisted in piling fuel upon the flames. Along in the night, Mr. Foster thinks it was near midnight, the heat of the flames and the dropping coals and embers thawed the snow underneath the fire until a deep, well-like cavity was formed about the fire. Suddenly, as if to intensify the dreadful horrors of the situation, the bottom of this well gave way, and the fire disappeared! The camp and the fire had been built over a stream of water, and the fire had melted through the overlying snow until it had fallen into the stream! Those who peered over the brink of the dark opening about which they were gathered, could hear, far down in the gloom, during the lull of the storm, the sound of running waters.

If there is anything lacking in this picture of despair, it is furnished in the groans and cries of the shivering, dying outcasts, and the demoniacal shrieks and ravings of Patrick Dolan, who was in the delirium which precedes death. It was not necessary that life should be taken by the members of the company. Death was busily at work, and before the wild winter night was ended, his ghastly victims were deaf to wind or storm.

When the fire disappeared, it became apparent that the entire forlorn hope would perish before morning if exposed to the cold and storm. W. H. Eddy says the wind increased until it was a perfect tornado. About midnight, Antoine, overcome by starvation, fatigue, and the bitter cold, ceased to breathe. Mr. F. W. Graves was dying. There was a point beyond which an iron nerve and a powerful constitution were unable to sustain a man. This point had been reached, and Mr. Graves was fast passing away. He was conscious, and calling his weeping, grief-stricken daughters to his side, exhorted them to use every means in their power to prolong their lives. He reminded them of their mother, of their little brothers and sisters in the cabin at the lake. He reminded Mrs. Pike of her poor babies. Unless these daughters succeeded in reaching Sutter's Fort, and were able to send back relief, all at the lake must certainly die. Instances had been cited in history, where, under less provocation, human flesh had been eaten, yet Mr. Graves well knew that his daughters had said they would never touch the loathsome food.

Was there not something noble and grand in the dying advice of this father? Was he not heroic when he counseled that all false delicacy be laid aside and that his body be sacrificed to support those that were to relieve his wife and children?

Earnestly pleading that these afflicted children rise superior to their prejudices and natural instincts—Franklin Ward Graves died. A sublimer death seldom is witnessed. In the solemn darkness, in the tempestuous storm, on the deep, frozen snow-drifts, overcome by pain and exposure, with the pangs of famine gnawing away his life, this unselfish father, with his latest breath urged that his flesh be used to prolong the lives of his companions. Truly, a soul that could prompt such utterances had no need, after death, for its mortal tenement—it had a better dwelling-place on high.

With two of their little number in the icy embraces of death, some plan to obtain warmth for the living was immediately necessary. W. H. Eddy proposed a frontiersman's method. It was for all to huddle closely together in a circle, lie down on a blanket with their heads outward, and be covered with a second blanket. Mr. Eddy arranged his companions, spread the blanket over them, and creeping under the coverlid, completed the circle. The wind swept the drifting snow in dense clouds over their heads. The chilling air, already white with falling snowflakes, became dense with the drifting masses. In a little while the devoted band were completely hidden from wind, or storm, or piercing cold, by a deep covering of snow. The warmth of their bodies, confined between the blankets, under the depth of snow, soon rendered them comfortably warm. Their only precaution now was to keep from being buried alive. Occasionally some member of the party would shake the rapidly accumulating snow from off their coverlid.

They no longer were in danger of freezing. But while the elements were vainly waging fierce war above their heads, hunger was rapidly sapping the fountains of life, and claiming them for its victims. When, for a moment, sleep would steal away their reason, in famished dreams they would seize with their teeth the hand or arm of a companion. The delirium of death had attacked one or two, and the pitiful wails and cries of these death-stricken maniacs were heart-rending. The dead, the dying, the situation, were enough to drive one crazy.

The next day was ushered in by one of the most furious storms ever witnessed on the Sierra. All the day long, drifts and the fast-falling snow circled above them under the force of the fierce gale. The air was a frozen fog of swift-darting ice-lances. The fine particles of snow and sleet, hurled by maddened storm-fiends, would cut and sting so that one's eyes could not be opened in the storm, and the rushing gale would hurl one prostrate on the snow. Once or twice the demented Dolan escaped from his companions and disappeared in the blinding storm. Each time he returned or was caught and dragged 'neath the covering, but the fatal exposure chilled the little life remaining in his pulses. During the afternoon he ceased to shriek, or struggle, or moan. Patrick Dolan, the warm-hearted Irishman, was starved to death.

Mr. Eddy states, in Thornton's work, that they entered this Camp of Death, Friday, December 25, Christmas. According to his version they started from the cabins on the sixteenth day of December, with scanty rations for six days. On the twenty-second they consumed the last morsel of their provisions. Not until

Sunday noon, December 27, did the storm break away. They had been over four days without food, and two days and a half without fire. They were almost dead.

Is there a mind so narrow, so uncharitable, that it can censure these poor dying people for the acts of this terrible day? With their loved ones perishing at Donner Lake, with the horror of a lingering death staring them in the face, can the most unfeeling heart condemn them?

Emerging from the dreary prison-house, they attempted to kindle a fire. Their matches were wet and useless. Their flint-lock gun would give forth a spark, but without some dry material that would readily ignite, it was of no avail.

On this morning of the twenty-seventh Eddy says that he blew up a powder-horn in an effort to strike fire under the blankets. His face and hands were much burned. Mrs. McCutchen and Mrs. Foster were also burned, but not seriously. For some time all efforts to obtain a fire proved fruitless. Their garments were drenched by the storm. Mrs. Pike had a mantle that was lined with cotton. The lining of this was cut open, and the driest portion of the cotton was exposed to the sun's rays, in the hope that it could be made to catch the spark from the flint. At last they were successful. A fire was kindled in a dead tree, and the flames soon leaped up to the loftiest branches. The famished, shivering wretches gathered round the burning tree. So weak and lifeless were they that when the great pine limbs burned off and fell crashing about them, neither man nor woman moved or attempted to escape the threatening danger. All felt that sudden death would be welcome. They were stunned and horrified by the dreadful alternative which it was evident they must accept.

The men finally mustered up courage to approach the dead. With averted eyes and trembling hand, pieces of flesh were severed from the inanimate forms and laid upon the coals. It was the very refinement of torture to taste such food, yet those who tasted lived. One could not eat. Lemuel Murphy was past relief. A boy about thirteen years old, Lemuel was dearly loved by his sisters, and, full of courage, had endeavored to accompany them on the fearful journey. He was feeble when he started from the cabins, and the overwhelming sufferings of the fatal trip had destroyed his remaining, strength. Starvation is agony during the first three days, apathy and inanition during the fourth and perhaps the fifth, and delirium from that time until the struggle ceases. When the delirium commences, hope ends. Lemuel was delirious Sunday morning, and when food was placed to his lips he either could not eat or was too near death to revive. All day Mrs. Foster held her brother's head in her lap, and by every means in her power sought to soothe his death agonies. The sunlight faded from the surrounding summits. Darkness slowly emerged from the canyons and enfolded forest and hill-slope in her silent embrace. The glittering stars appeared in the heavens, and the bright, full moon rose over the eastern mountain crests. The silence, the profound solitude, the ever-present wastes of snow, the weird moonlight, and above all the hollow moans of the dying boy in her lap, rendered this night the most impressive in the life of Mrs. Foster. She says she never beholds a bright moonlight without recurring with a shudder to this night on the Sierra. At two o'clock in the morning Lemuel Murphy ceased to breathe. The warm tears and kisses of the afflicted sisters were showered upon lips that would never more quiver with pain.

Until the twenty-ninth of December they remained at the "Camp of Death." Would you know more of the shuddering details? Does the truth require the narration of the sickening minutiæ of the terrible transactions of these days? Human beings were never called upon to undergo more trying ordeals. Dividing into groups, the members of each family were spared the pain of touching their own kindred. Days and perhaps weeks of starvation were awaiting them in the future, and they dare not neglect to provide as best they might. Each of the four bodies was divested of its flesh, and the flesh was dried. Although no person partook of kindred flesh, sights were often witnessed that were blood-curdling. Mrs. Foster, as we have seen, fairly worshiped her brother Lemuel. Has human pen power to express the shock of horror this sister received when she saw her brother's heart thrust through with a stick, and broiling upon the coals? No man can record or read such an occurrence without a cry of agony! What, then, did she endure who saw this cruel sight?

These are facts. They are given just as they came from the lips of Mrs. Foster, a noble woman, who would have died of horror and a broken heart but for her starving babe, her mother, and her little brothers and sisters who were at Donner Lake. Mary Graves corroborates Mrs. Foster, and W. H. Eddy gave a similar version to Judge Thornton.

The Indian guides, Lewis and Salvador, would not eat this revolting food. They built a fire away from the company, and with true Indian stoicism endured the agonies of starvation without so much as beholding the occurrences at the other camp-fire.

Starved bodies possess little flesh, and starving people could carry but light burdens through such snow-drifts. On these accounts, the provision which the Almighty seemed to have provided to save their lives, lasted only until the thirty-first On New Year's morning they ate their moccasins and the strings of their snow-shoes. On the night before, Lewis and Salvador caught the sound of ominous words, or perceived glances that were filled with dreadful import, and during the darkness they fled.

For several days past the party had been lost. The Indians could not recognize the country when it was hidden from thirty to fifty feet in snow. Blindly struggling forward, they gradually separated into three parties. On the fourth, W. H. Eddy and Mary Graves were in advance with the gun. A starved deer crossed their path and providentially was slain. Drinking its warm blood and feasting upon its flesh, this couple waited for the arrival of Mr. and Mrs. Foster, Mrs. McCutchen, and Mrs. Pike, who were some distance behind. Night came and passed and they did not arrive. Indeed, Foster was dying for lack of nourishment. Behind this party were Mr. and Mrs. Jay Fosdick. During the night, Mr. Fosdick perished, and the faithful wife, after remaining with him until morning, struggled forward and met Mrs. Foster and a companion. Mrs. Fosdick related the death of her husband, and upon being informed of Foster's condition, consented that her husband's body be converted into food. It was done. This was the first time that women's hands had used the knife, but by the act a life was saved. Mrs. Fosdick, although dying, would not touch the food, and but for the venison would not have lived to see the setting of the sun. But what was one small deer among so many famished people? Hide, head, feet, entrails, all were eaten. On the sixth, the last morsel was consumed. They were now without hope. Their journey was apparently interminable. Wearied, foot-sore, freezing at night and tortured by hunger during the day, life could not last many hours. Some one must die; else none could live and reach the long-talked-of relief. Would it be Eddy, whose wife and two children were behind? Would it be Mrs. Pike, who left two babes? Mrs. McCutchen, who left one? Mr. or Mrs. Foster, whose baby boy was at the cabin? Or would it be Mary Graves or Mrs. Fosdick, who had left mother and family? On the night of the seventh, they lay down upon the snow without having tasted a mouthful of food during the day. Continued famine and exhaustion had so weakened their frames that they could not survive another day. Yet, on the morning of the seventh, they arose and staggered onward. Soon they halted and gathered about some freshly made tracks. Tracks marked by blood! Tracks that they knew had been made by Lewis and Salvador, whose bare feet were sore and bleeding from cuts and bruises inflicted by the cruel, jagged rocks, the frozen snow, and flinty ice. These Indians had eaten nothing for nine days, and had been without fire or blankets for four days. They could not be far ahead.

CHAPTER VIII

STARVATION AT DONNER LAKE — PREPARING RAWHIDE FOR
FOOD — EATING THE FIRE-RUG — SHOVELING SNOW OFF THE
BEDS — PLAYING THEY WERE TEA-CUPS OF CUSTARD — A
STARVING BABY — PLEADING WITH SILENT ELOQUENCE —
PATRICK BREEN'S DIARY — JACOB DONNER'S DEATH — A
CHILD'S VOW — A CHRISTMAS DINNER — LOST ON THE SUM-
MITS — A STUMP TWENTY-TWO FEET HIGH — SEVEN NURSING
BABES AT DONNER LAKE — A DEVOUT FATHER — A DYING
BOY — SORROW AND SUFFERING AT THE CABINS.

How fared it with those left at Donner Lake? About the time the fifteen began their terrible journey, Baylis Williams starved to death. Such food as the rest had was freely given to him, but it did not satisfy the demands of his nature. Quietly, uncomplainingly, he had borne the pangs of famine, and when the company first realized his dreadful condition, he was in the delirium which preceded death. What words can portray the emotions of the starving emigrants, when they saw one of their number actually perish of hunger before their eyes! Williams died in the Graves cabin, and was buried near the house by W. C. Graves and John Denton.

All the Donner Party were starving. When the cattle were killed the hides had been spread over the cabins in lieu of shingles. These were now taken down and eaten. All the survivors describe the method of preparing this miserable substitute for food. The narration by Mrs. J. M. Murphy (Virginia E. Reed), of San Jose, is among the most vivid. She says the green rawhides were cut into strips and laid upon the coals, or held in the flames until the hair was completely singed off. Either side of the piece of hide was then scraped with a knife until comparatively clean, and was placed in a kettle and boiled until soft and pulpy. There was no salt, and only a little pepper, and yet this substance was all that was between them and starvation. When cold, the boiled hides and the water in which they were cooked, became jellied and exactly resembled glue. The tender stomachs, of many of the little children revolted at this disagreeable diet, and the loathing they acquired for the sight of this substance still exists in the minds of some of the survivors. To this day, Thomas K. Reed, of San Jose, who was then a tiny three-year-old, can not endure the sight of calf's-foot jelly, or of similar dishes, because of its resemblance to the loathed food which was all his mother could give him in the cabins at Donner Lake.

William G. Murphy describes how they gathered up the old, castaway bones of the cattle — bones from which all the flesh had been previously picked — and boiled, and boiled, and boiled them until they actually would crumble between the teeth, and were eaten. The little children, playing upon the fire-rug in his mother's cabin, used to cut off little pieces of the rug, toast them crisp upon the coals, and then eat them. In this manner, before any one was fairly aware of the fact, the fire-rug was entirely consumed.

The Donner families, at Prosser Creek, were, if possible, in even a sadder condition. In order to give a glimpse of the suffering endured in these two tents, the following is quoted from a letter written by Mrs. W. A. Babcock (Georgia A. Donner), now residing at Mountain View, Santa Clara County: "The families shared with one another as long as they had anything to share. Each one's portion was very small. The hides were boiled, and the bones were burned brown and eaten. We tried to eat a decayed buffalo robe, but it was too tough, and there was no nourishment in it. Some of the few mice that came into camp were caught and eaten. Some days we could not keep a fire, and many times, during both days and nights, snow was shoveled from off our tent, and from around it, that we might not be buried alive. Mother remarked one day that it had been two weeks that our beds and the clothing upon our bodies had been wet. Two of my sisters and myself spent some days at Keseberg's cabin. The first morning we were there they shoveled the snow from our bed before we could get up. Very few can believe it possible for human beings to live and suffer the exposure and hardships endured there."

Oh! how long and dreary the days were to the hungry children! Even their very plays and pastimes were pathetic, because of their piteous silent allusion to the pangs of starvation. Mrs. Frank Lewis (Patty Reed), of San Jose, relates that the poor, little, famishing girls used to fill the pretty porcelain tea-cups with freshly fallen snow, daintily dip it out with teaspoons and eat it, playing it was custard.

Dear Mrs. Murphy had the most sacred and pitiful charge. It was the wee nursing babe, Catherine Pike, whose mother had gone with the "Forlorn Hope," to try, if possible, to procure relief. All there was to give the tiny sufferer, was a little gruel made from snow water, containing a slight sprinkling of coarse flour. This flour was simply ground wheat, unbolted. Day after day the sweet little darling would lie helplessly upon its grandmother's lap, and seem with its large, sad eyes to be pleading for nourishment. Mrs. Murphy carefully kept the little handful of flour concealed — there was only a handful at the very beginning — lest some of the starving children might get possession of the treasure. Each day she gave Catherine a few teaspoonfuls of the gruel. Strangely enough, this poor little martyr did not often cry with hunger, but with tremulous, quivering mouth, and a low, subdued sob or moan, would appear to be begging for something to eat. The poor, dumb lips, if gifted with speech, could not have uttered a prayer half so eloquent, so touching. Could the mother, Mrs. Pike, have been present, it would have broken her heart to see her patient babe dying slowly, little by little. Starvation had dried the maternal breasts long before Mrs. Pike went away, so that no one can censure her for leaving her baby. She could only have done as Mrs. Murphy did, give it the plain, coarse gruel, and watch it die, day by day, upon her lap.

Up to this time, but little has been said of Patrick Breen. He was an invalid during the winter of 1846 and '47. A man of more than ordinary intelligence, a devout Catholic, a faithful and devoted father, his life furnishes a rare type of the pioneer Californian. To Mr. Breen we are indebted for the most faithful and authentic record of the days spent at the cabins. This record is in the form of a diary, in which the events of the day were briefly noted in the order of their occurrence. Lewis Keseberg kept a similar diary, but it was subsequently accidentally destroyed. Mrs. Tamsen Donner kept a journal, but this, with her paintings and botanical collections, disappeared at the fatal tent on Alder Creek. Mr. Breen's diary alone was preserved. He gave it into Col. McKinstry's possession in the spring of 1847, and on the fourth of September of that year it was published in the Nashville (Tenn.) Whig. A copy of the Whig of that date is furnished by Wm. G. Murphy, of Marysville. Other papers have published garbled extracts from this diary, but none have been reliable. The future history of the events which transpired at the cabins will be narrated in connection with this diary.

It must be remembered that the lake had always been known as "Truckee Lake," it having been named after an old Indian guide who had rendered much assistance to the Schallenberger party in 1844. The record appears without the slightest alteration. Even the orthography of the name of the lake is printed as it was written, "Truckey."

The diary commences as follows:

"TRUCKEY'S LAKE, November 20, 1846.

"Came to this place on the thirty-first of last month; went into the pass; the snow so deep we were unable to find the road, and when within three miles from the summit, turned back to this shanty on Truckey's Lake; Stanton came up one day after we arrived here; we again took our teams and wagons, and made another unsuccessful attempt to cross in company with Stanton; we returned to this shanty; it continued to snow all the time. We now have killed most part of our cattle, having to remain here until next spring, and live on lean beef, without bread or salt. It snowed during the space of eight days, with little intermission, after our arrival, though now clear and pleasant, freezing at night; the snow nearly gone from the valleys.

"November 21. Fine morning; wind northwest; twenty-two of our company about starting to cross the mountains this day, including Stanton and his Indians.

"Nov. 22. Froze last night; fine and clear to-day; no account from those on the mountains.

"Nov. 23. Same weather; wind west; the expedition across the mountains returned after an unsuccessful attempt.

"Nov. 25. Cloudy; looks like the eve of a snow-storm; our mountaineers are to make another trial to-morrow, if fair; froze hard last night.

"Nov. 26. Began to snow last evening; now rains or sleets; the party do not start to-day.

"Nov. 27. Still snowing; now about three feet deep; wind west; killed my last oxen to-day; gave another yoke to Foster; wood hard to be got.

"Nov. 30. Snowing fast; looks as likely to continue as when it commenced; no living thing without wings can get about.

"Dec. 1. Still snowing; wind west; snow about six or seven and a half feet deep; very difficult to get wood, and we are completely housed up; our cattle all killed but two or three, and these, with the horses and Stanton's mules, all supposed to be lost in the snow; no hopes of finding them alive.

"Dec. 3. Ceases snowing; cloudy all day; warm enough to thaw.

"Dec. 5. Beautiful sunshine; thawing a little; looks delightful after the long storm; snow seven or eight feet deep.

"Dec. 6. The morning fine and clear; Stanton and Graves manufacturing snow-shoes for another mountain scrabble; no account of mules.

"Dec. 8. Fine weather; froze hard last night; wind south-west; hard work to find wood sufficient to keep us warm or cook our beef.

"Dec. 9. Commenced snowing about eleven o'clock; wind northwest; took in Spitzer yesterday, so weak that he an not rise without help; caused by starvation. Some have scanty supply of beef; Stanton trying to get some for himself and Indians; not likely to get much.

"Dec. 10. Snowed fast all night, with heavy squalls of wind; continues to snow; now about seven feet in depth.

"Dec. 14. Snows faster than any previous day; Stanton and Graves, with several others, making preparations to cross the mountains on snow-shoes; snow eight feet on a level.

"Dec. 16. Fair and pleasant; froze hard last night; the company started on snow-shoes to cross the mountains; wind southeast.

"Dec. 17. Pleasant; William Murphy returned from the mountain party last evening; Baylis Williams died night before last; Milton and Noah started for Donner's eight days ago; not returned yet; think they are lost in the snow.

"Dec. 19. Snowed last night; thawing to-day; wind northwest; a little singular for a thaw.

"Dec. 20. Clear and pleasant; Mrs. Reed here; no account from Milton yet. Charles Burger started for Donner's; turned back; unable to proceed; tough times, but not discouraged. Our hope is in God. Amen.

"Dec. 21. Milton got back last night from Donner's camp. Sad news; Jacob Donner, Samuel Shoemaker, Rhinehart, and Smith are dead; the rest of them in a low situation; snowed all night, with a strong southwest wind."

Jacob Donner was the first to die at Prosser Creek. He expired while sitting at the table in his tent, with his head bowed upon his hands, as if in deep meditation. The following terse account is from the gifted pen of Mrs. S. O. Houghton (Eliza P. Donner), of San Jose: "Jacob Donner was a slight man, of delicate constitution, and was in poor health when we left Springfield, Illinois. The trials of the journey reduced his strength and exhausted his energy. When we reached the place of encampment in the mountains he was discouraged and gave up in despair. Not even the needs of his family could rouse him to action. He was utterly dejected and made no effort, but tranquilly awaited death."

"Dec. 23. Clear to-day; Milton took some of his meat away; all well at their camp. Began this day to read the 'Thirty Days' Prayers;' Almighty God, grant the requests of unworthy sinners!

"Dec. 24. Rained all night, and still continues; poor prospect for any kind of comfort, spiritual or temporal."

As will be seen by various references throughout this diary, Mr. Breen was a devout Catholic. During the darkest hour of trial the prayers were regularly read. That this might be done during the long weary evenings, as well as by day, pieces of pitch pine were split and laid carefully in one corner of the cabin, which would be lighted at the fire, and would serve as a substitute for candles. Those of the survivors who are living often speak of the times when they held these sticks while Mr. Breen read the prayers. So impressive were these religious observances that one girl, a bright, beautiful child, Virginia E. Reed, made a solemn vow that if God would hear these prayers, and deliver her family from the dangers surrounding them, she would become a Catholic. God did save her family, and she kept her vow. She is to-day a fervent Catholic.

"Dec. 25. Began to snow yesterday, snowed all night, and snows yet rapidly; extremely difficult to find wood; uttered our prayers to God this Christmas morning; the prospect is appalling, but we trust in Him."

What a desolate Christmas morning that was for the snow-bound victims! All were starving. Something to eat, something to satisfy the terrible cravings of appetite, was the constant wish of all. Sometimes the wishes were expressed aloud, but more frequently a gloomy silence prevailed. When anything was audibly wished for, it was invariably something whose size was proportional to their hunger. They never wished for a meal, or a mouthful, but for a barrel full, a wagon load, a house full, or a storehouse full.

On Christmas eve the children spoke in low, subdued tones, of the visits Santa Claus used to make them in their beautiful homes, before they started across the plains. Now they knew that no Santa Claus could find them in the pathless depths of snow.

One family, the Reeds, were in a peculiarly distressing situation. They knew not whether the father was living or dead. No tidings had reached them since his letters ceased to be found by the wayside. The meat they had obtained from the Breen and Graves families was now gone, and on Christmas morning their breakfast was a "pot of glue," as the boiled rawhide was termed. But Mrs. Reed, the dear, tender-hearted mother, had a surprise in store for her children this day. When the last ox had been purchased, Mrs. Reed had placed the frozen meat in one corner of the cabin, so that pieces could be chipped off with a knife or hatchet. The tripe, however, she cleaned carefully and hung on the outside of the cabin, on the end of a log, close to the ground. She knew that the snow would soon conceal this from view. She also laid away secretly, one teacupful of white beans, about half that quantity of rice, the same measure of dried apples, and a piece of bacon two inches square. She knew that if Christmas found them alive, they would be in a terribly destitute condition. She therefore resolved to lay these articles away, and give them to her starving children for a Christmas dinner. This was done. The joy and gladness of these poor little children knew no bounds when they saw the treasures unearthed and cooking on the fire. They were, just this one meal, to have all they could eat! They laughed, and danced, and cried by turns. They eagerly watched the dinner as it boiled. The pork and tripe had been cut in dice-like pieces. Occasionally one of these pieces would boil up to the surface of the water for an instant, then a bean would take a peep at them from the boiling kettle, then a piece of apple, or a grain of rice. The appearance of each tiny bit was hailed by the children with shouts of glee. The mother, whose eyes were brimming with tears, watched her famished darlings with emotions that can be imagined. It seemed too sad that innocent children should be brought to such destitution that the very sight of food should so affect them! When the dinner was prepared, the mother's constant injunction was, "Children, eat slowly, there is plenty for all." When they thought of the starvation of to-morrow, they could not repress a shade of sadness, and when the name of papa was mentioned all burst into tears. Dear, brave papa! Was he struggling to relieve his starving family, or lying stark and dead 'neath the snows of the Sierra? This question was constantly uppermost in the mother's mind.

"Dec. 27. Cleared off yesterday, and continues clear; snow nine feet deep; wood growing scarce; a tree, when felled, sinks into the snow, and is hard to be got at.

"Dec. 30. Fine clear morning; froze hard last night. Charles Burger died last evening about 10 o'clock.

"Dec. 31. Last of the year. May we, with the help of God, spend the coming year better than we have the past, which we propose to do if it is the will of the Almighty to deliver us from our present dreadful situation. Amen. Morning fair, but cloudy; wind east by south; looks like another snow-storm. Snow-storms are dreadful to us. The snow at present is very deep.

"Jan. 1, 1847. We pray the God of mercy to deliver us from our present calamity, if it be His holy will. Commenced snowing last night, and snows a little yet. Provisions getting very scanty; dug up a hide from under the snow yesterday; have not commenced on it yet.

"Jan. 3. Fair during the day, freezing at night. Mrs. Reed talks of crossing the mountains with her children.

"Jan. 4. Fine morning; looks like spring. Mrs. Reed and Virginia, Milton Elliott, and Eliza Williams started a short time ago with the hope of crossing the mountains; left the children here. It was difficult for Mrs. Reed to part with them."

This expedition was only one of many that the emigrants attempted. The suffering that was endured at these times was indescribable. The broken, volcanic nature of the summits rendered it extremely difficult to keep from getting lost. The white, snowy cliffs were everywhere the same. This party became bewildered and lost near the beautiful Lake Angeline, which is close to the present "Summit Station" of the Central Pacific. Had they attempted to proceed, all would undoubtedly have perished.

Within half a mile of the wagon road which now extends from Donner Lake to the Summit are places where rocks and cliffs are mingled in wildest confusion. Even in summer time it is difficult to find one's way among the broken, distorted mountain tops. In the mighty upheaval which produced the Sierra Nevada, these vast mounds or mountains of frowning granite were grouped into weird, fantastic labyrinths. Time has wrought little effect upon their bold precipitous sides, and made slight impress upon their lofty and almost inaccessible crests. Between these fragmentary mountains, in shapely, symmetrical bowls which have been delved by the fingers of the water nymphs and Undines, lie beautiful lakelets. Angeline is but one of a dozen which sparkle like a chain of gems between Donner Lake and the snowy, overhanging peaks of Mount Stanford. The clefts and fissures of the towering granite cliffs are filled, in summer, with dainty ferns, clinging mosses, and the loveliest of mountain wild flowers, and the rims of the lakelets are bordered with grasses, shrubbery, and a wealth of wild blossoms. But in winter this region exhibits the very grandeur of desolation. No verdure is visible save the dwarfed and shattered pines whose crushed branches mark the path of the rushing avalanche. The furious winds in their wild sport toss and tumble the snowdrifts here and there, baring the sterile peaks, and heaping the white masses a hundred feet deep into chasm and gorge. The pure, clear lakes, as if in very fear, hide their faces from the turbulent elements in mantles of ice. The sun is darkened by dense clouds, and the icy, shivering, shrieking storm-fiends hold undisturbed their ghastly revels. On every side are lofty battlements of rock, whose trembling burden of snow seems ever ready to slide from its glassy foundations of ice, and entomb the bewildered traveler.

Into this interminable maze of rocks and cliffs and frozen lakelets, the little party wandered. Elliott had a compass, but it soon proved worthless, and only added to their perplexed and uncertain state of mind. They were out five days. Virginia's feet became so badly frozen that she could not walk. This occurrence saved the party. Reluctantly they turned back toward the cabins, convinced that it was madness to attempt to go forward. They reached shelter just as one of the most terrible storms of all that dreadful winter broke over their heads. Had they delayed their return a few hours, the path they made in ascending the mountains, and by means of which they retraced their steps, would have been concealed, and death would have been certain.

"Jan. 6. Eliza came back yesterday evening from the mountains, unable to proceed; the others kept ahead.

"Jan. 8. Mrs. Reed and the others came back; could not find their way on the other side of the mountains. They have nothing but hides to live on.

"Jan. 10. Began to snow last night; still continues; wind west-north-west.

"Jan. 13. Snowing fast; snow higher than the shanty; it must be thirteen feet deep. Can not get wood this morning; it is a dreadful sight for us to look upon."

One of the stumps near the Graves-Reed cabin, cut while the snow was at its deepest, was found, by actual measurement, to be twenty-two feet in height. Part of this stump is standing to-day.

"Jan. 14. Cleared off yesterday. The sun, shining brilliantly, renovates our spirits. Praise be to the God of heaven.

"Jan. 15. Clear to-day again. Mrs. Murphy blind; Landrum not able to get wood; has but one ax between him and Keseberg. It looks like another storm; expecting some account from Sutter's soon.

"Jan. 17. Eliza Williams came here this morning; Landrum crazy last night; provisions scarce; hides our main subsistence. May the Almighty send us help.

"Jan. 21. Fine morning; John Baptiste and Mr. Denton came this morning with Eliza; she will not eat hides. Mrs. — sent her back to live or die on them."

The blanks which occasionally occur were in the original diary. The delicacy which prompted Patrick Breen to omit these names can not fail to be appreciated. What if there was sometimes a shade of selfishness, or an act of harshness? What if some families had more than their destitute neighbors? The best provided had little. All were in reality strangely generous. All divided with their afflicted companions. The Reeds had almost nothing to eat when they arrived at the cabins, yet this family is the only one which reached the settlements without some one member having to partake of human flesh.

"Jan. 22. Began to snow after sunrise; likely to continue; wind north.

"Jan. 23. Blew hard and snowed all night; the most severe storm we have experienced this winter; wind west.

"Jan. 26. Cleared up yesterday; to-day fine and pleasant; wind south; in hopes we are done with snow-storms. Those who went to Sutter's not yet returned; provisions getting scant; people growing weak, living on a small allowance of hides.

"Jan. 27. Commenced snowing yesterday; still continues to-day. Lewis Keseberg, Jr., died three days ago; food growing scarce; don't have fire enough to cook our hides.

"Jan. 30. Fair and pleasant; wind west; thawing in the sun. John and Edward Breen went to Graves' this morning. Mrs.—seized on Mrs.—'s goods until they would be paid; they also took the hides which herself and family subsisted upon. She regained two pieces only, the balance they have taken. You may judge from this what our fare is in camp. There is nothing to be had by hunting, yet perhaps there soon will be.

"Jan. 31. The sun does not shine out brilliant this morning; froze hard last night; wind north-west. Landrum Murphy died last night about ten o'clock; Mrs. Reed went to Graves' this morning to look after goods."

Landrum Murphy was a large and somewhat overgrown young man. The hides and burnt bones did not contain sufficient nourishment to keep him alive. For some hours before he died, he lay in a semi-delirious state, breathing heavily and seemingly in little or no pain. Mrs. Murphy went to the Breen camp, and asked Mrs. Breen for a piece of meat to save her starving boy. Mrs. Breen gave her the meat, but it was too late, Landrum could not eat. Finally he sank into a gentle slumber. His breathing grew less and less distinct, and ere they were fairly aware of it life was extinct.

"Feb. 4. Snowed hard until twelve o'clock last night; many uneasy for fear we shall all perish with hunger; we have but little meat left, and only three hides; Mrs. Reed has nothing but one hide, and that is on Graves' house; Milton lives there, and likely will keep that. Eddy's child died last night.

"Feb. 5. It snowed faster last night and to-day than it has done this winter before; still continues without intermission; wind south-west. Murphy's folks and Keseberg say they can not eat hides. I wish we had enough of them. Mrs. Eddy is very weak.

"Feb. 7. Ceased to snow at last; to-day it is quite pleasant. McCutchen's child died on the second of this month."

This child died and was buried in the Graves cabin. Mr. W. C. Graves helped dig the grave near one side of the cabin, and laid the little one to rest. One of the most heart-rending features of this Donner tragedy is the number of infants that suffered. Mrs. Breen, Pike, Foster, McCutchen, Eddy, Keseberg, and Graves each had nursing babes when the fatal camp was pitched at Donner Lake.

"Feb. 8. Fine, clear morning. Spitzer died last night, and we will bury him in the snow; Mrs. Eddy died on the night of the seventh.

"Feb. 9. Mrs. Pike's child all but dead; Milton is at Murphy's, not able to get out of bed; Mrs. Eddy and child were buried to-day; wind south-east.

"Feb. 10. Beautiful morning; thawing in the sun; Milton Elliott died last night at Murphy's cabin, and Mrs. Reed went there this morning to see about his effects. John Denton trying to borrow meat for Graves; had none to give; they had nothing but hides; all are entirely out of meat, but a little we have; our hides are nearly all eat up, but with God's help spring will soon smile upon us.

"Feb. 12. Warm, thawy morning.

"Feb. 14. Fine morning, but cold. Buried Milton in the snow; John Denton not well.

"Feb. 15. Morning cloudy until nine o'clock, then cleared off warm. Mrs.—refused to give Mrs.—any hides. Put Sutter's pack hides on her shanty, and would not let her have them.

"Feb. 16. Commenced to rain last evening, and turned to snow during the night, and continued until morning; weather change-able, sunshine and then light showers of hail, and wind at times. We all feel unwell. The snow is not getting much less at present."

CHAPTER IX

THE LAST RESORT — TWO REPORTS OF A GUN — ONLY TEM-
PORARY RELIEF — WEARY TRAVELING — THE SNOW BRIDGES
— HUMAN TRACKS! — AN INDIAN RANCHERIE — ACORN
BREAD — STARVING FIVE TIMES! — CARRIED SIX MILES —
BRAVERY OF JOHN RHODES — A THIRTY-TWO DAYS JOURNEY
— ORGANIZING THE FIRST RELIEF PARTY — ALCALDE SIN-
CLAIR'S ADDRESS — CAPTAIN R. P. TUCKER'S COMPANIONS.

IT is recorded of Lewis and Salvador that they came willingly to
the relief of the emigrants. Two of Sutter's best trained vaqueros,
faithful, honest, reliable, they seemed rather proud when chosen
to assist Stanton in driving the mules laden with provisions for
the starving train. Now they were dying! Horrified at the sight of
human beings eating the flesh of their comrades, they withdrew
from the whites at the "Camp of Death." After that they always
camped apart, but continued to act as guides until they became
certain that their own lives were in danger. Then they fled.
Starving, exhausted, with frozen and bleeding feet, the poor
wretches dragged their weary bodies onward until they reached a
little streamlet, and here they lay down to die. Nine days, with no
other food than they could find in the snow, was too much even
for their hardy natures. They were unable to move when the famished "Seven" passed. Yes, PASSED! for the starving emigrants
went on by the poor fellows, unable to deprive them of the little
spark of life left in their wasted bodies. Traveling was now slow
work for the dying whites. They only went about two hundred

yards. In a few more hours, perhaps that very night, they would die of starvation. Already the terrible phantasies of delirium were beginning to dance before their sunken eyes. Ere the Indians would cease breathing some of the Seven would be past relief. There were two men and five women. William Foster could see that his wife—the woman who was all the world to him—was fast yielding to the deadly grasp of the fiends of starvation. For the sake of his life she had stifled the most sacred instincts of her womanly nature, and procured him food from Fosdick's body. Should he see her die the most terrible of deaths without attempting to rescue her? Reader, put yourself in this man's place. Brave, generous, heroic, full of lion-like nobility, William Foster could not stoop to a base action. Contemplate his position! Lying there prostrate upon the snow was Mrs. Pike, the woman whom, accidentally, he had rendered a widow. Her babes were dying in the cabins. His own boy was at the cabins. His comrades, his wife, were in the last stages of starvation. He, also, was dying. Eddy had not nerve enough, the women could not, and William Foster must—what! Was it murder? No! Every law book, every precept of that higher law, self-preservation, every dictate of right, reason or humanity, demanded the deed. The Indians were past all hope of aid. They could not lift their heads from their pillow of snow. It was not simply justifiable—it was duty; it was a necessity.

He told them, when he got back, that he was compelled to take their lives. They did not moan or struggle, or appear to regret that their lingering pain was to cease. The five women and Eddy heard two reports of a gun.

The "Forlorn Hope" might yet save those who were dying at Donner Lake.

Even this relief was but temporary. Taking the wasted flesh from the bones, drying it, and staggering forward, the little band speedily realized that they were not yet saved. It was food for only a few days. Then they again felt their strength failing. Once more they endured the excruciating torments which precede starvation.

In the very complete account of this trip, which is kindly furnished by Mary Graves, are many interesting particulars concerning the suffering of these days. "Our only chance for camp-fire for the night," she says, "was to hunt a dead tree of some description, and set fire to it. The hemlock being the best and generally much the largest timber, it was our custom to select the driest we could find without leaving our course. When the fire would reach the top of the tree, the falling limbs would fall all around us and bury themselves in the snow, but we heeded them not. Sometimes the falling, blazing limbs would brush our clothes, but they never hit us; that would have been too lucky a hit. We would sit or lie on the snow, and rest our weary frames. We would sleep, only to dream of something nice to eat, and awake again to disappointment. Such was our sad fate! Even the reindeer's wretched lot was not worse! 'His dinner and his bed were snow, and supper he had not.' Our fare was the same! We would strike fire by means of the flint-lock gun which we had with us. This had to be carried by turns, as it was considered the only hope left in case we might find game which we could kill. We traveled over a ridge of mountains, and then descended a deep canyon, where one could scarcely see the bottom. Down, down we would go, or rather slide, for it is very slavish work going down hill, and in many cases we were compelled to slide on our shoes as sleds. On reaching the bottom we would plunge into the snow, so that it was difficult getting out, with the shoes tied to our feet, our packs lashed to our backs, and ourselves head and ears under the snow. But we managed to get out some way, and one by one reached the bottom of the canyon. When this was accomplished we had to ascend a hill as steep as the one we had descended. We would drive the toes of our shoes into the loose snow, to make a sort of step, and one by one, as if ascending stair-steps, we climbed up. It took us an entire day to reach the top of the mountain. Each time we attained the summit of a mountain, we hoped we should be able to see something like a valley, but each time came disappointment, for far ahead was always another and higher mountain. We found some springs, or, as we called them, wells, from five to twenty feet under ground, as you might say, for they were under the snow on which we walked. The water was so warm that it melted the snow, and from some of these springs were large streams of running water. We crossed numbers of these streams on bridges of snow, which would sometimes form upon a blade of grass hanging over the water; and from so small a foundation would grow a bridge from ten to twenty-five feet high, and from a foot and a half to three feet across the top. It would make you dizzy to look down at the water, and it was with much difficulty we could place our clumsy ox-bow snow-shoes one ahead of the other without falling. Our feet had been frozen and thawed so many times that they were bleeding and sore. When we stopped at night we would take off our shoes, which by this time were so badly rotted by constant wetting in snow, that there was very little left of them. In the morning we would push our shoes on, bruising and numbing the feet so badly that they would ache and ache with walking and the cold, until night would come again. Oh! the pain! It seemed to make the pangs of hunger more excruciating."

Thus the party traveled on day after day, until absolute starvation again stared them in the face. The snow had gradually grown less deep, until finally it disappeared or lay only in patches. Their strength was well-nigh exhausted, when one day Mary Graves says: "Some one called out, 'Here are tracks!' Some one asked, 'What kind of tracks — human?' 'Yes, human!' Can any one imagine the joy these footprints gave us? We ran as fast as our strength would carry us."

Turning a chaparral point, they came in full view of an Indian rancherie. The uncivilized savages were amazed. Never had they seen such forlorn, wretched, pitiable human beings, as the tattered, disheveled, skeleton creatures who stood stretching out their arms for assistance. At first, they all ran and hid, but soon they returned to the aid of these dying wretches. It is said that the Indian women and children cried, and wailed with grief at the affecting spectacle of starved men and women. Such food as they had was speedily offered. It was bread made of acorns. This was eagerly eaten. It was at least a substitute for food. Every person in the rancherie, from the toddling papooses to the aged chief, endeavored to aid them.

After what had recently happened, could anything be more touching than these acts of kindness of the Indians?

After briefly resting, they pressed forward. The Indians accompanied and even led them, and constantly supplied them with food. With food? No, it was not such food as their weakened, debilitated systems craved. The acorn bread was not sufficient to sustain lives already so attenuated by repeated starvations. All that the starved experience in the way of pain and torture before they die, had been experienced by these people at least four different times. To their horror, they now discovered that despite the acorn bread, they must die of hunger and exhaustion a fifth and last time. So sick and weak did they become, that they were compelled to lie down and rest every hundred yards. Finally, after being with the Indians seven days, they lay down, and felt that they never should have strength to take another step. Before them, in all its beauty and loveliness, spread the broad valley of the Sacramento. Behind them were the ever-pleading faces of their starving dear ones. Yet neither hope nor affection could give them further strength. They were dying in full view of the long-desired haven of rest.

One of the number was hardly so near death's door as his companions. It was W. H. Eddy. As a last resort, their faithful allies, the Indians, took him upon either side, and fairly carried him along. His feet moved, but they were frozen, and blistered, and cracked, and bleeding. Left alone, he would have fallen helplessly to the earth. It was as terrible a journey as ever mortal man performed. How far he traveled, he knew not. During the last six miles his path was marked by blood-stains from his swollen feet.

By making abridgments from valuable manuscript contributed by George W. Tucker, of Calistoga, this narrative may be appropriately continued. Mr. Tucker's father and relatives had reached Johnson's Ranch on the twenty-fifth of October, 1846. They had been with the Donner Party until Fort Bridger was reached, and then took the Fort Hall road. Their journey had been full of dangers and difficulties, and reaching Johnson's Ranch, the first settlement on the west side of the Sierra, they determined to remain during the winter.

One evening, about the last of January, Mr. Tucker says a man was seen coming down Bear River, accompanied by an Indian. His haggard, forlorn look showed he was in great distress. When he reached us, he said he was of the Donner Party. He told briefly how the train had been caught in the snow east of the mountains, and was unable to get back or forward. He told how the fifteen had started, and that six beside himself were still alive. That the six were back in the mountains, almost starved. R. P. Tucker and three other men started at once with provisions, the Indian acting as guide. They reached them, fifteen miles back, some time during the night, and brought them in the next day. The names of the seven were W. H. Eddy, William Foster, Mrs. S. A. C. Foster, Mrs. H. F. Pike, Mrs. William McCutchen, Mrs. Sarah Fosdick, and Mary Graves. It had been thirty-two days since they left Donner Lake!

At Johnson's Ranch there were only three or four families of poor emigrants. Nothing could be done toward relieving those at Donner Lake until help could arrive from Sutter's Fort. A rainy winter had flooded Bear River, and rendered the Sacramento plains a vast quagmire. Yet one man volunteered to go to Sacramento with the tale of horror, and get men and provisions. This man was John Rhodes. Lashing two pine logs together with rawhides, and forming a raft, John Rhodes was ferried over Bear River. Taking his shoes in his hands, and rolling his pants up above his knees, he started on foot through water that frequently was from one to three feet deep. Some time during the night he reached the Fort.

A train in the mountains! Men, women, and children starving! It was enough to make one's blood curdle to think of it! Captain Sutter, generous old soul, and Alcalde Sinclair, who lived at Norris' Ranch two and a half miles from the Fort, offered provisions, and five or six men volunteered to carry them over the mountains. In about a week, six men, fully provided with supplies, reached Johnson's Ranch. Meantime the Tuckers and their neighbors had slaughtered five or six fat cattle, and had dried or "jerked" the meat. The country was scoured for horses and mules, and for saddles and pack-saddles, but at last, in ten or twelve days, they were ready to start. Alcalde Sinclair had come up from the Fort, and when all were ready to begin their march, he made them a thrilling little address. They were, he said, starting out upon a hazardous journey. Nothing could justify them in attempting so perilous an undertaking except the obligations due to their suffering fellow-men. He urged them to do all in their power, without sacrificing their lives, to save the perishing emigrants from starvation and death. He then appointed Reasin P. Tucker, the father of our informant, captain of the company. With a pencil he carefully wrote down the name of each man in the relief party. The names were John Rhodes, Daniel Rhodes, Aquilla Glover, R. S. Mootrey, Joseph Foster, Edward Coffeemire, M. D. Ritchie, James Curtis, William H. Eddy, William Coon, R. P. Tucker, George W. Tucker, and Adolph Brueheim. Thus the first relief party started.

CHAPTER X

A LOST AGE IN CALIFORNIA HISTORY — THE CHANGE
WROUGHT BY THE DISCOVERY OF GOLD — THE START FROM
JOHNSON'S RANCH — A BUCKING HORSE — A NIGHT RIDE —
LOST IN THE MOUNTAINS — A TERRIBLE NIGHT — A FLOODED
CAMP — CROSSING A MOUNTAIN TORRENT — MULE SPRINGS —
A CRAZY COMPANION — HOWLINGS OF GRAY WOLVES — A
DEER RENDEZVOUS — A MIDNIGHT THIEF — FRIGHTENING
INDIANS — THE DIARY OF THE FIRST RELIEF PARTY.

CALIFORNIA, at this time, was sparsely settled, and it was a fearful undertaking to cross the snowy mountains to the relief of the storm-bound emigrants. A better idea of the difficulties to be encountered by the various relief parties can not be presented than by quoting from the manuscript of George W. Tucker. This gentleman was sixteen years old at the time of the occurrences narrated, and his account is vouched for as perfectly truthful and reliable. This sketch, like the remainder of this book, treats of an epoch in California history which has been almost forgotten. The scene of his adventures is laid in a region familiar to thousands of miners and early Californians. Along the route over which he passed with so much difficulty, scores of mining camps sprung up soon after the discovery of gold, and every flat, ravine, and hill-slope echoed to pick, and shovel, and pan, and to voices of legions of men. Truly, his narration relates to a lost, an almost unremembered era in the history of the famous mining counties, Placer and Nevada. In speaking of the first relief party, he says:

"We mounted our horses and started. The ground was very soft among the foothills, but we got along very well for two or three miles after leaving Johnson's ranch. Finally, one of our pack-horses broke through the crust, and down he went to his sides in the mud. He floundered and plunged until the pack turned underneath his body. He then came out of the mud, bucking and kicking; and he bucked and kicked, and kicked and bucked, till he cleared himself of the pack, pack-saddle and all, and away he went back to the ranch. We gathered up the pack, put it upon the horse Eddy was riding, and the party traveled on. Eddy and myself were to go back to the ranch, catch the horse, and returning, overtake them. We failed to find the horse that day, but the next morning an Indian got on my horse, and, about nine o'clock, succeeded in finding the missing animal. My horse, however, was pretty well run down when he got back. Eddy and myself started about ten o'clock. We had to travel in one day what the company had traveled in two days. About the time we started it commenced clouding up, and we saw we were going to have a storm. We went on until about one o'clock, when my horse gave out. It commenced raining and was very cold. Eddy said he would ride on and overtake the company, if possible, and have them stop. He did not overtake them until about dark, after they had camped.

"My horse could only go in a slow walk, so I walked and led him to keep from freezing. The rain continued to increase in volume, and by dark it was coming down in torrents. It was very cold. The little stream began to rise, but I waded through, though sometimes it came up to my armpits. It was very dark, but I kept going on in hopes I would come in sight of the camp-fire. But the darkness increased, and it was very difficult to find the road. I would get down on my knees and feel for the road with my hands. Finally, about nine o'clock, it became so dark that I could not see a tree until I would run against it, and I was almost exhausted dragging my horse after me. I had lost the road several times, but found it by feeling for the wagon-ruts. At last I came to where the road made a short turn around the point of a hill, and I went straight ahead until I got forty or fifty yards from the road. I crawled around for some time on my knees, but could not find it. I knew if the storm was raging in the morning as it was then, if I got very far from the road, I could not tell which was east, west, north, or south, I might get lost and perish before the storm ceased, so I concluded to stay right there until morning. I had no blanket, and nothing on me but a very light coat and pair of pants. I tied my horse to a little pine tree, and sitting down, leaned against the tree. The rain came down in sheets. The wind blew, and the old pine trees clashed their limbs together. It seemed to me that a second deluge had come. I would get so cold that I would get up and walk around for a while. It seemed to me I should surely freeze. Toward morning I began to get numb, and felt more comfortable, but that was the longest and hardest night I ever experienced.

"In the morning, when it became light enough so that I could see two or three rods, I got up, but my legs were so numb that I could not walk. I rolled around until I got up a circulation, and could stand on my feet. Leaving my horse tied to the tree, I found the road, went about a hundred yards around the point of a hill, and saw the camp-fire up in a little flat about a quarter of a mile from where I had spent the night. Going up to camp, I found the men all standing around a fire they had made, where two large pines had fallen across each other. They had laid down pine bark and pieces of wood to keep them out of the water. They had stood up all night. The water was running two or three inches deep all through the camp. When I got to the fire, and began to get warm, my legs and arms began to swell so that I could hardly move or get my hands to my face.

"It never ceased raining all that day nor the next night, and we were obliged to stand around the fire. Everything we had was wet. They had stacked up our dried beef and flour in a pile, and put the saddles and pack saddles over it as well as they could, but still it got more or less wet. The third morning it stopped raining about daylight, and the sun came out clear and warm. We made scaffolds and spread our meat all out, hung up our blankets and clothing on lines, and by keeping up fires and with the help of the sun, we managed to get everything dry by night. The next morning we packed up and started on until we came to a little valley, where we found some grass for our horses. We stayed there that night. The next day we got to Steep Hollow Creek, one of the branches of Bear River. This stream was not more than a hundred feet wide, but it was about twenty feet deep, and the current was very swift. We felled a large pine tree across it, but the center swayed down so that the water ran over it about a foot deep. We tied ropes together and stretched them across to make a kind of hand railing, and succeeded in carrying over all our things. We undertook to make our horses swim the creek, and finally forced two of them into the stream, but as soon as they struck the current they were carried down faster than we could run. One of them at last reached the bank and got ashore, but the other went down under the tree we had cut, and the first we saw of him he came up about twenty yards below, heels upward. He finally struck a drift about a hundred yards below, and we succeeded in getting him out almost drowned. We then tied ropes together, part of the men went over, and tying a rope to each horse, those on one side would force him into the water, and the others would draw him across. We lost a half day at this place. That night we climbed a high mountain, and came to snow. Camped that night without any feed for our horses. The next day, about noon, we reached Mule Springs. The snow was from three to four feet deep, and it was impossible to go any farther with the horses. Unpacking the animals, Joe Varro and Wm. Eddy started back with them to Johnson's Ranch. The rest of us went to work and built a brush tent in which to keep our provisions. We set forks into the ground, laid poles across, and covered them with cedar boughs. We finished them that evening, and the next morning ten of the men fixed up their packs, consisting of dried beef and flour, and started on foot, each one carrying about seventy-five pounds. They left Billy Coon and myself to watch the provisions until they returned. I have never been in that country since, but I think Mule Springs is on the opposite side of Bear River from Dutch Flat.

"After the men had all gone, I amused myself the first day by getting wood and cutting cedar limbs to finish our camp with. My companion, Billy Coon, was partially insane, and was no company at all. He would get up in the morning, eat his food, and then lie down and sleep for two or three hours. He would only talk when he was spoken to; and all he knew was to sleep and eat. I got very lonesome, and would sit for hours thinking of our situation. Sixty miles from any human habitation! Surrounded with wild Indians and wild beasts! Then, when I would look away at the snow-capped peaks of the Sierra, and think that my father and the rest of the men where there, toiling under the heavy loads which they carried, I became still more gloomy. When night would come, the big gray wolves that had collected on the mountains facing to the south, where the snow had melted off, would set up their howlings. This, with the dismal sound of the wind roaring through the tall pine trees, was almost unendurable. To this day, when I am in pine timber, and hear the wind sighing through the tree-tops, I always think of the Donner Party and of those lonely days in the mountains.

"The third day after the men left I became so lonesome that I took the gun and went down in the direction in which I had heard the wolves howling. When I got down out of the snow, I found the deer had collected there by the hundreds. I killed two deer; went up and got Billy Coon, and we carried them up to camp. We hung one on each corner of our brush tent, not more than six feet from our bed, and not more than four feet from the fire. Next morning one of the deer was gone! I supposed the Indians had found us out and stolen it; but when I looked for tracks I found the thief had been a California lion. I tracked him two or three hundred yards, but he had walked off with the deer so easily, I thought he might keep it. That afternoon I went down to kill another deer, but when I reached a point from which I could see down to the river, I saw the smoke of an Indian camp. I was afraid to shoot for fear the Indians would hear the gun, and finding out we were there, would come up and give us trouble. I started back, and when in sight of camp I sat down on a log to rest. While sitting there I saw three Indians coming up the hill. I sat still to see what they would do. They came up to within sight of the camp, and all crawled up behind a large sugar-pine tree, and sat there watching the camp. I did not like their movements, so thought I would give them a scare. I leveled the old gun at the tree, about six feet above their heads, and fired away. They got away from there faster than they came, and I never saw them afterwards.

"On the fifth day after the men left, three of them came back to the camp. They informed me they had been three days in traveling from Mule Springs to Bear Valley, a distance of twelve miles. These three had found it impossible to stand the journey, but the other seven had started on from Bear Valley. It was thought they could never get over to Truckee Lake, for the snow was so soft it was impossible to carry their heavy loads through from ten to thirty feet of it."

M. D. Ritchie and R. P. Tucker kept a diary of the journey of the first relief party, which, thanks to Patty Reed, now Mrs. Frank Lewis, is before us. It is brief, concise, pointed, and completes the narration of Mr. George W. Tucker. Mr. Ritchie's diary reads:

"Feb. 5, 1847. First day traveled ten miles. Bad roads; often miring down horses and mules. On the sixth and seventh traveled fifteen miles. Road continued bad; commenced raining before we got to camp, and continued to rain all that day and night very severe. Lay by here on the eighth to dry our provisions and clothing.

"Feb. 9. Travelled fifteen miles. Swam the animals over one creek, and carried the provisions over on a log.

"Feb. 10. Traveled four miles; came to the snow; continued about four miles further. Animals floundering in snow, and camped at the Mule Springs.

"Feb. 11. Mr. Eddy started back with the animals; left William Coon and George Tucker to guard what provisions were left in camp; the other ten men, each taking about fifty pounds, except

Mr. Curtis, who took about twenty-five pounds. Traveled on through the snow, having a very severe day's travel over mountains, making about six miles. Camped on Bear River, near a cluster of large pines.

"Feb. 12. Moved camp about two miles, and stopped to make snow-shoes; tried them on and found them of no benefit; cast them away.

"Feb. 13. Made Bear Valley. Upon digging for Curtis' wagon, found the snow ten feet deep, and the provisions destroyed by the bears. Rain and snow fell on us all night."

By Curtis' wagon is meant a cache made by Reed and McCutchen, which will be described in the next chapter.

"Feb. 14. Fine weather."

From this time forward, the journal was kept by Reasin P. Tucker.

"Feb. 15. Fine day. Three of our men decline going any further— W. D. Ritchie, A. Brueheim, and James Curtis. Only seven men being left, the party was somewhat discouraged. We consulted together, and under existing circumstances I took it upon myself to insure every man who persevered to the end, five dollars per day from the time they entered the snow. We determined to go ahead, and camped to-night on Yuba River, after traveling fifteen miles.

"Feb. 16. Traveling very bad, and snowing. Made but five miles, and camped in snow fifteen feet deep.

"Feb. 17. Traveled five miles.

"Feb. 18. Traveled eight miles, and camped on the head of the Yuba; on the pass we suppose the snow to be thirty feet deep."

The "pass" was the Summit. Relief was close at hand. Would it find the emigrants?

CHAPTER XI

HARDSHIPS OF REED AND HERRON — GENEROSITY OF
CAPTAIN SUTTER — ATTEMPTS TO CROSS THE MOUNTAINS
WITH PROVISIONS — CURTIS' DOG — COMPELLED TO
TURN BACK — HOSTILITIES WITH MEXICO — MEMORIAL
TO GOV. STOCKTON — YERBA BUENA'S GENEROSITY —
JOHNSON'S LIBERALITY — PITIFUL SCENES AT DONNER
LAKE — NOBLE MOTHERS — DYING RATHER THAN EAT
HUMAN FLESH — A MOTHER'S PRAYER — TEARS OF JOY —
EATING THE SHOESTRINGS.

JAMES F. Reed encountered the most disheartening trials after
leaving the Donner Party. He and Walter Herron were reduced to
the utmost verge of starvation while on the Sierra Nevada. At one
time they discovered five beans in the road, one after the other,
and at another time they ate of the rancid tallow which was found
in a tar bucket under an old wagon.

Mr. Reed has told the rest in an article contributed by him to
the Rural Press. It explains so well the difficulties of getting relief
to the emigrants, that it is copied:

"When I arrived at Captain Sutter's, making known my situation to him, asking if he would furnish me horses and saddles
to bring the women and children out of the mountains (I
expected to meet them at the head of Bear Valley by the time I
could return there), he at once complied with the request, also
saying that he would do everything possible for me and the
company. On the evening of my arrival at the Captain's, I found

Messrs. Bryant, Lippencott, Grayson, and Jacobs, some of the early voyagers in the Russel Company, they having left that company at Fort Laramie, most of them coming on horseback.

"During the evening a meeting was held, in which I participated, adopting a memorial to the commander of Sutter's Fort, to raise one or more companies of volunteers, to proceed to Los Angeles, we being at war with Mexico at this time. The companies were to be officered by the petitioners. Being requested to take command of one of the companies, I declined, stating that it would be necessary for the captain to stay with the company; also that I had to return to the mountains for the emigrants, but that I would take a lieutenancy. This was agreed to, and I was on my return to the emigrants to enlist all the men I could between there and Bear Valley. On my way up I enlisted twelve or thirteen.

"The second night after my arrival at Captain Sutter's, we had a light rain; next morning we could see snow on the mountains. The Captain stated that it was low down and heavy for the first fall of the season. The next day I started on my return with what horses and saddles Captain Sutter had to spare. He furnished us all the flour needed, and a hind quarter of beef, giving us an order for more horses and saddles at Mr. Cordway's, near where Marysville is located. In the mean time, Mr. McCutchen joined us, he being prevented from returning with Mr. Stanton on account of sickness. After leaving Mr. Johnson's ranch we had thirty horses, one mule, and two Indians to help drive.

"Nothing happened until the evening before reaching the head of Bear Valley, when there commenced a heavy rain and sleet, continuing all night. We drove on until a late hour before halting. We secured the flour and horses, the rain preventing us from kindling a fire. Next morning, proceeding up the valley to where we were to take the mountain, we found a tent containing a Mr. Curtis and wife. They hailed us as angels sent for their delivery, stating that they would have perished had it not been for our arrival. Mrs. Curtis stated that they had killed their dog, and at the time of our arrival had the last piece in the Dutch oven baking. We told them not to be alarmed about anything to eat, for we had plenty, both of flour and beef, and that they were welcome to all they needed. Our appetites were rather keen, not having eaten anything from the morning previous. Mr. Curtis remarked that in the oven was a piece of the dog and we could have it. Raising the lid of the oven, we found the dog well baked, and having a fine savory smell. I cut out a rib, smelling and tasting, found it to be good, and handed it over to McCutchen, who, after smelling it some time, tasted it and pronounced it very good dog. We partook of Curtis' dog. Mrs. Curtis immediately commenced making bread, and in a short time had supper for all.

"At the lower end of the valley, where we entered, the snow was eighteen inches in depth, and when we arrived at the tent, it was two feet. Curtis stated that his oxen had taken the back track, and that he had followed them by the trail through the snow. In the morning, before leaving, Mrs. Curtis got us to promise to take them into the settlement when on our return with the women and children. Before leaving, we gave them flour and beef sufficient to keep them until our return, expecting to do so in a few days.

"We started, following the trail made by the oxen, and camped a number of miles up the mountain. In the night, hearing some of the horses going down the trail, we went to where the Indians had lain down, and found them gone. McCutchen mounted his horse and rode down to Curtis' camp, and found that the Indians had been there, stopped and warmed themselves, and then started down the valley. He returned to camp about the middle of the night.

"Next morning we started, still on the trail of the oxen, but unfortunately, the trail turned off to the left from our direction. We proceeded on, the snow deepening rapidly, our horses struggling to get through; we pushed them on until they would rear upon their hind feet to breast the snow, and when they would alight they would, sink in it until nothing was seen of them but the nose and a portion of the head. Here we found that it was utterly impossible to proceed further with the horses. Leaving them, we proceeded further on foot, thinking that we could get in to the people, but found that impossible, the snow being soft and deep.

"I may here state that neither of us knew anything about snow-shoes, having always lived in a country where they never were used.

"With sorrowful hearts, we arrived that night at the camp of Mr. Curtis, telling them to make their arrangements for leaving with us in the morning. Securing our flour in the wagon of Mr. Curtis, so that we could get it on our return, we packed one horse with articles belonging to Mr. and Mrs. Curtis, and started down the valley to where the snow was light, and where there was considerable underbrush, so that our famished animals could browse, they not having eaten anything for several days.

"After packing Mr. Curtis' horse for him the next morning, we started; in a short time, Mr. and Mrs. Curtis proceeded ahead, leaving the pack-horse behind for us to drive, instead of his leading him; we having our hands full in driving the loose ones, they scattering in all directions. The pack turned on the horse. Mr. Curtis was requested to return and help repack and lead his horse, but he paid no attention to us. We stood this for some time; finally, McCutchen became angry, started after him, determined to bring him back; when he got with him he paid no attention to McCutchen's request to return; Mac becoming more exasperated, hit him several times over the shoulders with his riatta. This brought him to his senses. He said that if Mac would not kill him, he would come back and take care of the pack animal, and he did.

"As soon as we arrived at Captain Sutter's, I made a statement of all the circumstances attending our attempt to get into the mountains. He was no way surprised at our defeat. I also gave the Captain the number of head of cattle the company had when I left them. He made an estimate, and stated that if the emigrants would kill the cattle, and place the meat in the snow for preservation, there was no fear of starvation until relief could reach them. He further stated that there were no able-bodied men in that vicinity, all having gone down the country with and after Fremont to fight the Mexicans. He advised me to proceed to Yerba Buena, now San Francisco, and make my case known to the naval officer in command.

"I left Captain Sutter's, by the way of San Jose, for San Francisco, being unable to come by water. When I arrived at San Jose, I found the San Francisco side of the bay was occupied by the Mexicans. Here I remained, and was attached to a company of volunteers, commanded by Captain Webber, until after the fight at Santa Clara.

"The road now being clear, I proceeded to San Francisco with a petition from some of the prominent citizens of San Jose, asking the commander of the navy to grant aid to enable me to return to the mountains."

It is proper, perhaps, to interrupt the narrative in the Rural Press for the purpose of introducing the memorial referred to by Mr. Reed. The copy of the original document was recently found among his papers by his daughter, Patty Reed.

"To his Excellency, R. F. Stockton, Governor and Commander-in-Chief, by sea and land, of the United States Territory of California: We, the undersigned citizens and residents of the Territory of California, beg leave respectfully to present to your Excellency the following memorial, viz.: That, whereas, the last detachment of emigrants from the United States to California have been unable, from unavoidable causes, to reach the frontier settlements, and are now in the California mountains, seventy-five or one hundred miles east from the Sacramento Valley, surrounded by snow, most probably twenty feet deep, and being about eighty souls in number, a large proportion of whom are women and children, who must shortly be in a famishing condition from scarcity of provisions, therefore, the undersigned most earnestly beseech your Excellency to take into consideration the propriety of fitting out an expedition to proceed on snow-shoes immediately to the relief of the sufferers. Your memorialists beg leave to subscribe themselves, very respectfully, yours, etc.

"January, 1847."

The article in the Rural Press continues: "Arriving at San Francisco, I presented my petition to Commodore Hull, also making a statement of the condition of the people in the mountains as far as I knew, the number of them, and what would be needed in provisions and help to get them out. He made an estimate of the expense, and said that he would do anything within reason to further the object, but was afraid that the department at Washington would not sustain him if he made the general outfit. His sympathy was that of a man and a gentleman.

"I also conferred with several of the citizens of Yerba Buena; their advice was not to trouble the Commodore further; that they would call a meeting of the citizens and see what could be done. At the meeting, the situation of the people was made known, and committees were appointed to collect money. Over a thousand dollars was raised in the town, and the sailors of the fleet gave over three hundred dollars. At the meeting, Midshipman Woodworth volunteered to go into the mountains. Commodore Hull gave me authority to raise as many men, with horses, as would be required. The citizens purchased all the supplies necessary for the outfit, and placed them on board the schooner——, for Hardy's Ranch, mouth of Feather River. Midshipman Woodworth took charge of the schooner, and was the financial agent of the government.

"I left in a boat for Napa by way of Sonoma, to procure men and horses, and when I arrived at Mr. Gordon's, on Cache Creek, I had all the men and horses needed. From here I proceeded to the mouth of Feather River for the purpose of meeting Mr. Woodworth with the provisions. When we reached the river the boat had not arrived. The water was very high in the river, the tule lands being overflowed. From here I sent a man to a point on the Sacramento River opposite Sutter's Fort, to obtain information of the boat with our provisions; he returned and reported the arrival of the boat at the Fort."

"Before leaving Yerba Buena, news came of a party of fifteen persons having started from the emigrant encampment, and only seven getting to Johnson's. I was here placed in a quandary — no boat to take us across the river, and no provisions for our party to take into the mountains. We camped a short distance back from the river, where we killed a number of elk for the purpose of using the skins in covering a skeleton boat. Early next morning we started for the river, and to our delight saw a small schooner, belonging to Perry McCan, which had arrived during the night. We immediately crossed, McCutchen and myself, to the opposite bank of the river. I directed the men to cross and follow us to Johnson's Ranch. We arrived there early that day. Making known our situation, he drove his cattle up to the house, saying, 'There are the cattle, take as many as you need.' We shot down five head, staid up all night, and with the help of Mr. Johnson and his Indians, by the time the men arrived the next morning, we had the meat fire-dried and ready to be placed in bags. Mr. Johnson had a party of Indians making flour by hand mills, they making, during the night, nearly two hundred pounds.

"We packed up immediately and started. After reaching the snow, the meat and flour was divided into suitable packs for us to carry, we leaving the horses here. At Johnson's I learned that a relief party had passed in a few days previous, being sent by Captain Sutter and Mr. Sinclair."

This was the party commanded by Captain Reasin P. Tucker, whose journey over the mountains as far as the summit was described in the last chapter. Reed was faithful and energetic in endeavoring to recross the mountains. Mr. McCutchen, also, did all in his power to reach the wife and baby he left behind. The snow belt is about four times as wide on the west side of the summit as it is on the east side. It was almost impossible for relief parties to cross the mountains. Captain Tucker's party was composed of men of great nerve and hardihood, yet, as will be seen, the trip was almost as much as their lives were worth.

On the morning of the nineteenth of February, 1847, the relief party of Captain R. P. Tucker began the descent of the gorge leading to Donner Lake.

Let us glance ahead at the picture soon to be unfolded to their gaze. The mid-winter snows had almost concealed the cabins. The inmates lived subterranean lives. Steps cut in the icy snow led up from the doorways to the surface. Deep despair had settled upon all hearts. The dead were lying all around, some even unburied, and nearly all with only a covering of snow. So weak and powerless had the emigrants become, that it was hardly possible for them to lift the dead bodies up the steps out of the cabins. All were reduced to mere skeletons. They had lived on pieces of rawhide, or on old, castaway bones, which were boiled or burned until capable of being eaten. They were so reduced that it seemed as if only a dry, shriveled skin covered their emaciated frames. The eyes were sunken deep in their sockets, and had a fierce, ghastly, demoniacal look. The faces were haggard, woebegone, and sepulchral. One seldom heard the sound of a voice, and when heard, it was weak, tremulous, pitiful. Sometimes a child would moan and sob for a mouthful of food, and the poor, helpless mothers, with breaking hearts, would have to soothe them, as best they could, with kind words and tender caresses. Food, there was none. Oh! what words can fitly frame a tribute for those noble mothers! When strong men gave up, and passively awaited the delirium of death, the mothers were actively administering to the wants of the dying, and striving to cheer and comfort the living. Marble monuments never bore more heroic names than those of Margaret W. Reed, Lavina Murphy, Elizabeth Graves, Margaret Breen, Tamsen Donner, and Elizabeth Donner. Their charity, fortitude, and self-sacrifice failed not in the darkest hour. Death came so often now, that little notice was taken of his approach, save by these mothers. A dreadful want of consciousness precedes starvation. The actual death is not so terrible. The delirious would rave of feasts, and rich viands, and bountiful stores of food. As the shadows of death more closely enveloped the poor creatures, the mutterings grew unintelligible, and were interrupted, now and then, by startled cries of frenzy, which gradually grew fainter, until the victims finally slumbered. From this slumber there was no awakening. The breathing became feebler and more irregular, and finally ceased. It was not so terrible to the unconscious dying, as to the weeping mother who watched by the sufferer's side.

It was always dark and gloomy enough in the snow-covered cabins, but during the fierce, wild storms, the desolation became almost unendurable. The rushing gale, the furious storm, the lashing of storm-rent pine boughs, or the crash of giant trees overthrown by the hurricane, filled the souls of the imprisoned emigrants with nameless dread. Sometimes the silent darkness of the night would shudder with the howl of the great gray wolves which in those days infested the mountains. Too well did they know that these gaunt beasts were howling for the bodies of the living as well as of the dead.

Wood grew plentifully at short distances from the cabins, but for these weak, starving creatures to obtain it was a herculean task. To go out when the storms were raging, would be almost impossible for a well, strong man. To struggle through the deep, loose drifts, reaching frequently to the waist, required, at any time, fearful exertion. The numb, fleshless fingers could hardly guide, or even wield the ax. Near the site of the Breen cabin, to-day, stands a silent witness of the almost superhuman exertions that were made to procure fuel. On the side of a pine tree are old seams and gashes, which, by their irregular position, were evidently made by hands too weak to cut down a tree. Hundreds of blows, however, were struck, and the marks of the ax-blade extend up and down the side of the tree for a foot and a half. Bark seared with age has partly covered portions of the cuts, but in one place the incision is some inches deep. At the foot of this pine was found a short, decayed ax-handle, and a broad-bladed, old-fashioned ax-head. The mute story of these witnesses is unmistakable. The poor starved being who undertook the task, never succeeded.

Trees felled, frequently buried themselves out of sight in the loose snow, or at best, only the uppermost branches could be obtained. Without fire, without food, without proper shelter from the dampness occasioned by the melting snows, in the bitter, biting wintry weather, the men, women, and children were huddled together, the living and the dead. When Milton Elliott died, there were no men to assist in removing the body from the deep pit. Mrs. Reed and her daughter, Virginia, bravely undertook the task. Tugging, pushing, lifting as best they could, the corpse was raised up the icy steps. He died in the Murphy cabin by the rock. A few days before he died, he crawled over to the Breen cabin, where were Mrs. Reed and her children. For years be had been one of the members of this family. He worked for Mr. Reed in the mill and furniture establishment owned by the latter in Jamestown, Illinois. He drove the same yoke of oxen, "Bully" and "George," who were the wheel-oxen of Reed's family team on the plains. When Mr. Reed proposed crossing the plains, his wife and children refused to go, unless Milt could be induced to drive. He was a kind, careful man, and after Mr. Reed had been driven away from the company, Elliott always provided for them as best he was able. Now that he was going to die, he wanted to see "Ma" and the children once more. "Ma" was the term he always used in addressing Mrs. Reed. None realized better than he the sorrowful position in which she was placed by having no husband upon whom to lean in this time of great need. Poor Elliott! he knew that he was starving! starving! "Ma, I am not going to starve to death, I am going to eat of the bodies of the dead." This is what he told Mrs. Reed, yet when he attempted to do so, his heart revolted at the thought. Mrs. Reed accompanied him a portion of the way back to the Murphy cabin, and before leaving him, knelt on the snow and prayed as only a mother can, that the Good Father would help them in this hour of distress. It was a starving Christian mother praying that relief might come to her starving children, and especially to this, her starving boy. From the granite rocks, the solemn forests, and the snow-mantled mountains of Donner Lake, a more fervent prayer never ascended heavenward. Could Elliott have heard, in his dying moments, that this prayer was soon to be answered, so far as Mrs. Reed and her little ones were concerned, he would have welcomed death joyfully.

As time wore wearily on, another and more severe trial awaited Mrs. Reed. Her daughter Virginia was dying. The innutritions rawhide was not sufficient to sustain life in the poor, famished body of the delicate child. Indeed, toward the last, her system became so debilitated that she found it impossible to eat the loathsome, glue-like preparation which formed their only food. Silently she had endured her sufferings, until she was at the very portals of death. This beautiful girl was a great favorite of Mrs. Breen's. Oftentimes during the days of horror and despair, this good Irish mother had managed, unobserved, to slip an extra piece of meat or morsel of food to Virginia. Mrs. Breen was the first to discover that the mark of death was visible upon the girl's brow. In order to break the news to Mrs. Reed, without giving those in the cabin a shock which might prove fatal, Mrs. Breen asked the mother up out of the cabin on the crisp, white snow.

It was the evening of the nineteenth of February, 1847. The sun was setting, and his rays, in long, lance-like lines, sifted through the darkening forests. Far to the eastward, the summits of the Washoe mountains lay bathed in golden sunlight, while the deep gorges at their feet were purpling into night. The gentle breeze which crept over the bosom of the ice-bound lake, softly wafted from the tree-tops a muffled dirge for the dying girl. Ere another day dawned over the expanse of snow, her spirit would pass to a haven of peace where the demons of famine could never enter.

In the desolate cabin, all was silence. Living under the snow, passing an underground life, as it were, seldom visiting each other, or leaving the cabins, these poor prisoners learned to listen rather than look for relief. During the first days they watched hour after hour the upper end of the lake where the "fifteen" had disappeared. With aching eyes and weary hearts, they always turned back to their subterranean abodes disappointed. Hope finally deserted the strongest hearts. The brave mothers had constantly encouraged the despondent by speaking of the promised relief, yet this was prompted more by the necessities of the situation than from any belief that help would arrive. It was human nature, however, to glance toward the towering summits whenever they ascended to the surface of the snow, and to listen at all times for an unfamiliar sound or footstep. So delicate became their sense of hearing, that every noise of the wind, every visitor's tread, every sound that ordinarily occurred above their heads, was known and instantly detected.

On this evening, as the two women were sobbing despairingly upon the snow, the silence of the twilight was broken by a shout from near Donner Lake! In an instant every person forgot weakness and infirmity, and clambered up the stairway! It was a strange voice, and in the distance they discovered strange forms approaching. The Reed and the Breen children thought, at first, that it was a band of Indians, but Patrick Breen, the good old father, soon declared that the strangers were white men. Captain Tucker and his men had found the wide expanse of snow covering forest and lake, and had shouted to attract attention, if any of the emigrants yet survived. Oh! what joy! There were tears in other eyes than those of the little children. The strong men of the relief party sat down on the snow and wept with the rest. It is related of one or two mothers, and can readily be believed, that their first act was to fall upon their knees, and with faces turned to God, to pour out their gratitude to Him for having brought assistance to their dying children. Virginia Reed did not die.

Captain Reasin P. Tucker, who had been acquainted with the Graves family on the plains before the Donner Party took the Hastings Cut-off, was anxious to meet them. They lived in the lower cabin, half a mile further down Donner Creek. When he came close enough to observe the smoke issuing from the hole in the snow which marked their abode, he shouted, as he had done at the upper cabins. The effect was as electrical as in the former instance. All came up to the surface, and the same unrestrained gladness was manifested by the famished prisoners. Famished they were. Mrs. Graves is especially praised by the survivors for her unstinted charity. Instead of selfishly hoarding her stores and feeding only her own children, she was generous to a fault, and no person ever asked at her door for food who did not receive as good as she and her little ones had to eat.

Dear Mrs. Graves! How earnestly she asked about her husband and daughters! Did all reach the valley? Captain Tucker felt his heart rise in his throat. How could he tell this weak, starved woman of the terrible fate which had befallen her husband and her son-in-law! He could not! He answered with assumed cheerfulness in the affirmative. So, too, they deceived Mrs. Murphy regarding her dear boy Lemuel. It was best. Had the dreadful truth been told, not one of all this company would ever have had courage to attempt the dangerous journey.

Little sleep was there in the Donner cabins that night. The relief party were to start back in a couple of days, and such as were strong enough were to accompany them. Mrs. Graves had four little children, and told her son William C. Graves that he must remain with her to cut wood to keep the little ones from freezing. But William was anxious to go and help send back provisions to his mother. So earnestly did he work during the next two days, that he had two cords of wood piled up near the cabin. This was to last until he could return. His task was less difficult because this cabin was built in a dense grove of tamarack.

Food had been given in small quantities to the sufferers. Many of the snow-bound prisoners were so near death's door that a hearty meal would have proven fatal. The remnant of provisions brought by the relief party was carefully guarded lest some of the famished wretches should obtain more than was allotted them. This was rendered easier from the fact that the members of the relief party were unable to endure the scenes of misery and destitution in the cabins, and so camped outside upon the snow. So hungry were the poor people that some of them ate the strings of the snow-shoes which part of the relief company had brought along.

On the twentieth of February, John Rhodes, R. S. Mootry, and R. P. Tucker visited the Donner tents on Alder Creek, seven miles from the cabins. Only one ox-hide remained to these destitute beings. Here, as well as at the cabins, the all-important question was, who should go with the relief party and who remain. In each family there were little children who could not go unless carried. Few of the Donner Party had more than enough strength to travel unencumbered across the deep snows. Should a storm occur on the mountains, it was doubtful if even the members of the relief party could escape death. It was hopefully urged that other relief parties would soon arrive from California, and that these would bring over those who remained. In determining who should go and who stay, examples of heroism and devotion were furnished which were never surpassed in the history of man. Could their vision have penetrated the veil which interposed between them and the sad occurrences about to ensue, they would have known that almost every family, whose members separated, was bidding good-by to some member forever.

CHAPTER XII

A WIFE'S DEVOTION — TAMSEN DONNER'S EARLY LIFE — THE
EARLY SETTLERS OF SANGAMON COUNTY — AN INCIDENT IN
SCHOOL — TEACHING AND KNITTING — SCHOOL DISCIPLINE —
CAPTAIN GEORGE DONNER'S APPEARANCE — PARTING
SCENES AT ALDER CREEK — STARTING OVER THE MOUNTAINS —
A BABY'S DEATH — A MASON'S VOW — CROSSING THE SNOW
BARRIER — MORE PRECIOUS THAN GOLD OR DIAMONDS —
ELITHA DONNER'S KINDNESS.

MRS. Tamsen Donner was well and comparatively strong, and
could easily have crossed the mountains in safety with this party.
Her husband, however, was suffering from a serious swelling on
one of his hands. Some time before reaching the mountains he
had accidentally hurt this hand while handling a wagon. After
encamping at Alder Creek he was anxious to assist in the arrangements and preparations for winter, and while thus working the
old wound reopened. Taking cold in the hand, it became greatly
swollen and inflamed, and he was rendered entirely helpless.
Mrs. Donner was urged to go with the relief party, but resolutely
determined to heed the promptings of wifely devotion and
remain by her husband.

No one will ever read the history of the Donner Party without
greatly loving and reverencing the character of this faithful wife.
The saddest, most tear-stained page of the tragedy, relates to her
life and death in the mountains. A better acquaintance with the
Donner family, and especially with Mrs. Tamsen Donner, can not

fail to be desirable in view of succeeding chapters. Thanks to Mr. Allen Francis, the present United States Consul at Victoria, British Columbia, very complete, authentic, and interesting information upon this subject has been furnished. Mr. Francis was publisher of the Springfield (Illinois) Journal in 1846, and a warm personal friend of the family.

The Donners were among the first settlers of Sangamon County, Ill. They were North Carolinians, immigrants to Kentucky in 1818, subsequently to the State of Indiana, and from thence to what was known as the Sangamon Country, in the year 1828.

George Donner, at the time of leaving Springfield, Ill., was a large, fine-looking man, fully six feet in height, with merry black eyes, and the blackest of hair, lined with an occasional silver thread. He possessed a cheerful disposition, an easy temperament, industrious habits, sound judgment, and much general information. By his associates and neighbors he was called "Uncle George." To him they went for instructions relating to the management of their farms, and usually they returned feeling they had been properly advised. Twice had death bequeathed him a group of motherless children, and Tamsen was his third wife.

Her parents, William and Tamsen Eustis, were respected and well to do residents of Newburyport, Mass., where she was born in November, 1801. Her love of books made her a student at an early age; almost as soon as the baby-dimples left her cheeks, she sought the school-room, which afforded her reat enjoyment. Her mother's death occurred before she attained her seventh year, and for a time her childish hopes and desires were overshadowed with sadness by this, her first real sorrow. But the sympathy of friends soothed her grief, and her thirst for knowledge led her back to the school-room, where she pursued her studies with greater eagerness than before.

Her father married again, and little Tamsen's life was rendered happier by this event; for in her step-mother she found a friend who tenderly directed her thoughts and encouraged her work. At fifteen years of age she finished the course of study, and her proficiency in mathematics, geometry, philosophy, etc., called forth the highest praise of her teachers and learned friends. She, like many daughters of New England, felt that talents are intrusted to be used, and that each life is created for some definite purpose. She therefore resolved to devote herself to the instruction of the young, and after teaching at Newburyport for a short time, she accepted a call to fill a vacancy in the academy at Elizabeth City, N. C., where she continued an earnest and appreciated teacher for a number of years. She became a fluent French scholar while at that institution, and her leisure hours were devoted to the fine arts. Her paintings and drawings were much admired for their correctness in outline, subdued coloring, and delicacy in shading.

In Elizabeth City she met Mr. Dozier, a young man of education and good family, and they were married. He was not a man of means, but her forethought enabled them to live comfortably. For a few brief years she enjoyed all the happiness which wedded bliss and maternal love could confer, then death came, and in a few short weeks her husband and two babes were snatched from her arms. In her desolation and bereavement she thought of her old home, and longed for the sympathy of her childhood's friends. She returned to Newburyport, where she spent three years in retirement and rest. In 1836, she received a letter from her brother in Illinois, urging her to come to his afflicted household, and teach his motherless children. She remained with them one winter, but her field of action had been too wide to permit her to settle quietly on a farm. Besides, she had heard much of the manner in which country schools were conducted, and became desirous of testing her ability in controlling and teaching such a school. She obtained one in Auburn, and soon became the friend of her pupils. All agreed that Mrs. Dozier was a faithful teacher until the following little incident occurred. The worthy Board of School Trustees heard that Mrs. Dozier was in the habit of knitting during school hours. "Surely, she could not knit and instruct her pupils properly; therefore, she must either give up her knitting or her school." When Mrs. Dozier heard their resolution, she smiled, and said: "Before those gentlemen deny my ability to impart knowledge and work with my fingers at the same time, I would like them to visit my school, and judge me by the result of their observation."

A knock at the school-room door, a week later, startled the children, and a committee of trustees entered. Mrs. Dozier received them in the most ladylike manner, and after they were seated, she called each class at its appointed time. The recitations were heard, and lessons explained, yet no one seemed disturbed by the faint, but regular, click of knitting needles. For hours those gentlemen sat in silence, deeply interested in all that transpired. When the time for closing school arrived, the teacher invited the trustees to address her pupils, after which she dismissed school, thanked her visitor for their kind attention, and went home without learning their opinion.

The next morning she was informed that the Board of Trustees had met the previous evening, and after hearing the report of the visiting committee, had unanimously agreed that Mrs. Dozier might continue her school and her knitting also. This little triumph was much enjoyed by her friends.

The following year she was urged to take the school on Sugar Creek, where the children were older and further advanced than those at Auburn. Her connection with this school marked a new era for many of its attendants. Mr. J. Miller used to relate an incident which occurred a few days after she took charge of those unruly boys who had been in the habit of managing the teacher and school to suit themselves. "I will never forget," said Mr. Miller, "how Mrs. Dozier took her place at the table that morning, tapped for order, and in a kind, but firm, tone said: 'Young gentlemen and young ladies, as a teacher only, I can not criticise the propriety of your writing notes to each other when out of school; but as your teacher, with full authority in school, I desire and request you neither to write nor send notes to any one during school hours. I was surprised at your conduct yesterday, and should my wish be disregarded in the future, I will be obliged to chastise the offender.' She called the first class, and school began in earnest. I looked at her quiet face and diminutive form, and thought how easy it would be for me to pick up two or three such little bodies as she, and set them outside of the door! I wrote a note and threw it to the pupil in front of me, just to try Mrs. Dozier. When the recitation was finished, she stepped to the side of her table, and looked at me with such a grieved expression on her face, then said: 'Mr. Miller, I regret that my eldest scholar should be the first to violate my rule. Please step forward.' I quailed beneath her eye. I marched up to where she stood. The stillness of that room was oppressive. I held out my hand at the demand of that little woman, and took the punishment I deserved, and returned to my seat deeply humiliated, but fully determined to behave myself in the future, and make the other boys do likewise. Well, she had no more trouble while she was our teacher. Her pluck had won our admiration, and her quiet dignity held our respect, and we soon ceased wondering at the ease with which she overturned our plans and made us eager to adopt hers; for no teacher ever taught on Sugar Creek who won the affections or ruled pupils more easily or happily than she. We were expected to come right up to the mark; but if we got into trouble, she was always ready to help us out, and could do it in the quietest way imaginable."

She taught several young men the art of surveying, and had a wonderful faculty of interesting her pupils in the study of botany. She sought by creek and over plain for specimens with which to illustrate their lessons. It was while engaged in this place that Mrs. Dozier met George Donner, who at that time resided about two and a half miles from Springfield. Their acquaintance resulted in marriage. Her pupils always called her their "little teacher," for she was but five feet in height, and her usual weight ninety-six pounds. She had grayish-blue eyes, brown hair, and a face full of character and intelligence. She was gifted with fine conversational powers, and was an excellent reader. Her voice would hold in perfect silence, for hours, the circle of neighbors and friends who would assemble during the long winter evenings to hear her read. Even those who did not fail to criticise her ignorance of farm and dairy work, were often charmed by her voice and absence of display; for while her dress was always of rich material, it was remarkable for its Quaker simplicity.

Mr. Francis says: "Mrs. George Donner was a perfect type of an eastern lady, kind, sociable, and exemplary, ever ready to assist neighbors, and even the stranger in distress. Whenever she could spare time, she wielded a ready pen on various topics. She frequently contributed gems in prose and poetry to the columns of the Journal, that awakened an interest among its readers to know their author. Herself and husband were faithful members of the German Prairie Christian Church, situated a little north of their residence. Here they lived happily, and highly respected by all who knew them, until the spring of 1846, when they started for California."

Having said this much of the Donners, and especially of the noble woman who refused to leave her suffering husband, let us glance at the parting scenes at Alder Creek. It had been determined that the two eldest daughters of George Donner should accompany Captain Tucker's party. George Donner, Jr., and William Hook, two of Jacob Donner's sons, Mrs. Wolfinger, and Noah James were also to join the company. This made six from the Donner tents. Mrs. Elizabeth Donner was quite able to have crossed the mountains, but preferred to remain with her two little children, Lewis and Samuel, until another and larger relief party should arrive. These two boys were not large enough to walk, Mrs. Donner was not strong enough to carry them, and the members of Captain Tucker's party had already agreed to take as many little ones as they could carry.

Leanna C. Donner, now Mrs. John App, of Jamestown, Tuolumne County, Cal., gives a vivid description of the trip from George Donner's tent to the cabins at Donner Lake Miss Rebecca E. App, acting as her mother's amanuensis, writes:

"Mother says: Never shall I forget the day when my sister Elitha and myself left our tent. Elitha was strong and in good health, while I was so poor and emaciated that I could scarcely walk. All we took with us were the clothes on our backs and one thin blanket, fastened with a string around our necks, answering the purpose of a shawl in the day-time, and which was all we had to cover us at night. We started early in the morning, and many a good cry I had before we reached the cabins, a distance of about eight miles. Many a time I sat down in the snow to die, and would have perished there if my sister had not urged me on, saying, 'The cabins are just over the hill.' Passing over the hill, and not seeing the cabins, I would give up, again sit down and have another cry, but my sister continued to help and encourage me until I saw the smoke rising from the cabins; then I took courage, and moved along as fast as I could. When we reached the Graves cabin it was all I could do to step down the snow-steps into the cabin. Such pain and misery as I endured that day is beyond description."

In Patrick Breen's diary are found the following entries, which allude to Captain Tucker's relief party:

"Feb. 19. Froze hard last night. Seven men arrived from California yesterday with provisions, but left the greater part on the way. To-day it is clear and warm for this region; some of the men have gone to Donner's camp; they will start back on Monday.

"Feb. 22. The Californians started this morning, twenty-three in number, some in a very weak state. Mrs. Keseberg started with them, and left Keseberg here, unable to go. Buried Pike's child this morning in the snow; died two days ago."

Poor little Catherine Pike lingered until this time! It will be remembered that this little nursing babe had nothing to eat except a little coarse flour mixed in snow water. Its mother crossed the mountains with the "Forlorn Hope," and from the sixteenth of December to the twentieth of February it lived upon the miserable gruel made from unbolted flour. How it makes the heart ache to think of this little sufferer, wasting away, moaning with hunger, and sobbing for something to eat. The teaspoonful of snow water would contain only a few particles of the flour, yet how eagerly the dying child would reach for the pitiful food. The tiny hands grew thinner, the sad, pleading eyes sank deeper in their fleshless sockets, the face became hollow, and the wee voice became fainter, yet, day after day, little Catherine Pike continued to breathe, up to the very arrival of the relief party.

Patrick Breen says twenty-three started across the mountains. Their names were: Mrs. Margaret W. Reed and her children — Virginia E. Reed, Patty Reed, Thomas Reed, and James F. Reed, Jr.; Elitha C. Donner, Leanna C. Donner, Wm. Hook, and George Donner, Jr.; Wm. G. Murphy, Mary M. Murphy, and Naomi L. Pike; Wm. C. Graves, Eleanor Graves, and Lovina Graves; Mrs. Phillipine Keseberg, and Ada Keseberg; Edward J. and Simon P. Breen, Eliza Williams, John Denton, Noah James, and Mrs. Wolfinger.

In starting from the camps at Donner Lake, Mrs. Keseberg's child and Naomi L. Pike were carried by the relief party. In a beautiful letter received from Naomi L. Pike (now Mrs. Schenck, of the Dalles, Oregon), she says: "I owe my life to the kind heart of John Rhodes, whose sympathies were aroused for my mother. He felt that she was deserving of some relic of all she had left behind when she started with the first party in search of relief, and he carried me to her in a blanket." We have before spoken of this noble man's bravery in bearing the news of the condition of the "Forlorn Hope" and of the Donner Party to Sutter's Fort. Here we find him again exhibiting the nobility of his nature by saving this little girl from starvation by carrying her on his back over forty miles of wintry snow.

Before the party had proceeded two miles, a most sad occurrence took place. It became evident that Patty and Thomas Reed were unable to stand the fatigue of the journey. Already they exhibited signs of great weakness and weariness, and it was not safe to allow them to proceed. Mr. Aquila Glover informed Mrs. Reed that it was necessary that these two children go back. Who can portray the emotions of this fond mother? What power of language can indicate the struggle which took place in the minds of this stricken family? Mr. Glover promised to return as soon as he arrived at Bear Valley, and himself bring Patty and Thomas over the mountains. This promise, however, was but a slight consolation for the agonized mother or weeping children, until finally a hopeful thought occurred to Mrs. Reed. She turned suddenly to Mr. Glover, and asked, "Are you a Mason?" He replied, "I am." "Do you promise me," she said, "upon the word of a Mason, that when you arrive at Bear Valley, you will come back and get my children?" Mr. Glover made the promise, and the children were by him taken back to the cabins. The mother had remembered, in this gloomiest moment of life, that the father of her little ones was a Mason, and that he deeply reverenced the order. If her children must be left behind in the terrible snows, she would trust the promise of this Mason to return and save them. It was a beautiful trust in a secret order by a Mason's wife in deep distress.

Rebecca E. App, writing for her mother, gives a vivid description of this journey across the summits, from which is taken the following brief extract:

"It was a bright Sunday morning when we left the cabins. Some were in good health, while others were so poor and emaciated that they could scarcely walk. I was one of the weakest in the party, and not one in the train thought I would get to the top of the first hill. We were a sad spectacle to look upon as we left the cabins. We marched along in single file, the leader wearing snowshoes, and the others following after, all stepping in the leader's tracks. I think my sister and myself were about the rear of the train, as the strongest were put in front. My sister Elitha and I were alone with strangers, as it were, having neither father, mother, nor brothers, to give us a helping hand or a word of courage to cheer us onward. We were placed on short allowance of food from the start, and each day this allowance was cut shorter and shorter, until we received each for our evening and morning meal two small pieces of jerked beef, about the size of the index finger of the hand. Finally, the last ration was issued in the evening. This was intended for that evening and the next morning, but I was so famished I could not resist the temptation to eat all I had — the two meals at one time. Next morning, of course, I had nothing for breakfast. Now occurred an incident which I shall never forget. While I sat looking at the others eating their morsels of meat, which were more precious than gold or diamonds, my sister saw my distress, and divided her piece with me. How long we went without food after that, I do not know. I think we were near the first station."

CHAPTER XIII

DEATH OF ADA KESEBERG — DENTON DISCOVERING GOLD —
A POEM COMPOSED WHILE DYING — THE CACHES OF
PROVISIONS ROBBED BY FISHERS — THE SEQUEL TO THE
REED-SNYDER TRAGEDY — DEATH FROM OVER-EATING —
THE AGONY OF FROZEN FEET — AN INTERRUPTED PRAYER —
STANTON, AFTER DEATH, GUIDES THE RELIEF PARTY — THE
SECOND RELIEF PARTY ARRIVES — A SOLITARY INDIAN —
PATTY REED AND HER FATHER — STARVING CHILDREN
LYING IN BED — MRS. GRAVES' MONEY STILL BURIED AT
DONNER LAKE.

REASIN P. Tucker's relief party had twenty-one emigrants with
them after Patty and Thomas Reed returned to the desolate
cabins. On the evening of the first day, one of the twenty-one
died. It was the baby child of Lewis Keseberg. The mother had
fairly worshiped her girl. They buried the little one in the snow.
It was all they could do for the pallid form of the starved little
girl. Mrs. Keseberg was heart-broken over her baby's death. At
the very outset she had offered everything she possessed —
twenty-five dollars and a gold watch — to any one who would
carry her child over the mountains. After the starved band
resumed their weary march next morning, it is doubtful if
many thought of the niche hollowed out of the white snow, or
of the pulseless heart laid therein. Death had become fearfully
common, and his victims were little heeded by the perishing

company. The young German mother, however, was inconsolable. Her only boy had starved to death at the cabins, and now she was childless.

The next day the company reached Summit Valley. An incident of this day's travel illustrates the exhausted condition of the members of the Donner Party. John Denton, an Englishman, was missed when camp was pitched, and John Rhodes returned and found him fast asleep upon the snow. He had become so weary that he yielded to a slumber that would soon have proven fatal. With much labor and exertion he was aroused and brought to camp. Denton appreciated the kindness, but at the same time declared that it would be impossible for him to travel another day. Sure enough, after journeying a little way on the following morning, his strength utterly gave way. His companions built a fire for him, gave him such food as they were able, and at his earnest request continued their sorrowful march. If another relief came soon, he would, perhaps, be rescued. Denton was well educated and of good family, was a gun-smith by trade, and was skilled in metals. It is related, that while in the Reed cabin, he discovered in the earth, ashes, and burnt stones in the fireplace, some small pieces of yellowish metal, which he declared to be gold. These he made into a small lump, which he carefully preserved until he left the lake, and it was doubtless lost on the mountains at his death. This was in the spring of 1847, before the discovery of gold in California. The strange little metallic lump was exhibited to several who are yet living, and who think there is reason for believing it was really gold. A few years before the construction of the Central Pacific, Knoxville, about ten miles south of Donner Lake, and Elizabethtown, some six miles from Truckee, were famous mining camps. Gold never has been found on the very shore of Donner Lake, but should the discovery be made, and especially should gold be found in the rocks or earth near the Reed cabin, there would be reason to believe that this poor unfortunate man was in reality the first discoverer of the precious metal in California. Left alone in the snow-mantled forests of the Sierra, what were this man's emotions? In the California Star of 1847, a bound volume of which is in the State Library in Sacramento, appears the following poem. The second relief party found it written on the leaf of a memorandum book by the side of Denton's lifeless body. The pencil with which it was written lay also by the side of the unfortunate man. Ere the lethargy of death stole away his senses, John Denton's thoughts had been of his boyhood's beautiful home in merry England. These thoughts were woven into verse. Are they not strangely pathetic and beautiful? Judge Thornton, in 1849, published them with the following prefatory words: "When the circumstances are considered in connection with the calamities in which the unhappy Denton was involved, the whole compass of American and English poetry may be challenged to furnish a more exquisitely beautiful, a more touching and pathetic piece. Simple and inornate to the last degree, yet coming from the heart, it goes to the heart. Its lines are the last plaintive notes which wintry winds have wakened from an Æolian harp, the strings of which rude hands have sundered. Bring before your mind the picture of an amiable young man who has wandered far from the paternal roof, is stricken by famine, and left by his almost equally unhappy companions to perish among the terrible snows of the great Sierra Nevada. He knows that his last, most solemn hour is near. Reason still maintains her empire, and memory, faithful to the last, performs her functions. On every side extends a boundless waste of trackless snow. He reclines against a bank of it, to rise no more, and busy memory brings before him a thousand images of past beauty and pleasure, and of scenes he will never revisit. A mother's image presents itself to his mind, tender recollections crowd upon his heart, and the scenes of his boyhood and youth pass in review before him with an unwonted vividness. The hymns of praise and thanksgiving that in harmony swelled from the domestic circle around the family altar are remembered, and soothe the sorrows of the dying man, and finally, just before he expires, he writes:"

"Oh! after many roving years,
    How sweet it is to come
Back to the dwelling-place of youth,
    Our first and dearest home;
To turn away our wearied eyes
    From proud ambition's towers,
And wander in those summer fields,
    The scenes of boyhood's hours.

"But I am changed since last I gazed
    Upon that tranquil scene,
And sat beneath the old witch elm
    That shades the village green;
And watched my boat upon the brook —
    It was a regal galley —
And sighed not for a joy on earth,
    Beyond the happy valley.

"I wish I could once more recall
    That bright and blissful joy,
And summon to my weary heart
    The feelings of a boy.
But now on scenes of past delight
    I look, and feel no pleasure,
As misers on the bed of death
    Gaze coldly on their treasure."

When Captain Tucker's relief party were going to Donner
Lake, they left a portion of their provisions in Summit Valley, tied
up in a tree. They had found these provisions difficult to carry,
and besides, it was best to have something provided for their
return, in case the famished emigrants ate all they carried over the
summit. It was indeed true that all was eaten which they carried
over. All the scanty allowances were, one after another, consumed.
When the relief party, and those they were rescuing, reached the

place where the provisions had been cached, they were in great need of the reserve store which they expected to find. To their horror and dismay, they found that wild animals had gnawed the ropes by which the cache had been suspended, and had destroyed every vestige of these provisions! Death stared them in the face, and the strongest men trembled at the prospect.

Here comes the sequel to the Reed-Snyder tragedy. Had it not been for Reed's banishment, there is every reason to believe that these people would have died for want of food. It will be remembered, however, that the relief party organized by Reed was only a few days behind Captain Tucker's. On the twenty-seventh of February, just as the horror and despair of their dreadful situation began to be realized, Tucker, and those with him were relieved by the second relief party.

In order to better understand these events, let us return and follow the motions of Reed and the members of the second relief party. In the article quoted in a former chapter from the Rural Press, Reed traced their progress as far as Johnson's ranch. Patty Reed (Mrs. Frank Lewis) has in her possession the original diary kept by her father during this journey. This diary shows that on the very morning Capt. Tucker, and the company with him, left Donner Lake to return to the valleys, Reed and the second relief party started from Johnson's ranch to go to Donner Lake. All that subsequently occurred, is briefly and pointedly narrated in the diary.

"February 22, 1847. All last night I kept fire under the beef which I had drying on the scaffolds, and Johnson's Indians were grinding flour in a small hand-mill. By sunrise this morning I had about two hundred pounds of beef dried and placed in bags. We packed our horses and started with our supplies. Including the meat Greenwood had dried, we had seven hundred pounds of flour, and five beeves. Mr. Greenwood had three men, including himself. Traveled this day about ten miles.

"Feb. 23. Left camp early this morning, and pushed ahead, but camped early on account of grass. To-morrow we will reach the snow.

"Feb. 24. Encamped at Mule Springs this evening. Made arrangements to take to the snow in the morning, having left in camp our saddles, bridles, etc.

"Feb. 25. Started with eleven horses and mules lightly packed, each having about eighty pounds. Traveled two miles, and left one mule and his pack. Made to-day, with hard labor for the horses, in the snow, about six miles. Our start was late.

"Feb. 26. Left our encampment, Cady thinking the snow would bear the horses. Proceeded two hundred yards with difficulty, when we were compelled to unpack the horses and take the provisions on our backs. Usually the men had kept in the best of spirits, but here, for a few moments, there was silence. When the packs were ready to be strung upon their backs, however, the hilarity and good feeling again commenced. Made the head of Bear Valley, a distance of fifteen miles. We met in the valley, about three miles below the camp, Messrs. Glover and Rhodes, belonging to the party that went to the lake. They informed me they had started with twenty-one persons, two of whom had died, John Denton, of Springfield, Ill., and a child of Mr. and Mrs. Keseberg. Mr. Glover sent two men back to the party with fresh provisions. They are in a starving condition, and all have nearly given out. I have lightened our packs with a sufficient quantity of provisions to do the people when they shall arrive at this place.

"Feb. 27. I sent back two men to our camp of night before last, to bring forward provisions. They will return to-morrow. I also left one man to prepare for the people who were expected to-day. Left camp on a fine, hard snow, and proceeded about four miles, when we met the poor, unfortunate, starved people. As I met them scattered along the snow-trail, I distributed some bread that I had baked last night. I gave in small quantities to each. Here I met my wife and two of my little children. Two of my children are still in the mountains. I can not describe the death-like look all these people had. 'Bread!' 'Bread!' 'Bread!' 'Bread!' was the begging cry of every child and grown person. I gave all I dared to them, and set out for the scene of desolation at the lake. I am now camped within twenty-five miles of the place, which I hope to reach by traveling to-night and to-morrow. We had to camp early this evening, on account of the softness of the snow, the men sinking in to their waists, The party who passed us to-day were overjoyed when we told them there was plenty of provision at camp. I made a cache, to-day, after we had traveled about twelve miles, and encamped three miles further eastward, on the Yuba. Snow about fifteen feet deep."

The meeting between Reed and his family can better be imagined than described. For months they had been separated. While the father was battling with fate in endeavoring to reach California and return with assistance, the mother had been using every exertion to obtain food for her starving children. Now they met in the mountains, in the deep snows, amid pathless forests, at a time when the mother and children, and all with them, were out of provisions and ready to perish.

Meantime, the first relief, with their little company, now reduced to nineteen, passed forward toward the settlements. At Bear Valley, another cache of provisions had been made, and this was found unmolested. Camping at this place, the utmost precaution was taken to prevent the poor starved people from overeating. After a sufficient quantity of food had been distributed, the remainder of the provisions was hung up in a tree. Of course, the small portion distributed to each did not satisfy the cravings of hunger. Some time during the night, Wm. Hook quietly crept to the tree, climbed up to the food, and ate until his hunger was appeased. Poor boy, it was a fatal act. Toward morning it was discovered that he was dying. All that the company could do to relieve his sufferings was done, but it was of no avail. Finding that the poor boy was past relief, most of the emigrants moved on toward the settlements. Wm. G. Murphy's feet had been badly frozen, and he was suffering such excruciating agony that he could not travel and keep up with the others. At his request, his sister Mary had cut his shoes open, in order to get them off, and his feet thereupon swelled up as if they had been scalded. Because he could not walk, the company left him with William Hook. A camp-keeper also remained. This boy's death is thus described by Mr. Murphy, who writes:

"William Hook went out on the snow and rested on his knees and elbows. The camp-keeper called to him to come in. He then told me to make him come into camp. I went and put my hand on him, speaking his name, and he fell over, being already dead. He did not die in great agony, as is usually alleged. No groan, nor signs of dying, were manifested to us. The camp-keeper and myself took the biscuits and jerked beef from his pockets, and buried him just barely under the ground, near a tree which had been fired, and from around which the snow had melted." Those who were in the company thought Wm. G. Murphy could not possibly walk, but when all had gone, and Hook was dead, and no alternative remained but to walk or die, he did walk. It took him two days to go barefooted over the snow to Mule Springs, a journey which the others had made in one day. The agony which he endured during that trip can better be imagined than described. Nothing but an indomitable will could have sustained him during those two days.

All the members of this relief party suffered greatly, and several came near perishing. Little James F. Reed, Jr., was too small to step in the tracks made by the older members of the party. In order to travel with the rest he had to partly use his knees in walking. When one foot was in a track he would place the other knee on the untrodden snow, and was thus enabled to put his foot in the next track. John Denton was left with a good fire, and when last seen was reclining smoking, on a bed of freshly gathered pine boughs. He looked so comfortable that the little timid boy James begged hard to be allowed to remain with him. Mrs. Reed had hard work to coax him to come. Among other things, she promised that when he reached California he should have a horse "all for himself," and that he should never have to walk any more. This promise was literally fulfilled. James F. Reed, Jr., since reaching California, has always had a horse of his own. No matter what vicissitudes of fortune have overtaken him, he has always kept a saddle horse.

Sad scenes were occurring at the cabin at Donner Lake and the tents at Alder Creek. Starvation was fast claiming its victims. The poor sufferers tried to be brave and trust God, but sometimes hope well-nigh disappeared. The evening prayers were always read in Patrick Breen's cabin, and all the inmates knelt and joined in the responses. Once when they were thus praying, they heard the cries of wild geese flying over the cabin. With one accord all raised their heads and listened for a moment to the soul-inspiring sound. "Thank God, the spring is coming," was all Patrick Breen said, and again bowing their heads, the prayer was resumed.

Charles L. Cady, writing from Calistoga, says that Commodore Stockton employed Greenwood and Turner to guide the second relief party over the mountains to Donner Lake. Cady, Stone, and Clark, being young, vigorous men, left their companions, or were sent forward by Reed, and reached the cabins some hours in advance of the party. At one time, near the present station of Summit Valley, Cady and Stone became bewildered, thought they were lost, and wanted to return. Mr. dark, however, prevailed upon them to press forward, agreeing that if they did not catch some glimpse of Donner Lake when they reached a certain mountain top in the distance, he would give up and return with them. Had they reached the mountain top they could not have seen the lake, and so would have turned back, but while they were ascending, they came to the lifeless body of C. T. Stanton sitting upright against a tree. There was no longer room for doubting that they were going in the right direction to reach Donner Lake. Poor Stanton! even in death he pointed out to the relief party the way to the starving emigrants, to save whom he had sacrificed his life.

Reed's diary continues:

"Feb. 28. Left camp about twelve o'clock at night, but was compelled to camp about two o'clock, the snow still being soft. Left again about four o'clock, all hands, and made this day fourteen miles. Encamped early; snow very soft. The snow here is thirty feet deep. Three of my men, Cady, Clark, and Stone, kept on during the night to within two miles of the cabins, where they halted, and remained without fire during the night, on account of having seen ten Indians. The boys did not have any arms, and supposed these Indians had taken the cabins and destroyed the people. In the morning they started, and reached the cabins. All were alive in the houses. They gave provisions to Keseberg, Breen, Graves, and Mrs. Murphy, and the two then left for Donner's, a distance of seven miles, which they made by the middle of the day.

"March 1. I came up with the remainder of my party, and told the people that all who were able should start day after to-morrow. Made soup for the infirm, washed and clothed afresh Eddy's and Foster's children, and rendered every assistance in my power. I left Mr. Stone with Keseberg's people to cook, and to watch the eating of Mrs. Murphy, Keseberg, and three children."

In Patrick Breen's diary is found the following:

"Feb. 23. Froze hard last night. To-day pleasant and thawy; has the appearance of spring, all but the deep snow. Wind south-south-east. Shot a dog to-day and dressed his flesh.

"Feb. 25. To-day Mrs. Murphy says the wolves are about to dig up the dead bodies around her shanty, and the nights are too cold to watch them, but we hear them howl.

"Feb. 26. Hungry times in camp; plenty of hides, but the folks will not eat them; we eat them with tolerably good appetite, thanks to the Almighty God. Mrs. Murphy said here yesterday that she thought she would commence on Milton and eat him. I do not think she has done so yet; it is distressing. The Donners told the California folks four days ago that they would commence on the dead people if they did not succeed that day or the next in finding their cattle, then ten or twelve feet under the snow, and they did not know the spot or near it; they have done it ere this.

"Feb. 28. One solitary Indian passed by yesterday; came from the lake; had a heavy pack on his back; gave me five or six roots resembling onions in shape; tasted some like a sweet potato; full of tough little fibers.

"March 1. Ten men arrived this morning from Bear Valley, with provisions. We are to start in two or three days, and cache our goods here. They say the snow will remain until June."

This closes Patrick Breen's diary. Its record has always been considered reliable. None of the statements made in this diary have ever been controverted.

The Indian spoken of refused to be interviewed. To quote the language of Mr. John Breen, "he did not seem to be at all curious as to how or why there was a white man alone (as it must have seemed to him) in the wilderness of snow." The Indian was trudging along with a heavy pack on his back. As soon as he saw Mr. Breen, he halted and warned him with a gesture not to approach. Taking from the pack a few of the fibrous roots, he laid them on the snow, still cautioning with his hand not to approach until he was well out of reach. As soon as the Indian was gone, Mr. Breen went out and got the roots, which were very palatable. It is probable that this was one of the band of Indians seen by Clark, Cady, and Stone.

When Patty and Thomas Reed had been returned to the cabins by Aquila Glover, they had been received by the Breen family, where they remained all the time until their father came. The Breen cabin was the first one at which Mr. Reed arrived. His meeting with his daughter is thus described by Mr. Eddy, in Thornton's work: "At this camp Mr. Reed saw his daughter Patty sitting on the top of the snow with which the cabin was covered. Patty saw her father at some distance, and immediately started to run and meet him, but such was her weakness that she fell. Her father took her up, and the affectionate girl, bathed in tears, embraced and kissed him, exclaiming: 'Oh, papa! I never expected to see you again when the cruel people drove you out of camp. But I knew that God was good, and would do what was best. Is dear mamma living? Is Mr. Glover living? Did you know that he was a Mason? Oh, my dear papa, I am so happy to see you. Masons must be good men. Is Mr. Glover the same sort of Mason we had in Springfield? He promised mamma upon the word of a Mason that he would bring me and Tommy out of the mountains.' Mr. Reed told Patty that Masons were everywhere the same, and that he had met her mother and Mr. Glover, and had relieved him from his pledge, and that he himself had come to her and little Tommy to redeem that pledge and to take out all that were able to travel."

The greatest precaution was taken to keep the suffering emigrants from overeating. Cady, Stone, and Clark had distributed a small portion of food to each of the famished beings. Patty Reed was intrusted with the task of giving to each person a single biscuit. Taking the biscuits in her apron she went in turn to each member of the company. Who shall describe the rejoicings that were held over those biscuits? Several of the survivors, in speaking of the subject, say that to their hungry eyes these small pieces of bread assumed gigantic proportions. Never did the largest loaves of bread look half so large. Patty Reed says that some of the little girls cut their portions into thin slices, so as to eat them slowly and enjoy them more completely.

The names of the members of this second relief party were James F. Reed, Charles Cady, Charles Stone, Nicholas Clark, Joseph Jondro, Mathew Dofar, John Turner, Hiram Miller, Wm. McCutchen, and Brit. Greenwood. A portion of the party went to the Donner tents, and the remainder assisted the emigrants in preparing to start over the mountains. The distress and suffering at each camp was extreme. Even after the children had received as much food as was prudent, it is said they would stretch out their little arms and with cries and tears beg for something to eat. Mrs. Murphy informed Mr. Reed that some of the children had been confined to their beds for fourteen days. It was clearly to be seen that very few of the sufferers could cross the Sierra without being almost carried. They were too weak and helpless to walk. The threatening appearance of the weather and the short supply of provisions urged the party to hasten their departure, and it was quickly decided who should go, and who remain. Those who started from Donner Lake on the third of March with Mr. Reed and his party were Patrick Breen, Mrs. Margaret Breen, John Breen, Patrick Breen, Jr., James F. Breen, Peter Breen, and Isabella M. Breen, Patty Reed and Thomas Reed, Isaac Donner and Mary

M. Donner, Solomon Hook, Mrs. Elizabeth Graves, Nancy Graves, Jonathan Graves, Franklin Graves, and Elizabeth Graves, Jr. Many of the younger members of this party had to be carried. All were very much weakened and emaciated, and it was evident that the journey over the mountains would be slow and painful. In case a storm should occur on the summits, it was fearfully apparent that the trip would be exceedingly perilous.

Reed's party encamped the first night near the upper end of Donner Lake. They had scarcely traveled three miles. Upon starting from the Graves cabin, Mrs. Graves had taken with her a considerable sum of money. This money, Mr. McCutchen says, had been ingeniously concealed in auger-holes bored in cleats nailed to the bed of the wagon. These cleats, as W. C. Graves informs us, were ostensibly placed in the wagon-bed to support a table carried in the back part of the wagon. On the under side of these cleats, however, were the auger-holes, carefully filled with coin. The sum is variously stated at from three to five hundred dollars. At the camping-ground, near the upper end of Donner Lake, one of the relief party jokingly proposed to another to play a game of euchre to see who should have Mrs. Graves' money. The next morning, Mrs. Graves remained behind when the party started, and concealed her money. All that is known is, that she buried it behind a large rock on the north side of Donner Lake. So far as is known, this money has never been recovered, but still lies hidden where it was placed by Mrs. Graves.

CHAPTER XIV

LEAVING THREE MEN IN THE MOUNTAINS — THE EMIGRANTS
QUITE HELPLESS — BEAR TRACKS IN THE SNOW — THE CLUMPS
OF TAMARACK — WOUNDING A BEAR — BLOOD-STAINS UPON
THE SNOW — A WEARY CHASE — A MOMENTOUS DAY — STONE
AND CADY LEAVE THE SUFFERERS — A MOTHER OFFERING FIVE
HUNDRED DOLLARS — MRS. DONNER PARTING FROM HER
CHILDREN — "GOD WILL TAKE CARE OF YOU" — BURIED IN
THE SNOW, WITHOUT FOOD OR FIRE — PINES UPROOTED BY
THE STORM — A GRAVE CUT IN THE SNOW — THE CUB'S CAVE —
FIRING AT RANDOM — A DESPERATE UNDERTAKING — PREPARING
FOR A HAND-TO-HAND BATTLE — PRECIPITATED INTO THE
CAVE — SEIZING THE BEAR — MRS. ELIZABETH DONNER'S
DEATH — CLARK AND BAPTISTE ATTEMPT TO ESCAPE — A
DEATH MORE CRUEL THAN STARVATION.

BEFORE Reed's party started to return, a consultation was held, and it was decided that Clark, Cady, and Stone should remain at the mountain camps. It was intended that these men should attend to procuring wood, and perform such other acts as would assist the almost helpless sufferers. It was thought that a third relief party could be sent out in a few days to get all the emigrants who remained.

Nicholas Clark, who now resides in Honey Lake Valley, Lassen County, California, says that as he and Cady were going to the Donner tents, they saw the fresh tracks of a bear and cub crossing the road. In those days, there were several little clumps of tamarack along Alder Creek, just below the Donner tents, and as the tracks led towards these, Mr. Clark procured a gun and started for an evening's hunt among the tamaracks. He found the bear and her cub within sight of the tents, and succeeded in severely wounding the old bear. She was a black bear, of medium size. For a long distance, over the snow and through the forests, Clark followed the wounded animal and her cub. The approach of darkness at last warned him to desist, and returning to the tents, he passed the night. Early next morning, Clark again set out in pursuit of the bear, following her readily by the blood-stains upon the snow. It was another windy, cloudy, threatening day, and there was every indication that a severe storm was approaching. Eagerly intent upon securing his game, Mr. Clark gave little heed to weather, or time, or distance. The endurance of the wounded animal was too great, however, and late in the afternoon he realized that it was necessary for him to give up the weary chase, and retrace his steps. He arrived at the tents hungry, tired, and footsore, long after dark.

That day, however, had been a momentous one at the Donner tents. Stone had come over early in the morning, and he and Cady concluded that it was sheer madness for them to remain in the mountains. That a terrible storm was fast coming on, could not be doubted. The provisions were almost exhausted, and if they remained, it would only be to perish with the poor emigrants. They therefore concluded to attempt to follow and overtake Reed and his companions.

Mrs. Tamsen Donner was able to have crossed the mountains with her children with either Tucker's or Reed's party. On account of her husband's illness, however, she had firmly refused all entreaties, and had resolutely determined to remain by his bedside. She was extremely anxious, however, that her children should reach California; and Hiram Miller relates that she offered five hundred dollars to any one in the second relief party, who would take them in safety across the mountains. When Cady and Stone decided to go, Mrs. Donner induced them to attempt the rescue of these children, Frances, Georgia, and Eliza. They took the children as far as the cabins at the lake, and left them. Probably they became aware of the impossibility of escaping the storm, and knew that it would be sure death, for both themselves and the children, should they take them any farther. In view of the terrible calamity which befell Reed's party on account of this storm, and the fact that Cady and Stone had a terrible struggle for life, every one must justify these men in leaving the children at the cabins. The parting between the devoted mother and her little ones is thus briefly described by Georgia Donner, now Mrs. Babcock: "The men came. I listened to their talking as they made their agreement. Then they took us, three little girls, up the stone steps, and stood us on the bank. Mother came, put on our hoods and cloaks, saying, as if she was talking more to herself than to us: 'I may never see you again, but God will take care of you.' After traveling a few miles, they left us on the snow, went ahead a short distance, talked one to another, then came back, took us as far as Keseberg's cabin, and left us."

Mr. Cady recalls the incident of leaving the children on the snow, but says the party saw a coyote, and were attempting to get a shot at the animal.

When Nicholas Clark awoke on the morning of the third day, the tent was literally buried in freshly fallen snow. He was in what is known as Jacob Donner's tent. Its only occupants besides himself were Mrs. Elizabeth Donner, her son Lewis, and the Spanish boy, John Baptiste. George Donner and wife were in their own tent, and with them was Mrs. Elizabeth Donner's youngest child, Samuel. Mr. Clark says he can not remember how long the storm lasted, but it seems as if it must have been least a week. The snow was so deep that it was impossible to procure wood, and during all those terrible days and nights there was no fire in either of the tents. The food gave out the first day, and the dreadful cold was rendered more intense by the pangs of hunger. Sometimes the wind would blow like a hurricane, and they could plainly hear the great pines crashing on the mountain side above them, as the wind uprooted them and hurled them to the ground. Sometimes the weather would seem to moderate, and the snow would melt and trickle in under the sides of the tent, wetting their clothes and bedding, and increasing the misery of their situation.

When the storm cleared away, Clark found himself starving like the rest. He had really become one of the Donner Party, and was as certain to perish as were the unfortunates about him. It would necessarily be several days before relief could possibly arrive, and utter despair seemed to surround them. Just as the storm was closing, Lewis Donner died, and the poor mother was well-nigh frantic with grief. As soon as she could make her way to the other tent, she carried her dead babe over and laid it in Mrs. George Donner's lap. With Clark's assistance, they finally laid the child away in a grave cut out of the solid snow.

In going to a tamarack grove to get some wood, Mr. Clark was surprised to find the fresh track of the bear cub, which had recrossed Alder Creek and ascended the mountain behind the tents. It was doubtless the same one whose mother he had wounded. The mother had probably died, and after the storm the cub had returned. Mr. Clark at once followed it, tracking it far up the mountain side to a cliff of rocks, and losing the trail at the mouth of a small, dark cave. He says that all hope deserted him when he found that the cub had gone into the cave. He sat down upon the snow in utter despair. It was useless to return to the tents without food; he might as well perish upon the mountain side. After reflecting for some time upon the gloomy situation, he concluded to fire his gun into the cave, and see if the report might not frighten out the cub. He placed the muzzle of the gun as far down into the cave as he could, and fired. When the hollow reverberation died away among the cliffs, no sound disturbed the brooding silence. The experiment had failed. He seriously meditated whether he could not watch the cave day and night until the cub should be driven out by starvation. But suddenly a new idea occurred to him. Judging from the track, and from the size of the cub he had seen, Mr. Clark concluded that it was possible he might be able to enter the cave and kill the cub in a hand-to-hand fight. It was a desperate undertaking, but it was preferable to death from starvation. He approached the narrow opening, and tried again to peer into the cave and ascertain its depth. As he was thus engaged the snow suddenly gave way, and he was precipitated bodily into the cave. He partly fell, partly slid to the very bottom of the hole in the rocks. In endeavoring to regain an erect posture, his hand struck against some furry animal. Instinctively recoiling, he waited for a moment to see what it would do. Coming from the dazzling sunlight into the darkness, he could see nothing whatever. Presently he put out his foot and again touched the animal. Finding that it did not move, he seized hold of it and found that it was the cub — dead! His random shot had pierced its brain, and it had died without a struggle. The cave or opening in the rocks was not very deep, and after a long time he succeeded in dragging his prize to the surface.

There was food in the Donner tents from this time forward. It came too late, however, to save Mrs. Elizabeth Donner or her son Samuel. This mother was quite able to have crossed the mountains with either of the two relief parties; but, as Mrs. E. P. Houghton writes: "Her little boys were too young to walk through the deep snows, she was not able to carry them, and the relief parties were too small to meet such emergencies. She stayed with them, hoping some way would be provided for their rescue. Grief, hunger, and disappointed hopes crushed her spirit, and so debilitated her that death came before the required help reached her or her children. For some days before her death she was so weak that Mrs. George Donner and the others had to feed her as if she had been a child. At last, one evening, as the sun went down, she closed her eyes and awoke no more. Her life had been sacrificed for her children. Could words be framed to express a more fitting tribute to her memory! Does not the simple story of this mother's love wreathe a chaplet of glory about her brow far holier than could be fashioned by human hands!

Samuel Donner lingered but a few days longer. Despite the tenderest care and attention, he grew weaker day by day, until he slept by the side of his mother and brother in their snowy grave.

All this time Mrs. Tamsen Donner was tortured with fear and dread, lest her children had perished in the dreadful storm on the summits. At last Clark yielded to her importunities, and decided to visit the cabins at Donner Lake, and see if there was any news from beyond the Sierra. Clark found the children at Keseberg's cabin, and witnessed such scenes of horror and suffering that he determined at once to attempt to reach California. Returning to Alder Creek, he told Mrs. Donner of the situation of her children, and says he informed her that he believed their lives were in danger of a death more violent than starvation. He informed her of his resolution to leave the mountains, and taking a portion of the little meat that was left, he at once started upon his journey. John Baptiste accompanied him.

The cub would have weighed about seventy pounds when killed; and now that its flesh was nearly gone, there was really very little hope for any one unless relief came speedily. In attempting to make their way across the mountains, Clark and Baptiste did the wisest thing possible, yet they well knew that they would perish by the way unless they met relief.

Mrs. Tamsen Donner did not dare to leave her husband alone during the night, but told Clark and Baptiste that she should endeavor to make the journey to the cabins on the following day. It was a long, weary walk over the pitiless snow, but she had before her yearning eyes not only the picture of her starving children, but the fear that they were in danger of a more cruel death than starvation.

CHAPTER XV

A MOUNTAIN STORM — PROVISIONS EXHAUSTED — BATTLING
THE STORM — FIENDS — BLACK DESPAIR — ICY COLDNESS —
A PICTURE OF DESOLATION — THE SLEEP OF DEATH — A
PITEOUS FAREWELL — FALLING INTO THE FIRE-WELL —
ISAAC DONNER'S DEATH — LIVING UPON SNOW-WATER —
EXCRUCIATING PAIN — A VISION OF ANGELS — "PATTY IS
DYING" — THE THUMB OF A MITTEN — A CHILD'S TREASURES —
THE "DOLLY" OF THE DONNER PARTY.

ON the evening of the second day after leaving Donner Lake,
Reed's party and the little band of famished emigrants found
themselves in a cold, bleak, uncomfortable hollow, somewhere
near the lower end of Summit Valley. Here the storm broke in all
its fury upon the doomed company. In addition to the cold, sleet-
like snow, a fierce, penetrating wind seemed to freeze the very
marrow in their bones. The relief party had urged the tired, hungry, enfeebled emigrants forward at the greatest possible speed all
day, in order to get as near the settlements as they could before
the storm should burst upon them. Besides, their provisions were
exhausted, and they were anxious to reach certain caches of supplies which they had made while going to the cabins. Fearing that
the storm would prevent the party from reaching these caches, Mr.
Reed sent Joseph Jondro, Matthew Dofar, and Hiram Turner forward to the first cache, with instructions to get the provisions and
return to the suffering emigrants. That very night the storm came,
and the three men had not been heard from.

The camp was in a most inhospitable spot. Exposed to the fury of the wind and storm, shelterless, supperless, overwhelmed with discouragements, the entire party sank down exhausted upon the snow. The entire party? No! There was one man who never ceased to work. When a fire had been kindled, and nearly every one had given up, this one man, unaided, continued to strive to erect some sort of shelter to protect the defenseless women and children. Planting large pine boughs in the snow, he banked up the snow on either side of them so as to form a wall. Hour after hour, in the darkness and raging storm, he toiled on alone, building the sheltering breastwork which was to ward off death from the party who by this time had crept shiveringly under its protection. But for this shelter, all would have perished before morning. At midnight the man was still at work. The darting snow particles seemed to cut his eye-balls, and the glare of the fire and the great physical exhaustion under which he was laboring, gradually rendered him blind. Like his companions, he had borne a child in his arms all day over the soft, yielding snow. Like them, he was drenched to the skin, and his clothing was frozen stiff and hard with ice. Yet he kept up the fire, built a great sheltering wall about the sufferers, and went here and there amongst the wailing and dying. With unabated violence the storm continued its relentless fury. The survivors say it was the coldest night they ever experienced. There is a limit to human endurance. The man was getting stone-blind. Had he attempted to speak, his tongue would have cloven to the roof of his mouth. His senses were chilled, blunted, dead. Sleep had stilled the plaintive cries of those about him. All was silent save the storm. Without knowing it, this heroic man was yielding to a sleep more powerful than that which had overcome his companions. While trying to save those who were weaker than himself, he had been literally freezing. Sightless, benumbed, moving half unconsciously about his work, he staggered, staggered, staggered, and finally sank in the snow. All slept! As he put no more fuel upon the fire, the flames died down. The logs upon which the fire had rested gave way, and most of the coals fell upon the snow. They were in almost total darkness.

Presently some one awoke. It was Mrs. Breen, whose motherly watchfulness prevented more than a few consecutive moments' sleep. The camp was quickly aroused. All were nearly frozen. Hiram Miller's hands were so cold and frosted that the skin on the fingers cracked open when he tried to split some kindlings. At last the fire was somehow renewed. Meantime they had discovered their leader—he who had been working throughout the night—lying cold, speechless, and apparently dead upon the snow. Hiram Miller and Wm. McCutchen carried the man to the fire, chafed his hands and limbs, rubbed his body vigorously, and worked with him as hard as they could for two hours before he showed signs of returning consciousness. Redoubling their exertions, they kept at work until the cold, gray morning dawned, ere the man was fully restored. Would you know the name of this man, this hero? It was James Frazier Reed.

From this time forward, all the toil, all the responsibility devolved upon Wm. McCutchen and Hiram Miller. Jondro, Dofar, and Turner were caught in the drifts ahead. The fishers or other wild animals had almost completely devoured the first cache of provisions, and while these men were trying to reach the second cache, the storm imprisoned them. They could neither go forward nor return. Cady and Stone were between Donner Lake and Starved Camp, and were in a like helpless condition. McCutchen and Miller were the only ones able to do anything toward saving the poor creatures who were huddled together at the miserable camp. All the other men were completely disheartened by the fearful calamity which had overtaken them. But for the untiring exertions of these two men, death to all would have been certain. McCutchen had on four shirts, and yet he became so chilled while trying to kindle the fire, that in getting warm he burned the back out of his shirts. He only discovered the mishap by the scorching and burning of his flesh.

What a picture of desolation was presented to the inmates of Starved Camp during the next three days! It stormed incessantly. One who has not witnessed a storm on the Sierra can not imagine the situation. A quotation from Bret Harte's "Gabriel Conroy" will afford the best idea of the situation:

"Snow. Everywhere. As far as the eye could reach—fifty miles, looking southward from the highest white peak. Filling ravines and gulches, and dropping from the walls of canyons in white shroud-like drifts, fashioning the dividing ridge into the likeness of a monstrous grave, hiding the bases of giant pines, and completely covering young trees and larches, rimming with porcelain the bowl-like edges of still, cold lakes, and undulating in motionless white billows to the edge of the distant horizon. Snow lying everywhere on the California Sierra, and still falling. It had been snowing in finely granulated powder, in damp, spongy flakes, in thin, feathery plumes; snowing from a leaden sky steadily, snowing fiercely, shaken out of purple-black clouds in white flocculent masses, or dropping in long level lines like white lances from the tumbled and broken heavens. But always silently! The woods were so choked with it, it had so cushioned and muffled the ringing rocks and echoing hills, that all sound was deadened. The strongest gust, the fiercest blast, awoke no sigh or complaint from the snow-packed, rigid files of forest. There was no cracking of bough nor crackle of underbrush; the overladen branches of pine and fir yielded and gave away without a sound. The silence was vast, measureless, complete!"

In alluding to these terrible days, in his diary, Mr. Reed says, under date of March 6:

"With the snow there is a perfect hurricane. In the night there is a great crying among the children, and even with the parents there is praying, crying, and lamentation on account of the cold and the dread of death from hunger and the howling storm. The men up nearly all night making fires. Some of the men began praying. Several of them became blind. I could not see the light of the fire blazing before me, nor tell when it was burning. The light of heaven is, as it were, shut out from us. The snow blows so thick and fast that we can not see twenty feet looking against the wind. I dread the coming night. Three of my men only, able to get wood. The rest have given out for the present. It is still snowing, and very cold. So cold that the few men employed in cutting the dry trees down, have to come and warm about every ten minutes. 'Hungry!' 'Hungry!' is the cry with the children, and nothing to give them. 'Freezing!' is the cry of the mothers who have nothing for their little, starving, freezing children. Night closing fast, and with it the hurricane increases.

"Mar. 7. Thank God day has once more appeared, although darkened by the storm. Snowing as fast as ever, and the hurricane has never ceased for ten minutes at a time during one of the most dismal nights I have ever witnessed. I hope I shall never witness another such in a similar situation. Of all the praying and crying I ever heard, nothing ever equaled it. Several times I expected to see the people perish of the extreme cold. At one time our fire was nearly gone, and had it not been for McCutchen's exertions it would have entirely disappeared. If the fire had been lost, two thirds of the camp would have been out of their misery before morning; but, as God would have it, we soon had it blazing comfortably, and the sufferings of the people became less for a time. Hope began to animate the bosoms of many, young and old, when the cheering blaze rose through the dry pine logs we had piled together. One would say, 'Thank God for the fire!' Another, 'How good it is!' The poor, little, half-starved, half-frozen children would say, 'I'm glad, I'm glad we have got some fire! Oh, how good it feels! It is good our fire didn't go out!' At times the storm would burst forth with such fury that I felt alarmed for the safety of the people on account of the tall timber that surrounded us."

Death entered the camp on the first night. He came to claim one who was a true, faithful mother. One who merits greater praise than language can convey. Though comparatively little has been told concerning her life by the survivors, doubt not that Mrs. Elizabeth Graves was one of the noblest of the mothers of the

Donner Party. Her charity is kindly remembered by all who have spoken her name. To her companions in misfortune she always gave such food as she possessed; for her children she now gave her life. The last morsels of food, the last grain of flour, she had placed in the mouths of her babes, though she was dying of starvation.

Mrs. Farnham, who talked personally with Mrs. Breen, gives the following description of that terrible night:

"Mrs. Breen told me that she had her husband and five children together, lying with their feet to the fire, and their heads under shelter of the snow breast-work. She sat by them, with only moccasins on her feet, and a blanket drawn over her shoulders and head, within which, and a shawl she constantly wore, she nursed her poor baby on her knees. Her milk had been gone several days, and the child was so emaciated and lifeless that she scarcely expected at any time on opening the covering to find it alive. Mrs. Graves lay with her babe and three or four older children at the other side of the fire. The storm was very violent all night, and she watched through it, dozing occasionally for a few minutes, and then rousing herself to brush the snow and flying sparks from the covering of the sleepers. Toward morning she heard one of the young girls opposite call to her mother to cover her. The call was repeated several times impatiently, when she spoke to the child, reminding her of the exhaustion and fatigue her mother suffered in nursing and carrying the baby, and bidding her cover herself, and let her mother rest. Presently she heard the mother speak, in a quiet, unnatural tone, and she called to one of the men near her to go and speak to her. He arose after a few minutes and found the poor sufferer almost past speaking. He took her infant, and after shaking the snow from her blanket, covered her as well as might be. Shortly after, Mrs. Breen observed her to turn herself slightly, and throw one arm feebly up, as if to go to sleep. She waited a little while, and seeing her remain quite still, she walked around to her. She was already cold in death. Her poor starving child wailed and moaned piteously in the arms of its young sister, but the mother's heart could no more warm or nourish it."

The members of the second relief party realized that they were themselves in imminent danger of death. They were powerless to carry the starving children over the deep, soft, treacherous snow, and it was doubtful if they would be able to reach the settlements unincumbered. Isaac Donner, one of the sons of Jacob and Elizabeth Donner, perished during one of the stormy nights. He was lying on the bed of pine boughs between his sister Mary and Patty Reed, and died so quietly that neither of the sleeping girls awoke.

The relief party determined to set out over the snow, hasten to the settlements, and send back relief. Solomon Hook, Jacob Donner's oldest boy, insisted that he was able to walk, and therefore joined the party. Hiram Miller, an old friend of the Reed family, took little Thomas Reed in his arms, and set out with the others. Patty Reed, full of hope and courage, refused to be carried by her father, and started on foot.

With what emotions did the poor sufferers in Starved Camp watch the party as it disappeared among the pines! There was no food in camp, and death had already selected two of their number. What a pitiable group it was! Could a situation more desolate or deplorable be imagined? Mr. Breen, as has been heretofore mentioned, was feeble, sickly, and almost as helpless as the children. Upon Mrs. Breen devolved the care, not only of her husband, but of all who remained in the fatal camp, for all others were children. John Breen, their eldest son, was the strongest and most vigorous in the family, yet the following incident shows how near he was to death's door. It must have occurred the morning the relief party left. The heat of the fire had melted a deep, round hole in the snow. At the bottom of the pit was the fire. The men were able to descend the sides of this cavity, and frequently did so to attend to the fire. At one time, while William McCutchen was down by the fire, John Breen was sitting on the end of one of the logs on which the fire had originally been kindled. Several logs had been laid side by side, and the fire had been built in the middle of the floor thus constructed. While the central logs had burned out and let the fire descend, the outer logs remained with their ends on the firm snow. On one of these logs John Breen was sitting. Suddenly overcome by fatigue and hunger, he fainted and dropped headlong into the fire-pit. Fortunately, Mr. McCutchen caught the falling boy, and thus saved him from a horrible death. It was some time before the boy was fully restored to consciousness. Mrs. Breen had a small quantity of sugar, and a little was placed between his clenched teeth. This seemed to revive him, and he not only survived, but is living to-day, the head of a large family, in San Benito County.

Mrs. Breen's younger children, Patrick, James, Peter, and the nursing babe, Isabella, were completely helpless and dependent. Not less helpless were the orphan children of Mr. and Mrs. Graves. Nancy was only about nine years old, and upon her devolved the task of caring for the babe, Elizabeth. Nancy Graves is now the wife of the earnest and eloquent divine. Rev. R. W. Williamson, of Los Gatos, Santa Clara County. To her lasting honor be it said, that although she was dying of hunger in Starved Camp, yet she faithfully tended, cared for, and saved her baby sister. Aside from occasional bits of sugar, this baby and Mrs. Breen's had nothing for an entire week, save snow-water. Besides Nancy and Elizabeth, there were of the Graves children, Jonathan, aged seven, and Franklin, aged five years. Franklin soon perished. Starvation and exposure had so reduced his tiny frame, that he could not endure these days of continual fasting.

Mary M. Donner, whom all mention as one of the most lovely girls in the Donner Party, met with a cruel accident the night before the relief party left Starved Camp. Her feet had become frozen and insensible to pain. Happening to lie too near the fire, one of her feet became dreadfully burned. She suffered excruciating agony, yet evinced remarkable fortitude. She ultimately lost four toes from her left foot, on account of this sad occurrence.

Seven of the Breens, Mary Donner, and the three children of Mr. and Mrs. Graves, made the eleven now waiting for relief at Starved Camp. Mrs. Graves, her child Franklin, and the boy, Isaac Donner, who lay stark in death upon the snow, completed the fourteen who were left by the relief party.

Meantime, how fared it with those who were pressing forward toward the settlements? At each step they sank two or three feet into the snow. Of course those who were ahead broke the path, and the others, as far as possible, stepped in their tracks. This, Patty Reed could not do, because she was too small. So determined was she, however, that despite the extra exertion she was compelled to undergo, she would not admit being either cold or fatigued. Patty Reed has been mentioned as only eight years old. Many of the survivors speak of her, however, in much the same terms as John Breen, who says: "I was under the impression that she was older. She had a wonderful mind for one of her age. She had, I have often thought, as much sense as a grown person." Over Patty's large, dark eyes, on this morning, gradually crept a film. Previous starvation had greatly attenuated her system, and she was far too weak to endure the hardship she had undertaken. Gradually the snow-mantled forests, the forbidding mountains, the deep, dark canyon of Bear River, and even the forms of her companions, faded from view. In their stead came a picture of such glory and brightness as seldom comes to human eyes. It was a vision of angels and of brilliant stars. She commenced calling her father, and those with him, and began talking about the radiant forms that hovered over her. Her wan, pale face was illumined with smiles, and with an ecstasy of joy she talked of the angels and stars, and of the happiness she experienced. "Why, Reed," exclaimed McCutchen, "Patty is dying!" And it was too true.

For a few moments the party forgot their own sufferings and trials, and ministered to the wants of the spirituelle child, whose entrance into the dark valley had been heralded by troops of white-winged angels. At Starved Camp, Reed had taken the hard, frozen sacks in which the provisions had been carried, and by holding them to the fire had thawed out the seams, and scraped therefrom about a teaspoonful of crumbs. These he had placed in the thumb of his woolen mitten to be used in case of emergency. Little did he suppose that the emergency would come so soon. Warming and moistening these crumbs between his own lips, the father placed them in his child's mouth. Meantime they had wrapped a blanket around her chilled form, and were busily chafing her hands and feet. Her first return to consciousness was signaled by the regrets she expressed at having been awakened from her beautiful dream. To this day she cherishes the memory of that vision as the dearest, most enchanting of all her life. After this, some of the kind-hearted Frenchmen in the party took turns with Reed in carrying Patty upon their backs.

Past-midshipman S. E. Woodworth is a name that in most published accounts figures conspicuously among the relief parties organized to rescue the Donner Party. At the time Reed and his companions were suffering untold horrors on the mountains, and those left at Starved Camp were perishing of starvation, Woodworth, with an abundance of supplies, was lying idle in camp at Bear Valley. This was the part that Selim E. Woodworth took in the relief of the sufferers.

The three men who had been sent forward to the caches, left the remnant of the provisions which had not been destroyed, where it could easily be seen by Reed and his companions. Hurrying forward, they reached Woodworth's. camp, and two men, John Stark and Howard Oakley, returned and met Reed's party. It was quite time. With frozen feet and exhausted bodies, the members of the second relief were in a sad plight. They left the settlements strong, hearty men. They returned in a half-dead condition. Several lost some of their toes on account of having them frozen, and one or two were crippled for life. They had been three days on the way from Starved Camp to Woodworth's. Cady and Stone overtook Reed and his companions on the second day after leaving Starved Camp. On the night of the third day, they arrived at Woodworth's.

When Patty Reed reached Woodworth's and had been provided with suitable food, an incident occurred which fully illustrates the tenderness and womanliness of her nature. Knowing that her mother and dear ones were safe, knowing that relief would speedily return to those on the mountains, realizing that for her there was to be no more hunger, or snow, and that she would no longer be separated from her father, her feelings may well be imagined. In her quiet joy she was not wholly alone. Hidden away in her bosom, during all the suffering and agony of the journey over the mountains, were a number of childish treasures. First, there was a lock of silvery gray hair which her own hand had cut from the head of her Grandmother Keyes way back on the Big Blue River. Patty had always been a favorite with her grandma, and when the latter died, Patty secured this lock of hair. She tied it up in a little piece of old-fashioned lawn, dotted with wee blue flowers, and always carried it in her bosom. But this was not all. She had a dainty little glass salt-cellar, scarcely larger than the inside of a humming-bird's nest, and, what was more precious than this, a tiny, wooden doll. This doll had been her constant companion. It had black eyes and hair, and was indeed very pretty. At Woodworth's camp, Patty told "Dolly" all her joy and gladness, and who can not pardon the little girl for thinking her dolly looked happy as she listened?

Patty Reed is now Mrs. Frank Lewis, of San Jose, Cal. She has a pleasant home and a beautiful family of children. Yet oftentimes the mother, the grown-up daughters, and the younger members of the family, gather with tear-dimmed eyes about a little sacred box. In this box is the lock of hair in the piece of lawn, the tiny salt-cellar, the much loved "Dolly," and an old woolen mitten, in the thumb of which are yet the traces of fine crumbs.

CHAPTER XVI

A MOTHER AT STARVED CAMP — REPEATING THE LITANY —
HOPING IN DESPAIR — WASTING AWAY — THE PRECIOUS
LUMP OF SUGAR — "JAMES IS DYING" — RESTORING A LIFE —
RELENTLESS HUNGER — THE SILENT NIGHT-VIGILS — THE
SIGHT OF EARTH — DESCENDING THE SNOW-PIT — THE
FLESH OF THE DEAD — REFUSING TO EAT — THE MORNING
STAR — THE MERCY OF GOD — THE MUTILATED FORMS —
THE DIZZINESS OF DELIRIUM — FAITH REWARDED — "THERE
IS MRS. BREEN!"

VERY noble was the part which Mrs. Margaret Breen performed in this Donner tragedy, and very beautifully has that
part been recorded by a woman's hand. It is written so tenderly,
so delicately, and with so much reverence for the maternal love
which alone sustained Mrs. Breen, that it can hardly be
improved. This account was published by its author, Mrs.
Farnham, in 1849, and is made the basis of the following
sketch. With alterations here and there, made for the sake of
brevity, the article is as it was written:

There was no food in Starved Camp. There was nothing to eat
save a few seeds, tied in bits of cloth, that had been brought along
by some one, and the precious lump of sugar. There were also a
few teaspoonfuls of tea. They sat and lay by the fire most of the
day, with what heavy hearts, who shall know! They were upon
about thirty feet of snow. The dead lay before them, a ghastlier
sight in the sunshine that succeeded the storm, than when the

149

dark clouds overhung them. They had no words of cheer to speak to each other, no courage or hope to share, but those which pointed to a life where hunger and cold could never come, and their benumbed faculties were scarcely able to seize upon a consolation so remote from the thoughts and wants that absorbed their whole being.

A situation like this will not awaken in common natures religious trust. Under such protracted suffering, the animal outgrows the spiritual in frightful disproportion. Yet the mother's sublime faith, which had brought her thus far through her agonies, with a heart still warm toward those who shared them, did not fail her now. She spoke gently to one and another; asked her husband to repeat the litany, and the children to join her in the responses; and endeavored to fix their minds upon the time when the relief would probably come. Nature, as unerringly as philosophy could have done, taught her that the only hope of sustaining those about her, was to set before them a termination to their sufferings.

What days and nights were those that went by while they waited! Life waning visibly in those about her; not a morsel of food to offer them; her own infant—and the little one that had been cherished and saved through all by the mother now dead—wasting hourly into the more perfect image of death; her husband worn to a skeleton; it needed the fullest measure of exalted faith, of womanly tenderness and self-sacrifice, to sustain her through such a season. She watched by night as well as by day. She gathered wood to keep them warm. She boiled the handful of tea and dispensed it to them, and when she found one sunken and speechless, she broke with her teeth a morsel of the precious sugar, and put it in his lips. She fed her babe freely on snow-water, and scanty as was the wardrobe she had, she managed to get fresh clothing next to its skin two or three times a week. Where, one asks in wonder and reverence, did she get the strength and courage for all this? She sat all night by her family, her elbows on her knees, brooding over the meek little victim that lay there, watching those who slept, and occasionally dozing with a fearful consciousness of their terrible condition always upon her. The sense of peril never slumbered. Many times during the night she went to the sleepers to ascertain if they all still breathed. She put her hand under their blankets; and held it before the mouth. In this way she assured herself that they were yet alive. But once her blood curdled to find, on approaching her hand to the lips of one of her own children, there was no warm breath upon it. She tried to open his mouth, and found the jaws set. She roused her husband, "Oh! Patrick, man! arise and help me! James is dying!" "Let him die!" said the miserable father, "he will be better off than any of us." She was terribly shocked by this reply. In her own expressive language, her heart stood still when she heard it. She was bewildered, and knew not where to set her weary hands to work, but she recovered in a few moments and began to chafe the breast and hands of the perishing boy. She broke a bit of sugar, and with considerable effort forced it between his teeth with a few drops of snow-water. She saw him swallow, then a slight convulsive motion stirred his features, he stretched his limbs feebly, and in a moment more opened his eyes and looked upon her. How fervent were her thanks to the Great Father, whom she forgot not day or night.

Thus she went on. The tea leaves were eaten, the seeds chewed, the sugar all dispensed. The days were bright, and compared with the nights, comfortable. Occasionally, when the sun shone, their voices were heard, though generally they sat or lay in a kind of stupor from which she often found it alarmingly difficult to arouse them. When the gray evening twilight drew its deepening curtain over the cold glittering heavens and the icy waste, and when the famishing bodies had been covered from the frost that pinched them with but little less keenness than the unrelenting hunger, the solitude seemed to rend her very brain. Her own powers faltered. But she said her prayers over many times in the darkness as well as the light, and always with renewed trust in Him who had not yet forsaken her, and thus she sat out her weary watch. After the turning of the night she always sat watching for the morning star, which seemed every time she saw it rise clear in the cold eastern sky, to renew the promise, "As thy day is, so shall thy strength be."

Their fire had melted the snow to a considerable depth, and they were lying on the bank above. Thus they had less of its heat than they needed, and found some difficulty in getting the fuel she gathered placed so it would burn. One morning after she had hailed her messenger of promise, and the light had increased so as to render objects visible in the distance, she looked as usual over the white expanse that lay to the south-west, to see if any dark moving specks were visible upon its surface. Only the tree-tops, which she had scanned so often as to be quite familiar with their appearance, were to be seen. With a heavy heart she brought herself back from that distant hope to consider what was immediately about her. The fire had sunk so far away that they had felt but little of its warmth the last two nights, and casting her eyes down into the snow-pit, whence it sent forth only a dull glow, she thought she saw the welcome face of beloved mother Earth. It was such a renewing sight after their long, freezing separation from it! She immediately aroused her eldest son, John, and with a great deal of difficulty, and repeating words of cheer and encouragement, brought him to understand that she wished him to descend by one of the tree-tops which had fallen in so as to make a sort of ladder, and see if they could reach the naked earth, and if it were possible for them all to go down. She trembled with fear at the vacant silence in which he at first gazed at her, but at length, after she had told him a great many times, he said "Yes, mother," and went.

He reached the bottom safely, and presently spoke to her. There was naked, dry earth under his feet; it was warm, and he wished her to come down. She laid her baby beside some of the sleepers, and descended. Immediately she determined upon taking them all down. How good, she thought, as she descended the boughs, was the God whom she trusted. By perseverence, by entreaty, by encouragement, and with her own aid, she got them into this snug shelter.

Relief came not, and as starvation crept closer and closer to himself and those about him, Patrick Breen determined that it was his duty to employ the means of sustaining life which God seemed to have placed before them. The lives of all might be saved by resorting to such food as others, in like circumstances, had subsisted upon. Mrs. Breen, however, declared that she would die, and see her children die, before her life or theirs should be preserved by such means. If ever the father gave to the dying children, it was without her consent or knowledge. She never tasted, nor knew of her children partaking. Mrs. Farnham says that when Patrick Breen ascended to obtain the dreadful repast, his wife, frozen with horror, hid her face in her hands, and could not look up. She was conscious of his return, and of something going on about the fire, but she could not bring herself to uncover her eyes till all had subsided again into silence. Her husband remarked that perhaps they were wrong in rejecting a means of sustaining life of which others had availed themselves, but she put away the suggestion so fearfully that it was never renewed, nor acted upon by any of her family. She and her children were now, indeed, reaching the utmost verge of life. A little more battle with the grim enemies that had pursued them so relentlessly, twenty-four, or at most forty-eight hours of such warfare, and all would be ended. The infants still breathed, but were so wasted they could only be moved by raising them bodily with the hands. It seemed as if even their light weight would have dragged the limbs from their bodies. Occasionally, through the day, she ascended the tree to look out. It was an incident now, and seemed to kindle more life than when it only required a turn of the head or a glance of the eye to tell that there was no living thing near them. She could no longer walk on the snow, but she had still strength enough to crawl from tree to tree to gather a few boughs, which she threw along before her to the pit, and piled them in to renew the fire. The eighth day was passed. On the ninth morning she ascended to watch for her star of mercy. Clear and bright it stood over against her beseeching gaze, set in the light liquid blue that overflows the pathway of the opening day. She prayed earnestly as she gazed, for she knew that there were but few hours of life in those dearest to her. If human aid came not that day, some eyes, that would soon look imploringly into hers, would be closed in death before that star would rise again. Would she herself, with all her endurance and resisting love, live to see it? Were they at length to perish? Great God! should it be permitted that they, who had been preserved through so much, should die at last so miserably?

Her eyes were dim, and her sight wavering. She could not distinguish trees from men on the snow, but had they been near, she could have heard them, for her ear had grown so sensitive that the slightest unaccustomed noise arrested her attention. She went below with a heavier heart than ever before. She had not a word of hope to answer the languid, inquiring countenances that were turned to her face, and she was conscious that it told the story of her despair. Yet she strove with some half-insane words to suggest that somebody would surely come to them that day. Another would be too late, and the pity of men's hearts and the mercy of God would surely bring them. The pallor of death seemed already to be stealing over the sunken countenances that surrounded her, and, weak as she was, she could remain below but a few minutes together. She felt she could have died had she let go her resolution at any time within the last forty-eight hours. They repeated the Litany. The responses came so feebly that they were scarcely audible, and the protracted utterances seemed wearisome. At last it was over, and they rested in silence.

The sun mounted high and higher in the heavens, and when the day was three or four hours old she placed her trembling feet again upon the ladder to look out once more. The corpses of the dead lay always before her as she reached the top—the mother and her son, and the little boy, whose remains she could not even glance at since they had been mutilated. The blanket that covered them could not shut out the horror of the sight.

The rays of the sun fell on her with a friendly warmth, but she could not look into the light that flooded the white expanse. Her eyes lacked strength and steadiness, and she rested herself against a tree and endeavored to gather her wandering faculties in vain. The enfeebled will could no longer hold rule over them. She had broken perceptions, fragments of visions, contradictory and mixed— former mingled with latter times. Recollections of plenty and rural peace came up from her clear, tranquil childhood, which seemed to have been another state of existence; flashes of her latter life—its comfort and abundance—gleams of maternal pride in her children who had been growing up about her to ease and independence.

She lived through all the phases which her simple life had ever worn, in the few moments of repose after the dizzy effort of ascending; as the thin blood left her whirling brain and returned to its shrunken channels, she grew more clearly conscious of the terrible present, and remembered the weary quest upon which she came. It was not the memory of thought, it was that of love, the old tugging at the heart that had never relaxed long enough to say, "Now I am done; I can bear no more!" The miserable ones down there—for them her wavering life came back; at thought of them she turned her face listlessly the way it had so often gazed. But this time something caused it to flush as if the blood, thin and cold as it was, would burst its vessels! What was it? Nothing that she saw, for her eyes were quite dimmed by the sudden access of excitement! It was the sound of voices! By a superhuman effort she kept herself from falling! Was it reality or delusion? She must at least live to know the truth. It came again and again. She grew calmer as she became more assured, and the first distinct words she heard uttered were,"There is Mrs. Breen alive yet, anyhow!" Three men were advancing toward her. She knew that now there would be no more starving. Death was repelled for this time from the precious little flock he had so long threatened, and she might offer up thanksgiving unchecked by the dreads and fears that had so long frozen her.

CHAPTER XVII

THE RESCUE — CALIFORNIA AROUSED — A YERBA BUENA
NEWSPAPER — TIDINGS OF WOE — A CRY OF DISTRESS —
NOBLE GENEROSITY — SUBSCRIPTIONS FOR THE DONNER
PARTY — THE FIRST AND SECOND RELIEFS — ORGANIZATION
OF THE THIRD — THE DILEMMA — VOTING TO ABANDON A
FAMILY — THE FATAL AYES — JOHN STARK'S BRAVERY —
CARRYING THE STARVED CHILDREN — A PLEA FOR THE
RELIEF PARTY.

FOSTER and Eddy, it will be remembered, were of the fifteen who composed the "Forlorn Hope." Foster was a man of strong, generous impulses, and great determination. His boy was at Donner Lake, and his wife's mother and brother. He hardly took time to rest and recruit his wasted strength before he began organizing a party to go to their rescue. His efforts were ably seconded by W. H. Eddy, whose wife and daughter had perished, but whose boy was still alive at the cabins.

California was thoroughly aroused over tidings which had come from the mountains. It was difficult to get volunteers to undertake the journey over the Sierra, but horses, mules, provisions, and good wages were allowed all who would venture the perilous trip. The trouble with Mexico had caused many of the able-bodied citizens of California to enlist in the service. Hence it was that it was so difficult to organize relief parties.

The following extracts are made from the California Star, a newspaper published at "Yerba Buena," as San Francisco was then called. They do justice to the sentiment of the people of

California, and indicate something of the willingness of the pioneers to aid the Donner Party. From the Star of January 16, 1847, is taken the following article, which appeared as an editorial:

"EMIGRANTS ON THE MOUNTAINS.

"It is probably not generally known to the people that there is now in the California mountains, in a most distressing situation, a party of emigrants from the United States, who were prevented from crossing the mountains by an early, heavy fall of snow. The party consists of about sixty persons—men, women, and children. They were almost entirely out of provisions when they reached the foot of the mountains, and but for the timely succor afforded them by Capt. J. A. Sutter, one of the most humane and liberal men in California, they must have all perished in a few days. Capt. Sutter, as soon as he ascertained their situation, sent five mules loaded with provisions to them. A second party was dispatched with provisions for them, but they found the mountains impassable in consequence of the snow. We hope that our citizens will do something for the relief of these unfortunate people."

From the same source, under date of February 6, 1847, is taken the following:

"PUBLIC MEETING.

"It will be recollected that in a previous number of our paper, we called the attention of our citizens to the situation of a company of unfortunate emigrants now in the California mountains. For the purpose of making their situation more fully known to the people, and of adopting measures for their relief, a public meeting was called by the Honorable Washington A. Bartlett, alcalde of the town, on Wednesday evening last. The citizens generally attended, and in a very short time the sum of $800 was subscribed to purchase provisions, clothing, horses, and mules to bring the emigrants in. Committees were appointed to call on those who could not attend the meeting, and there is no doubt but that $500 or $600 more will be raised. This speaks well for Yerba Buena."

One other extract is quoted from the Star of February 13, 1847:

"COMPANY LEFT.

"A company of twenty men left here on Sunday last for the California mountains, with provisions, clothing, etc., for the suffering emigrants now there. The citizens of this place subscribed about $1,500 for their relief, which was expended for such articles as the emigrants would be most likely to need. Mr. Greenwood, an old mountaineer, went with the company as pilot. If it is possible to cross the mountains, they will get to the emigrants in time to save them."

These three articles may aid the reader in better understanding what has heretofore been said about the organization of the relief parties. It will be remembered that James F. Reed and William McCutchen first procured animals and provisions from Capt. Sutter, attempted to cross the mountains, found the snow impassable, cached their provisions, and returned to the valleys. Reed, as described in his letter to the Rural Press, went to San Jose, Cal., and thence to Yerba Buena. McCutchen went to Napa and Sonoma, and awakened such an interest that a subscription of over $500 was subscribed for the emigrants, besides a number of horses and mules. Lieut. W. L. Maury and M. G. Vallejo headed this subscription, and $500 was promised to Greenwood if he succeeded in raising a company, and in piloting them over the mountains. In order to get men, Greenwood and McCutchen went to Yerba Buena, arriving there almost at the same time with Reed. The above notices chronicle the events which succeeded the announcement of their mission. The funds and supplies contributed were placed in charge of Lieut. Woodworth. This party set out immediately, and their journey has been described. They form the second relief party, because immediately upon the arrival of the seven who survived of the "Forlorn Hope," Capt. Tucker's party had been organized at Johnson's and Sutter's, and had reached Donner Lake first.

When Foster and Eddy attempted to form a relief party, they found the same difficulty in securing volunteers which others had encountered. It was such a terrible undertaking, that no man cared to risk his life in the expedition.

Captain J. B. Hull, of the United States navy, and Commander of the Northern District of California, furnished Foster and Eddy with horses and provisions. Setting out from Johnson's ranch, they arrived at Woodworth's camp in the afternoon. During that very night two of Reed's men came to the camp, and brought news that Reed and a portion of his party were a short distance back in the mountains. When Reed and his companions were brought into camp, and it was ascertained that fourteen people had been left in the snow, without food, the third relief party was at once organized. The great danger and suffering endured by those who had composed the first and second relief parties, prevented men from volunteering. On this account greater honor is due those who determined to peril their lives to save the emigrants. Hiram Miller, although weak and exhausted with the fatigues and starvation he had just undergone in the second relief party, joined Messrs. Foster and Eddy. These three, with Wm. Thompson, John Stark, Howard Oakley, and Charles Stone, set out from Woodworth's camp the next morning after Reed's arrival. It was agreed that Stark, Oakley, and Stone were to remain with the sufferers at Starved Camp, supply them with food, and conduct them to Woodworth's camp. Foster, Eddy, Thompson, and Miller were to press forward to the relief of those at Donner Lake. The three men, therefore, whose voices reached Mrs. Breen, were Stark, Oakley, and Stone.

When these members of the third relief party reached the deep, well-like cavity in which were the seven Breens, the three Graves children, and Mary Donner, a serious question arose. None of the eleven, except Mrs. Breen and John Breen, were able to walk. A storm appeared to be gathering upon the mountains, and the supply of provisions was very limited. The lonely situation, the weird, desolate surroundings, the appalling scenes at the camp, and above all, the danger of being overtaken by a snow-storm, filled the minds of Oakley and Stone with terror. When it was found that nine out of the eleven people must be carried over the snow, it is hardly to be wondered at that a proposition was made to leave a portion of the sufferers. It was proposed to take the three Graves children and Mary Donner. These four children would be quite a sufficient burden for the three men, considering the snow over which they must travel. The Breens, or at least such of them as could not walk, were to be abandoned. This was equivalent to leaving the father, mother, and five children, because the mother would not abandon any member of her family, and John, who alone could travel, was in a semi-lifeless condition. The members of the third relief party are said to have taken a vote upon the question. This scene is described in the manuscript of Hon. James F. Breen: "Those who were in favor of returning to the settlements, and leaving the Breens for a future relief party (which, under the circumstances, was equivalent to the death penalty), were to answer 'aye.' The question was put to each man by name, and as the names were called, the dreadful 'aye' responded. John Stark's name was the last one called, because he had, during the discussion of the question, strongly opposed the proposition for abandonment, and it was naturally supposed that when he found himself in so hopeless a minority he would surrender. When his name was called, he made no answer until some one said to him: 'Stark, won't you vote?' Stark, during all this proceeding of calling the roll, had stood apart from his companions with bowed head and folded arms. When he was thus directly appealed to, he answered quickly and decidedly: "No, gentlemen, I will not abandon these people. I am here on a mission of mercy, and I will not half do the work. You can all go if you want to, but I shall stay by these people while they and I live."

It was nobly said. If the Breens had been left at Starved Camp, even until the return of Foster, Eddy, Miller, and Thompson from the lake, none would have ever reached the settlements. In continuation of the above narration, the following is taken from the manuscript of John Breen: "Stark was finally left alone. To his great bodily strength, and unexcelled courage, myself and others owe our lives. There was probably no other man in California at that time, who had the intelligence, determination, and what was absolutely necessary in that emergency, the immense physical powers of John Stark. He was as strong as two ordinary men. On his broad shoulders, he carried the provisions, most of the blankets, and most of the time some of the weaker children. In regard to this, he would laughingly say that he could carry them all, if there was room on his back, because they were so light from starvation."

By every means in his power, Stark would cheer and encourage the poor sufferers. Frequently he would carry one or two ahead a little way, put them down, and return for the others. James F. Breen says; "I distinctly remember that myself and Jonathan Graves were both carried by Stark, on his back, the greater part of the journey." Others speak similarly.

Regarding this brave man, Dr. J. C. Leonard has contributed much valuable information, from which is selected the following:

"John Stark was born in 1817, in Wayne County, Indiana. His father, William Stark, came from Virginia, and was one of the first settlers of Kentucky, arriving there about the same time as Daniel Boone. He married a cousin of Daniel Boone, and they had a family of eight children. T. J. Stark, the oldest son, now lives at French Corral, Nevada County, California. John Stark, the younger brother, started from Monmouth County, Illinois, in the spring of 1846, but taking the Fort Hall road, reached California in safety. He was a powerfully built man, weighing two hundred and twenty pounds. He was sheriff of Napa County for six years, and in 1852 represented that county in the State Legislature. He died near Calistoga, in 1875, of heart disease.

His death was instantaneous, and occurred while pitching hay from a wagon. He was the father of eleven children, six of whom, with his wife, are now living."

Each one of the persons who were taken from Starved Camp by this man and his two companions, reached Sutter's Fort in safety. James F. Breen had his feet badly frozen, and afterwards burned while at the camp. No one had any hope that they could be saved, and when the party reached the fort, a doctor was sought to amputate them. None could be found, and kind nature effected a cure which a physician would have pronounced impossible.

In concluding this chapter, it is quite appropriate to quote the following, written by J. F. Breen: "No one can attach blame to those who voted to leave part of the emigrants. It was a desperate case. Their idea was to save as many as possible, and they honestly believed that by attempting to save all, all would be lost. But this consideration—and the further one that Stark was an entire stranger to every one in the camps, not bound to them by any tie of blood or kindred, nor having any hope of reward, except the grand consciousness of doing a noble act—makes his conduct shine more lustrously in the eyes of every person who admires nature's true and only nobility."

CHAPTER XVIII

ARRIVAL OF THE THIRD RELIEF — THE LIVING AND THE
DEAD — CAPTAIN GEORGE DONNER DYING — MRS. MURPHY'S
WORDS — FOSTER AND EDDY AT THE LAKE — TAMSEN DONNER
AND HER CHILDREN — A FEARFUL STRUGGLE — THE HUS-
BAND'S WISHES — WALKING FOURTEEN MILES — WIFELY
DEVOTION — CHOOSING DEATH — THE NIGHT JOURNEY —
AN UNPARALLELED ORDEAL — AN HONORED NAME — THREE
LITTLE WAIFS — "AND OUR PARENTS ARE DEAD."

EDDY, Foster, Thompson, and Miller passed Nicholas Clark and
John Baptiste near the head of Donner Lake. These starving fugi-
tives had journeyed thus far in their desperate effort to cross the
mountains. Of all those encamped at Alder Creek the sole survivors now were George Donner, the captain of the Donner Party,
and his faithful wife, Tamsen Donner. Under the snow-drifts
which covered the valley, lay Jacob Donner, Elizabeth Donner,
Lewis Donner, Samuel Donner, Samuel Shoemaker, Joseph
Rhinehart, and James Smith. One more was soon to be added to
the number. It was the man whose name had been given to the
company; the only one who died of a lingering, painful disease.
The injury of George Donner's hand had grown into a feverish,
virulent ulceration, which must have partaken of the nature of
erysipelas. At all events, mortification had set in, and when the
third relief party arrived it had reached his shoulder. In a few
hours at most he must die.

Foster's party found that much suffering had occurred at Donner Lake during the tearful days which elapsed between Reed's departure and their own arrival. Mrs. Lavina Murphy had charge of her son, Simon Murphy, her grandchild, George Foster, of the child James Eddy, and of the three little Donner girls, Frances, Georgia, and Eliza. All dwelt in the same cabin, and with them was Lewis Keseberg. Foster and Eddy found all there, save their own children. They were both dead. Keseberg has generally been accused of the murder of little George Foster. Except Mrs. Murphy, the oldest of those who were with Keseberg was only nine years of age. All that the children know is that Keseberg took the child to bed with him one night, and that it was dead next morning. One of the little ones who survived—one whose memory has proven exceedingly truthful upon all points wherein her evidence could be possibly substantiated—and who is now Mrs. Georgia A. Babcock—gives the mildest version of this sad affair which has ever appeared in print. She denies the story, so often reiterated, that Keseberg took the child to bed with him and ate it up before morning; but writes the following: "In the morning the child was dead. Mrs. Murphy took it, sat down near the bed where my sister and myself were lying, laid the little one on her lap, and made remarks to other persons, accusing Keseberg of killing it. After a while he came, took it from her, and hung it up in sight, inside the cabin, on the wall."

Foster, Eddy, Thompson, and Miller remained but a little while at the mountain camp. During this time Mr. Foster had no opportunity to talk with Mrs. Murphy save in Keseberg's presence. Afterwards, when the children told him of the suspicions expressed in their presence by Mrs. Murphy, Foster deeply regretted that he had not sought a private interview with her, for the purpose of learning the reasons for her belief.

In the morning the relief party was to start back to the settlements. Eddy was to carry Georgia Donner; Thompson, Frances Donner; Miller, Eliza Donner; and Foster was to carry Simon Murphy. John Baptiste and Nicholas Clark remained at the head of Donner Lake, and were to accompany the party. This left Mr. and

Mrs. Donner at Alder Creek, and Keseberg and Mrs. Murphy at the cabins. Mrs. Murphy had cared for her children and her grandchildren, and ministered to the wants of those around her, until she was sick, exhausted, and utterly helpless. She could not walk. She could scarcely rise from her bed. With all the tenderness of a son, Mr. Foster gave her such provisions as he could leave, procured her wood, and did whatever he was able to do to render her comfortable. He also promised to return speedily, and with such assistance that he could carry her over the summits to her children.

The very afternoon that the third relief party reached the cabins, Simon Murphy discovered a woman wandering about in the snow as if lost. It proved to be Mrs. Tamsen Donner. She had wearily traveled over the deep snows from Alder Creek, as narrated in a previous chapter, to see her children, and, if necessary, to protect their lives. Oh! the joy and the pain of the meeting of those little ones and their mother. As they wound their arms about her neck, kissed her lips, laughed in her eyes, and twined their fingers in her hair, what a struggle must have been taking place in her soul. As the pleading, upturned faces of her babies begged her not to leave them, her very heart-strings must have been rent with agony. Well may the voice quiver or the hand tremble that attempts to portray the anguish of this mother during that farewell interview. From the very first moment, her resolution to return to her husband remained unshaken. The members of the relief party entreated her to go with her children and save her own life. They urged that there could only be a few hours of life left in George Donner. This was so true that she once ventured the request that they remain until she could return to Alder Creek, and see if he were yet alive. The gathering storm-clouds, which had hovered over the summit for days, compelled them to refuse this request. An hour's delay might be fatal to all.

George Donner knew that he was dying, and had frequently urged his wife to leave him, cross the mountains, and take care of her children. As she held her darlings in her arms, it required no prophetic vision to disclose pictures of sadness, of lonely childhood, of longing girlhood, of pillows wet with tears, if these three little waifs were left to wander friendless in California. She never expressed a belief that she would see that land of promise beyond the Sierra. Often had her calm, earnest voice told them of the future which awaited them, and so far as possible had she prepared them to meet that future without the counsel or sympathy of father or mother.

The night-shadows, creeping through the shivering pines, warned her of the long, dreary way over which her tired feet must pass ere she reached her dying husband's side. She is said to have appeared strangely composed. The struggle was silent. The poor, bleeding heart brought not a single moan to the lips. It was a choice between life, hope, and her clinging babes, or a lonely vigil by a dying husband, and an unknown, shroudless death in the wintry mountains. Her husband was sixty-three; he was well stricken in years, and his life was fast ebbing away. If she returned through the frosty night-winds, over the crisp, freezing snow, she would travel fourteen miles that day. The strong, healthy men composing the relief parties frequently could travel but five or six miles in a day. If she made the journey, and found her husband was dead, she could have no hope of returning on the morrow. She had suffered too long from hunger and privation to hope to be able to return and overtake the relief party. It was certain life or certain death. On the side of the former was maternal love; on the side of the latter, wifely devotion. The whole wide range of history can not produce a parallel example of adherence to duty, and to the dictates of conjugal fidelity. With quick, convulsive pressure of her little ones to her heart; with a hasty, soul-throbbing kiss upon the lips of each; with a prayer that was stifled with a sob of agony, Tamsen Donner hurried away to her husband. Through the gathering darkness, past the shadowy sentinels of the forest, they watched with tearful eyes her retreating form. As if she dared not trust another sight of the little faces—as if to escape the pitiful wail of her darlings—she ran straight forward until out of sight and hearing. She never once looked back.

There are mental struggles which so absorb the being and soul that physical terrors or tortures are unnoticed. Tamsen Donner's mind was passing through such an ordeal. The fires of Moloch, the dreadful suttee, were sacrifices which long religious education sanctioned, and in which the devotees perished amidst the plaudits of admiring multitudes. This woman had chosen a death of solitude, of hunger, of bitter cold, of pain-racked exhaustion, and was actuated by only the pure principles of wifely love. Already the death-damp was gathering on George Donner's brow. At the utmost, she could hope to do no more than smooth the pillow of the dying, tenderly clasp the fast-chilling hand, press farewell kisses upon the whitening lips, and finally close the dear, tired eyes. For this, only this, she was yielding life, the world, and her darling babes. Fitted by culture and refinement to be an ornament to society, qualified by education to rear her daughters to lives of honor and usefulness, how it must have wrung her heart to allow her little ones to go unprotected into a wilderness of strangers. But she could not leave her husband to die alone. Rather solitude, better death, than desert the father of her children. O, Land of the Sunset! let the memory of this wife's devotion be ever enshrined in the hearts of your faithful daughters! In tablets thus pure, engrave the name of Tamsen Donner.

When the June sunshine gladdened the Sacramento Valley, three little barefooted girls walked here and there among the houses and tents of Sutter's Fort. They were scantily clothed, and one carried a thin blanket. At night they said their prayers, lay down in whatever tent they happened to be, and, folding the blanket about them, fell asleep in each other's arms. When they were hungry, they asked food of whomsoever they met. If any one inquired who they were, they answered as their mother had taught them: "We are the children of Mr. and Mrs. George Donner." But they added something they had learned since. It was, "And our parents are dead."

CHAPTER XIX

FALSE IDEAS ABOUT THE DONNER PARTY — ACCUSED OF SIX MURDERS — INTERVIEWS WITH LEWIS KESEBERG — HIS STATEMENT — AN EDUCATED GERMAN — A PREDESTINED FATE — KESEBERG'S LAMENESS — SLANDEROUS REPORTS — COVERED WITH SNOW — "LOATHSOME, INSIPID, AND DISGUSTING" — LONGINGS TOWARD SUICIDE — TAMSEN DONNER'S DEATH — GOING TO GET THE TREASURE — SUSPENDED OVER A HIDDEN STREAM — "WHERE IS DONNER'S MONEY?" — EXTORTING A CONFESSION.

KESEBERG is one of the leading characters in the Donner Party. Usually, his part in the tragedy has been considered the entire story. Comparatively few people have understood that any except this one man ate human flesh, or was a witness of any scene of horror. He has been loathed, execrated, abhorred as a cannibal, a murderer, and a heartless fiend. In the various published sketches which have from time to time been given to the world, Lewis Keseberg has been charged with no less than six murders. His cannibalism has been denounced as arising from choice, as growing out of a depraved and perverted appetite, instead of being the result of necessity. On the fourth of April, 1879, this strange man granted an interview to the author, and in this and succeeding interviews he reluctantly made a statement which was reduced to writing. "What is the use," he would urge, "of my making a statement? People incline to believe the most horrible reports concerning a man, and they will not credit what I say in my own defense. My conscience is clear. I am an old man, and am calmly awaiting my death. God is my judge, and it long ago ceased to trouble me that people shunned and slandered me."

Keseberg is six feet in height, is well proportioned, and weighs from one hundred and seventy-five to one hundred and eighty pounds. He is active, vigorous, and of an erect, manly carriage, despite his years and his many afflictions. He has clear blue eyes, regular features, light hair and beard, a distinct, rapid mode of enunciation, a loud voice, and a somewhat excited manner of speech. In conversing he looks one squarely and steadily in the eye, and appears like an honest, intelligent German. He speaks and writes German, French, Spanish, and English, and his selection of words proves him a scholar. His face generally wears a determined, almost fierce expression, but one is impressed with the thought that this appearance is caused by his habitually standing on the defensive as against his fellow-men. Since he has never before had an opportunity of speaking in his own defense, it is perhaps fitting that his statement should be given in his own language:

"My name is Lewis Keseberg. I was born in the city of Berleburg, Province of Westphalia, in the Kingdom of Prussia, on the twenty-second of May, 1814. I am therefore almost sixty-three years of age. I was married June 22, 1842, came to the United States May 22, 1844, and emigrated to California in 1846 with the Donner Party. I never have made a statement concerning my connection with that Party to any one connected with the press. It is with the utmost horror that I revert to the scenes of suffering and unutterable misery endured during that journey. I have always endeavored to put away from me all thoughts or recollections of those terrible events. Time is the best physician, and would, I trusted, heal the wounds produced by those days of torture; yet my mind to-day recoils with undiminished horror as I endeavor to speak of this dreadful subject. Heretofore I have never attempted to refute the villainous slanders which have been circulated and published about me. I feel it my duty to make this statement, however, because I am convinced of your willingness to do justice to all who were concerned in that dreadful affair, and heretofore I have been treated with gross injustice.

"If I believe in God Almighty having anything to do with the affairs of men, I believe that the misfortune which overtook the Donner Party, and the terrible part I was compelled to take in the great tragedy, were predestined. On the Hastings Cut-off we were twenty-eight days in going twenty-one miles. Difficulty and disaster hovered about us from the time we entered upon this cut-off.

"One day, while we were traveling on Goose Creek, we saw so many wild geese that I took my shotgun and went hunting. Ordinarily I am not superstitious, but on this morning I felt an overwhelming sense of impending calamity. I mentioned my pre-monitions to Mrs. Murphy before starting on the hunt. Becoming excited with the sport, and eagerly watching the game, I stepped down a steep bank. Some willows had been burned off, and the short, sharp stubs were sticking up just where I stepped. I had on buckskin moccasins, and one of these stubs ran into the ball of my foot, between the bones and the toes. From this time, until we arrived at Donner Lake, I was unable to walk, or even to put my foot to the ground. The foot became greatly swollen and inflamed, and was exceedingly painful. One day, at Donner Lake, one of my companions, at my earnest request, lanced my foot on the top. It discharged freely, and some days afterwards, in washing it, I found a hard substance protruding from the wound, and obtaining a pair of forceps, succeeded in extracting a piece of the willow stub, one and a half inches in length. It had literally worked up through my foot. I mention this particularly, because I have been frequently accused of remaining at the Donner cabins from selfish or sinister motives, when in fact I was utterly unable to join the relief parties."

It is proper to mention, in corroboration of Keseberg's state-ment regarding his lameness, that several of the survivors remembered, and had related the circumstance prior to the interview. It is a well-authenticated fact that he was very lame, and could not walk, yet, as a specimen of the abuse which has been heaped upon the man, a quotation is introduced from Thornton's "Oregon and California." In speaking of the departure of Foster and Eddy, Thornton says: "There were in camp Mrs. Murphy, Mr. and Mrs. George Donner, and Keseberg—the latter, it was believed, having far more strength to travel than others who had arrived in the settlements. But he would not travel, for the reason, as was suspected, that he wished to remain behind for the purpose of obtaining the property and money of the dead." Keseberg's statement continues:

"When we reached the lake, we lost our road, and owing to the depth of the snow on the mountains, were compelled to abandon our wagons, and pack our goods upon oxen. The cattle, unused to such burdens, caused great delay by 'bucking' and wallowing in the snow. There was also much confusion as to what articles should be taken and what abandoned. One wanted a box of tobacco carried along; another, a bale of calico, and some one thing and some another. But for this delay we would have passed the summit and pressed forward to California. Owing to my lameness, I was placed on horseback, and my foot was tied up to the saddle in a sort of sling. Near evening we were close to the top of the dividing ridge. It was cold and chilly, and everybody was tired with the severe exertions of the day. Some of the emigrants sat down to rest, and declared they could go no further. I begged them for God's sake to get over the ridge before halting. Some one, however, set fire to a pitchy pine tree, and the flames soon ascended to its topmost branches. The women and children gathered about this fire to warm themselves. Meantime the oxen were rubbing off their packs against the trees. The weather looked very threatening, and I exhorted them to go on until the summit was reached. I foresaw the danger plainly and unmistakably. Only the strongest men, however, could go ahead and break the road, and it would have taken a determined man to induce the party to leave the fire. Had I been well, and been able to push ahead over the ridge, some, if not all, would have followed. As it was, all lay down on the snow, and from exhaustion were soon asleep. In the night, I felt something impeding my breath. A heavy weight seemed to be resting upon me. Springing up to a sitting posture, I found myself covered with freshly-fallen snow. The camp, the cattle, my companions, had all disappeared. All I could see was snow everywhere. I shouted at the top of my voice. Suddenly, here and there, all about me, heads popped up through the snow. The scene was not unlike what one might imagine at the resurrection, when people rise up out of the earth. The terror amounted to a panic. The mules were lost, the cattle strayed away, and our further progress rendered impossible. The rest you probably know. We returned to the lake, and prepared, as best we could, for the winter. I was unable to build a cabin, because of my lameness, and so erected a sort of brush shed against one side of Breen's cabin.

"When Reed's relief party left the cabins, Mr. Reed left me a half teacupful of flour, and about half a pound of jerked beef. It was all he could give. Mrs. Murphy, who was left with me, because too weak and emaciated to walk, had no larger portion. Reed had no animosity toward me. He found me too weak to move. He washed me, combed my hair, and treated me kindly. Indeed, he had no cause to do otherwise. Some of my portion of the flour brought by Stanton from Sutter's Fort I gave to Reed's children, and thus saved their lives. When he left me, he promised to return in two weeks and carry me over the mountains. When this party left, I was not able to stand, much less to walk.

"A heavy storm came on in a few days after the last relief party left. Mrs. George Donner had remained with her sick husband in their camp, six or seven miles away. Mrs. Murphy lived about a week after we were left alone. When my provisions gave out, I remained four days before I could taste human flesh. There was no other resort—it was that or death. My wife and child had gone on with the first relief party. I knew not whether they were living or dead. They were penniless and friendless in a strange land. For their sakes I must live, if not for my own. Mrs. Murphy was too weak to revive. The flesh of starved beings contains little nutriment. It is like feeding straw to horses. I can not describe the unutterable repugnance with which I tasted the first mouthful of flesh. There is an instinct in our nature that revolts at the thought of touching, much less eating, a corpse. It makes my blood curdle to think of it! It has been told that I boasted of my shame—said that I enjoyed this horrid food, and that I remarked that human flesh was more palatable than California beef. This is a falsehood. It is a horrible, revolting falsehood. This food was never otherwise than loathsome, insipid, and disgusting. For nearly two months I was alone in that dismal cabin. No one knows what occurred but myself—no living being ever before was told of the occurrences. Life was a burden. The horrors of one day succeeded those of the preceding. Five of my companions had died in my cabin, and their stark and ghastly bodies lay there day and night, seemingly gazing at me with their glazed and staring eyes. I was too weak to move them had I tried. The relief parties had not removed them. These parties had been too hurried, too horror-stricken at the sight, too fearful lest an hour's delay might cause them to share the same fate. I endured a thousand deaths. To have one's suffering prolonged inch by inch, to be deserted, forsaken, hopeless; to see that loathsome food ever before my eyes, was almost too much for human endurance. I am conversant with four different languages. I speak and write them with equal fluency; yet in all four I do not find words enough to express the horror I experienced during those two months, or what I still feel when memory reverts to the scene. Suicide would have been a relief, a happiness, a godsend! Many a time I had the muzzle of my pistol in my mouth and my finger on the trigger, but the faces of my helpless, dependent wife and child would rise up before me, and my hand would fall powerless. I was not the cause of my misfortunes, and God Almighty had provided only this one horrible way for me to subsist."

Did you boil the flesh?

"Yes! But to go into details—to relate the minutiæ—is too agonizing! I can not do it! Imagination can supply these. The necessary mutilation of the bodies of those who had been my friends, rendered the ghastliness of my situation more frightful. When I could crawl about and my lame foot was partially recovered, I was chopping some wood one day and the ax glanced and cut off my heel. The piece of flesh grew back in time, but not in its former position, and my foot is maimed to this day.

"A man, before he judges me, should be placed in a similar situation; but if he were, it is a thousand to one he would perish. A constitution of steel alone could endure the deprivation and misery. At this time I was living in the log-cabin with the fireplace. One night I was awakened by a scratching sound over my head. I started up in terror, and listened intently for the noise to be repeated. It came again. It was the wolves trying to get into the cabin to eat me and the dead bodies.

"At midnight, one cold, bitter night, Mrs. George Donner came to my door. It was about two weeks after Reed had gone, and my loneliness was beginning to be unendurable. I was most happy to hear the sound of a human voice. Her coming was like that of an angel from heaven. But she had not come to bear me company. Her husband had died in her arms. She had remained by his side until death came, and then had laid him out and hurried away. He died at nightfall, and she had traveled over the snow alone to my cabin. She was going, alone, across the mountains. She was going to start without food or guide. She kept saying, 'My children! I must see my children!' She feared she would not survive, and told me she had some money in her tent. It was too heavy for her to carry. She said, 'Mr. Keseberg, I confide this to your care.' She made me promise sacredly that I would get the money and take it to her children in case she perished and I survived. She declared she would start over the mountains in the morning. She said, 'I am bound to go to my children.' She seemed very cold, and her clothes were like ice. I think she had got in the creek in coming. She said she was very hungry, but refused the only food I could offer. She had never eaten the loathsome flesh. She finally lay down, and I spread a feather-bed and some blankets over her. In the morning she was dead. I think the hunger, the mental suffering, and the icy chill of the preceding night, caused her death. I have often been accused of taking her life. Before my God, I swear this is untrue! Do you think a man would be such a miscreant, such a damnable fiend, such a caricature on humanity, as to kill this lone woman? There were plenty of corpses lying around. He would only add one more corpse to the many!

"Oh! the days and weeks of horror which I passed in that camp! I had no hope of help or of being rescued, until I saw the green grass coming up by the spring on the hillside, and the wild geese coming to nibble it. The birds were coming back to their breeding grounds, and I felt that I could kill them for food. I had plenty of guns and ammunition in camp. I also had plenty of tobacco and a good meerschaum pipe, and almost the only solace I enjoyed was smoking. In my weak condition it took me two or three hours every day to get sufficient wood to keep my fire going.

"Some time after Mrs. Donner's death, I thought I had gained sufficient strength to redeem the pledge I had made her before her death. I started to go to the camps at Alder Creek to get the money. I had a very difficult journey. The wagons of the Donners were loaded with tobacco, powder, caps, shoes, school-books, and dry-goods. This stock was very valuable, and had it reached California, would have been a fortune to the Donners. I searched carefully among the bales and bundles of goods, and found five hundred and thirty-one dollars. Part of this sum was silver, part gold. The silver I buried at the foot of a pine tree, a little way from the camp. One of the lower branches of another tree reached down close to the ground, and appeared to point to the spot. I put the gold in my pocket, and started to return to my cabin. I had spent one night at the Donner tents. On my return I became lost. When it was nearly dark, in crossing a little flat, the snow suddenly gave way under my feet, and I sank down almost to my armpits. By means of the crust on top of the snow, I kept myself suspended by throwing out my arms. A stream of water flowed underneath the place over which I had been walking, and the snow had melted on the underside until it was not strong enough to support my weight. I could not touch bottom with my feet, and so could form no idea of the depth of the stream. By long and careful exertion I managed to draw myself backward and up on the snow. I then went around on the hillside, and continued my journey. At last, just at dark, completely exhausted and almost dead, I came in sight of the Graves cabin. I shall never forget my joy at sight of that log-cabin. I felt that I was no longer lost, and would at least have shelter. Some time after dark I reached my own cabin. My clothes were wet by getting in the creek, and the night was so cold that my garments were frozen into sheets of ice. I was so weary, and chilled, and numbed, that I did not build up a fire, or attempt to get anything to eat, but rolled myself up in the bed-clothes and tried to get warm. Nearly all night I lay there shivering with cold; and when I finally slept, I slept very soundly. I did not wake up until quite late the next morning. To my utter astonishment my camp was in the most inexplicable confusion. My trunks were broken open, and their contents were scattered everywhere. Everything about the cabin was torn up and thrown about the floor. My wife's jewelry, my cloak, my pistol and ammunition were missing. I supposed Indians had robbed my camp during my absence. Suddenly I was startled by the sound of human voices. I hurried up to the surface of the snow, and saw white men coming toward the cabin. I was overwhelmed with joy and gratitude at the prospect of my deliverance. I had suffered so much, and for so long a time, that I could scarcely believe my senses. Imagine my astonishment upon their arrival to be greeted, not with a 'good morning' or a kind word, but with the gruff, insolent demand, 'Where is Donner's money?'

"I told them they ought to give me something to eat, and that I would talk with them afterwards, but no, they insisted that I should tell them about Donner's money. I asked them who they were, and where they came from, but they replied by threatening to kill me if I did not give up the money. They threatened to hang or shoot me, and at last I told them I had promised Mrs. Donner that I would carry her money to her children, and I proposed to do so, unless shown some authority by which they had a better claim. This so exasperated them, that they acted as though they were going to kill me. I offered to let them bind me as a prisoner, and take me before the alcalde at Sutter's Fort, and I promised that I would then tell all I knew about the money. They would listen to nothing, however, and finally I told them where they would find the silver buried, and gave them the gold. After I had done this, they showed me a document from Alcalde Sinclair, by which they were to receive a certain proportion of all moneys and property which they rescued."

The men spoken of by Keseberg, were the fourth relief party. Their names were, Captain Fallon, William M. Foster, John Rhodes, J. Foster, R. P. Tucker, E. Coffeemire, and —— Keyser. William M. Foster had recrossed the mountains the second time, hoping to rescue his wife's mother, Mrs. Murphy. Alas! he found only her mutilated remains.

CHAPTER XX

DECEMBER 16, 1846, the fifteen composing the "Forlorn Hope,"
left Donner Lake. January 17, 1847, they reached Johnson's
ranch; and February 5th Capt. Tucker's party started to the assistance of the emigrants. This first relief arrived February 19th at
the cabins; the second relief, or Reed's party, arrived March 1st;
the third, or Foster's, about the middle of March; and the fourth,
or Fallen's, on the seventeenth of April. Upon the arrival of Capt.
Fallen's company, the sight presented at the cabins beggars all
description. Capt. R. P. Tucker, now of Goleta, Santa Barbara
County, Cal., endeavors, in his correspondence, to give a slight
idea of the scene. Human bodies, terribly mutilated, legs, arms,
skulls, and portions of remains, were scattered in every direction
and strewn about the camp. Mr. Foster found Mrs. Murphy's body
with one of her limbs sawed off, the saw still lying by her remains.
It was such scenes as these which gave this party their first abhor-

rence for Keseberg. The man was nowhere to be seen, but a fresh track was discovered in the snow leading away from the cabins toward the Donner tents. The party pressed forward to Alder Creek. Captain Tucker writes: "The dead bodies lay moldering around, being all that was left to tell the tale of sorrow. On my first trip we had cut down a large pine tree, and laid the goods of the Donners on this tree to dry in the sun. These goods lay there yet, with the exception of those which Reed's party had taken away."

George Donner was wealthy. His wealth consisted not merely of goods, as many claim, but of a large amount of coin. Hiram Miller, of the relief parties, is authority for the statement that Mr. Donner owned a quarter section of land within the present city limits of Chicago. This land was sold for ten thousand dollars, shortly before Mr. Donner started for California. Mr. Allen Francis, who has been mentioned as the very best authority concerning this family, camped with them on the evening of their first night's journey out of Springfield, Illinois, saw Mr. Donner's money, and thinks there was ten thousand dollars. Mrs. F. E. Bond, of Elk Grove, Sacramento County, California, does not remember the exact amount, but knows that Mr. Donner started with a great deal of gold, because she helped make the belts in which it was to be carried in crossing the plains. The relief parties always understood there was at Donner's camp a large sum of money, estimated at from six to fourteen thousand dollars. It is not disputed that Halloran left about fifteen hundred dollars to this family. Yet Capt. Fallon's party could find no money. It was clear to their minds that some one had robbed the Donner tents.

Remaining over night, thoroughly searching in every place where the supposed money could be concealed, this party returned to Donner Lake. On their way they found the same mysterious track, also returning to the cabins. They probably discovered Keseberg in about the manner described. It is plain to be seen that they regarded him as the murderer of Mrs. Donner. In forcing him to tell what he had done with the money, they, too, claim to have choked him, to have put a rope around his neck, and to have threatened to hang him. On the other hand, if Keseberg's statement be accepted as truth, it is easy to understand why he refused to surrender the money to men who treated him from the outset as a murderer and a robber.

Let the God to whom Lewis Keseberg appeals be his judge. It is not the part of this book to condemn or acquit him. Most of the fourth relief party have already gone before the bar at which Keseberg asks to be tried. Capt. Tucker is about the only available witness, and his testimony is far more lenient than the rumors and falsehoods usually published.

If Keseberg be guilty of any or of all crimes, it will presently be seen that the most revengeful being on earth could not ask that another drop be added to his cup of bitterness. His statement continues:

"These men treated me with the greatest unkindness. Mr. Tucker was the only one who took my part or befriended me. When they started over the mountains, each man carried two bales of goods. They had silks, calicoes, and delaines from the Donners, and other articles of great value. Each man would carry one bundle a little way, lay it down, and come back and get the other bundle. In this way they passed over the snow three times. I could not keep up with them because I was so weak, but managed to come up to their camp every night. One day I was dragging myself slowly along behind the party, when I came to a place which had evidently been used as a camping-ground by some of the previous parties. Feeling very tired, I thought it would be a good place to make some coffee. Kindling a fire, I filled my coffee-pot with fresh snow and sat waiting for it to melt and get hot. Happening to cast my eyes carelessly around, I discovered a little piece of calico protruding from the snow. Half thoughtlessly, half out of idle curiosity, I caught hold of the cloth, and finding it did not come readily, I gave it a strong pull. I had in my hands the body of my dead child Ada! She had been buried in the snow, which, melting down, had disclosed a portion of her clothing. I thought I should go frantic! It was the first intimation I had of her death, and it came with such a shock!

"Just as we were getting out of the snow, I happened to be sitting in camp alone one afternoon. The men were hunting, or attending to their goods. I was congratulating myself upon my escape from the mountains, when I was startled by a snuffling, growling noise, and looking up, I saw a large grizzly bear only a few feet away. I knew I was too weak to attempt to escape, and so remained where I sat, expecting every moment he would devour me. Suddenly there was the report of a gun, and the bear fell dead. Mr. Foster had discovered the animal, and slipping up close to camp, had killed it."

When the party arrived at Sutter's Fort, they took no pains to conceal their feelings toward Keseberg. Some of the men openly accused him of Mrs. Donner's murder. Keseberg, at the suggestion of Captain Sutter, brought action against Captain Fallon, Ned Coffeemire, and the others, for slander. The case was tried before Alcalde Sinclair, and the jury gave Keseberg a verdict of one dollar damages. The old alcalde records are not in existence, but some of the survivors remember the circumstance, and Mrs. Samuel Kyburz, now of Clarksville, El Dorado County, was a witness at the trial. If Keseberg was able to vindicate himself in an action for slander against the evidence of all the party, it is clear that such evidence was not adduced as has frequently appeared in books. For instance, in Captain Fallon's report of this trip, he alleges that "in the cabin with Keseberg were found two kettles of human blood, in all supposed to be over one gallon." Had this been proven, no jury would have found for Keseberg. Fresh blood could not have been obtained from starved bodies, and had the blood been found, Keseberg would have been adjudged a murderer.

Speaking upon this point, Keseberg denies the assertion that any blood was discovered, calls attention to the length of time Mrs. Donner had been dead, to the readiness with which blood coagulates, and adds that not a witness testified to such a circumstance at the trial. Why should Keseberg murder Mrs. Donner? If he wanted her money, it was only necessary to allow her to go out into the mountains alone, without provisions, without any one to point out the way, and perish in the trackless snows. She could not carry any considerable portion of her money with her, and he had only to go back to Alder Creek and secure the treasure. He bears witness that she never tasted human flesh; that she would not partake of the food he offered; how reasonable, then, the story of her death. The fourth relief party expected to find a vast sum of money. One half was to be given them for their trouble. They regarded the man Keseberg as the murderer of George Foster, because of the reports given by the little children brought out by the third relief. The father of this child was with both the third and fourth reliefs. Arriving at the cabins, they were amazed and horrified at the dreadful sights. Hastening to the tents, they found no money. Their idea that Keseberg was a thief was confirmed by his disgorging the money when threatened with death. There was much reason for their hatred of the man who crossed the mountains with them, and this was intensified by their being brought before Alcalde Sinclair and proven slanderers. Out of this hatred has grown reports which time has magnified into the hideous falsehoods which greet the ear from all directions. Keseberg may be responsible for the death of Hardcoop, but urges in his defense that all were walking, even to the women and the children. He says Hardcoop was not missed until evening, and that it was supposed the old man would catch up with the train during the night. The terrible dangers surrounding the company, the extreme lateness of the season, the weakness of the oxen, and the constant fear of lurking, hostile Indians, prevented him or any one else from going back. Keseberg may be responsible for the death of Wolfinger, of George Foster, of James Eddy, of Mrs. Murphy, and of Mrs. Tamsen Donner, but the most careful searcher for evidence can not find the slightest trace of proofs. In his own mournful language, he comes near the truth when he say:

"I have been born under an evil star! Fate, misfortune, bad luck, compelled me to remain at Donner Lake. If God would decree that I should again pass through such an ordeal, I could not do otherwise than I did. My conscience is free from reproach. Yet that camp has been the one burden of my life. Wherever I have gone, people have cried, 'Stone him! stone him!' Even the little children in the streets have mocked me and thrown stones at me as I passed. Only a man conscious of his innocence, and clear in the sight of God, would not have succumbed to the terrible things which have been said of me—would not have committed suicide! Mortification, disgrace, disaster, and unheard-of misfortune have followed and overwhelmed me. I often think that the Almighty has singled me out, among all the men on the face of the earth, in order to see how much hardship, suffering, and misery a human being can bear!

"Soon after my arrival at the Fort, I took charge of the schooner Sacramento, and conveyed wheat from Sacramento to San Francisco, in payment of Capt. Sutter's purchase of the Russian possessions. I worked seven months for Sutter; but, although he was kind to me, I did not get my money. I then went to Sonoma, and worked about the same length of time for Gen. Vallejo. I had a good position and good prospects, but left for the gold mines. Soon afterward I was taken sick, and for eight months was an invalid. I then went to Sutter's Fort and started a boarding-house. I made money rapidly. After a time I built a house south of the Fort, which cost ten thousand dollars. In 1851 I purchased the Lady Adams hotel, in Sacramento. It was a valuable property, and I finally sold it at auction for a large sum of money. This money was to be paid the next day. The deeds had already passed. That night the terrible fire of 1852 occurred, and not only swept away the hotel, but ruined the purchaser, so that I could not collect one cent. I went back to Sutter's Fort and started the Phoenix Brewery. I succeeded, and acquired considerable property. I finally sold out for fifty thousand dollars. I had concluded to take this money, go back to Germany, and live quietly the rest of my days. The purchaser went to San Francisco to draw the money. The sale was effected eight days before the great flood of 1861–2. The flood came, and I lost everything."

Thus, throughout his entire career, have business reverses followed Lewis Keseberg. Several times he has been wealthy and honorably situated. At one time he was a partner of Sam. Brannan, in a mammoth distillery at Calistoga; and Mr. Brannan is one among many who speak in highest terms of his honesty, integrity, and business capacity. On the thirtieth of January, 1877, Phillipine Keseberg, his faithful wife, died. This was the severest loss of all, as will presently be seen.

Eleven children were born to them, and four are now living. One of these, Lillie, now lives in Sacramento with her husband. Another, Paulina, a widow, resides in San Rafael. Bertha and Augusta live with the father at Brighton, Sacramento County. Both these children are hopelessly idiotic. Bertha is twenty-six years of age, and has never uttered an intelligible word. Augusta is fifteen years old, weighs two hundred and five pounds, and possesses only slight traces of intelligence. Teething spasms, occurring when they were about two years old, is the cause of their idiocy. Both are subject to frequent and violent spasms or epileptic fits. They need constant care and attention. Should Bertha's hand fall into the fire, she has not sufficient intelligence to withdraw it from the flames. Both are helpless as children. The State provides for insane, but not for idiots. Keseberg says a bill setting aside a ward in the State Asylum for his two children, passed the Legislature, but received a pocket veto by the Governor. Sacramento County gives them eighteen dollars a month. Their helplessness and violence render it impossible to keep any nurse in charge of them longer than a few days. Keseberg is very poor. He has employment for perhaps three months during the year. While his wife lived, she took care of these children; but now he has personally to watch over them and provide for their necessities. While at work, he is compelled to keep them locked in a room in the same building. They scream so loudly while going into the spasms that he can not dwell near other people. He therefore lives isolated, in a plain little house back of his brewery. Here he lives, the saddest, loneliest, most pitiable creature on the face of the earth. He traces all his misfortunes to that cabin on Donner Lake, and it is little wonder that he says: "I beg of you, insert in your book a fervent prayer to Almighty God that He will forever prevent the recurrence of a similar scene of horror."

CHAPTER XXI

ZEALOUS in sending supplies and relief to the suffering Donner Party, earnest in providing shelter, clothing, and food to all who were rescued, Captain John A. Sutter merits more than a passing mention in this history. From the arrival of Stanton at Sutter's Fort with the tidings that a destitute emigrant train was *en route* for California until the return of the fourth relief party with Lewis Keseberg, Captain Sutter's time, wealth, and influence were enlisted in behalf of the party. Actuated only by motives of benevolence and humanity, he gave Stanton and the various relief parties full and free access to whatever he possessed, whether of money, provisions, clothing, mules, cattle, or guides. With all due deference to the generosity of Yerba Buena's citizens, and to the heroic endeavors of the noble men who risked their lives in rescuing the starving emigrants, it is but just and right that this warm-hearted philanthropist should be accorded the honor of being first among the benefactors of the Donner Party. His kindness did not cease with the arrival of the half-starved survivors at Sutter's Fort, but continued until all had found places of employment, and means of subsistance. Pitiful and unworthy is the reward which history can bestow upon such a noble character, yet since he never received any remuneration for his efforts and sacrifices, the reward of a noble name is the least and the most that earth can now bestow. In view of his good deeds, the survivors of the Donner Party have almost unanimously requested that a brief biographical sketch of the man be inserted in these pages.

At midnight on the twenty-eighth of February (or first of March), 1803, John A. Sutter was born in the city of Baden. He was of Swiss parentage, and his father and mother were of the Canton Berne. Educated in Baden, we find him at the age of thirty a captain in the French army. Filled with enthusiasm, energy, and love of adventure, his eyes turned toward America as his "land of promise," and in July, 1834, he arrived in New York. Again breaking away from the restraints of civilized life, he soon made his way to the then almost unknown regions west of the Mississippi. For some years he lived near St. Charles, in Missouri. At one time he entertained the idea of establishing a Swiss colony at this point, and was only prevented by the sinking of his vessel of supplies in the Mississippi River. During this time he accompanied an exploring party into the sultry, sand-covered wastes of New Mexico. Here he met hunters and trappers from California, and listened to tales of its beauty, fertility, and grandeur which awoke irresistible longings in his breast. In March, 1838, with Captain Tripp, of the American Fur Company, he traveled westward as far as the Rocky Mountains, and thence journeying with a small party of trappers, finally reached Fort Vancouver. Finding no land route to California, he embarked in a vessel belonging to the Hudson Bay Company, which was ready for a voyage to the Sandwich Islands. From Honolulu he thought there would be little difficulty in finding passage in a trading vessel for the Coast of

California. Disappointed in this, he remained at the Islands some months, and finally shipped as supercargo of a ship bound for Sitka. In returning, the vessel entered the Bay of San Francisco, but was not allowed to land, and Monterey was reached before Sutter was permitted to set foot upon California soil. From Governor Alvarado he obtained the right of settling in the Sacramento Valley. After exploring the Sacramento, Feather, and American Rivers, finally, on the sixteenth of August, 1839, he landed near the present site of Sacramento City, and determined to permanently locate. Soon afterward he began the construction of the famous Sutter's Fort. He took possession of the surrounding country, naming it New Helvetia. One of the first difficulties to be overcome was the hostility of the Indian tribes who inhabited the Sacramento and San Joaquin valleys. Kindness and humane treatment were generally sufficient to cause these Indians to become his allies, yet in more than one instance he was obliged to resort to arms. Considering the size of his army, there is a sort of grim heroism in the fact that he successfully waged at times a defensive and at times an aggressive warfare. His entire army was composed of six white men, who had been collected from different parts of the world, and eight Kanakas.

Dunbar, in describing Sutter's situation, says: "This portion of upper California, though fair to look upon, was peculiarly solitary and uninviting in its isolation and remoteness from civilization. There was not even one of those cattle ranches, which dotted the coast at long intervals, nearer to Sutter's locality than Suisun and Martinez, below the mouth of the Sacramento. The Indians of the Sacramento were known as 'Diggers.' The efforts of the Jesuit Fathers, so extensive on this continent, and so beneficial to the wild Indians wherever missions were established among them, never reached the wretched aborigines of the Sacramento country. The valley of the Sacramento had not yet become the pathway of emigrants from the East, and no civilized human being lived in this primitive and solitary region, or roamed over it, if we except a few trappers of the Hudson Bay Company."

Out of this solitude and isolation, Sutter, as if with a magician's wand, brought forth wealth and evolved for himself a veritable little kingdom. Near the close of the year 1839, eight white men joined his colony, and in 1840 his numbers were increased by five others. About this time the Mokelumne Indians became troublesome, and were conquered. Other tribes were forced into submission, and Sutter was practically monarch of the Sacramento and San Joaquin. The old pioneers speak with pride of the wonderful power he exerted over these Indians, teaching them the arts of civilization, forming them into military companies, drilling them in the use of fire-arms, teaching them to till the soil, and making them familiar with the rudiments of husbandry. The vast herds of cattle which in process of time he acquired, were tended and herded principally by these Indians, and the cannon which ultimately came into his possession were mounted upon the Fort, and in many instances were manned by these aborigines. Hides were sent to Yerba Buena, a trade in furs and supplies was established with the Hudson Bay Company, and considerable attention was given to mechanical and agricultural pursuits.

In 1841, Sutter obtained grants from Governor Alvarado of the eleven leagues of land comprised in his New Helvetia, and soon afterwards negotiated a purchase of the Russian possessions known as "Ross and Bodega." By this purchase, Sutter acquired vast real and personal property, the latter including two thousand cattle, one thousand horses, fifty mules, and two thousand five hundred sheep. In 1845 Sutter acquired from Gov. Manuel Micheltorena the grant of the famous *Sobrante,* which comprised the surplus lands over the first eleven leagues included within the survey accompanying the Alvarado grant.

As early as 1844 a great tide of emigration began flowing from the Eastern States toward California, a tide which, after the discovery of gold, became a deluge. Sutter's Fort became the great terminal point of emigration, and was far-famed for the generosity and open-heartedness of its owner. Relief and assistance were rendered so frequently and so abundantly to distressed emigrants, and aid and succor were so often sent over the Sierra to feeble or disabled trains, that Sutter's charity and generosity became proverbial. In the sunny hillslopes and smiling valleys, amidst the graceful groves and pleasant vineyards of this Golden State, it would be difficult to find localities where pioneers have not taught their children to love and bless the memory of the great benefactor of the pioneer days, John A. Sutter. With his commanding presence, his smiling face, his wealth, his power, and his liberality, he came to be regarded in those days as a very king among men. What he did for the Donner Party is but an instance of his unvarying kindness toward the needy and distressed. During this time he rendered important services to the United States, and notably in 1841, to the exploring expedition of Admiral Wilkes. The *Peacock*, a vessel belonging to the expedition, was lost on the Columbia bar, and a part of the expedition forces, sent overland in consequence, reached Sutter's Fort in a condition of extreme distress, and were relieved with princely hospitality. Later on he gave equally needed and equally generous relief to Colonel Fremont and his exploring party. When the war with Mexico came on, his aid and sympathy enabled Fremont to form a battalion from among those in Sutter's employ, and General Sherman's testimony is, "that to him (Sutter) more than any single person are we indebted for the conquest of California with all its treasures."

In 1848, when gold was discovered at Sutter's Mill, near Coloma, quoting again from Dunbar: "We find that Captain Sutter was the undisputed possessor of almost boundless tracts of land, including the former Russian possessions of Ross and Bodega, and the site of the present city of Sacramento. He had performed all the conditions of his land grants, built his fort, and completed many costly improvements. At an expense of twenty-five thousand dollars he had cut a mill-race three miles long, and nearly finished a new flouring mill. He had expended ten thousand dollars in the erection of a saw-mill near Coloma; one thousand acres of virgin soil were laid down to wheat, prom-

ising a yield of forty thousand bushels, and extensive preparations had been made for other crops. He owned eight thousand
cattle, two thousand horses and mules, two thousand sheep, and
one thousand swine. He was the military commander of the district, Indian agent of the territory, and Alcalde by appointment
of Commodore Stockton. Respected and honored by all, he was
the great man of the country."

Subsequently he was a member of the Constitutional Convention
at Monterey, and was appointed Major General of militia. Would that
the sketch of his life might end here; but, alas! there is a sad, sad closing to the chapter. This can not be told more briefly and eloquently
than in the language of the writer already mentioned:

"As soon as the discovery of gold was known, he was immediately deserted by all his mechanics and laborers, white, Kanaka,
and Indian. The mills were abandoned, and became a dead loss.
Labor could not be hired to plant, to mature the crops, or reap
and gather the grain that ripened.

"At an early period subsequent to the discovery, an immense
emigration from overland poured into the Sacramento Valley,
making Sutter's domains their camping-ground, without the
least regard for the rights of property. They occupied his culti-
vated fields, and squatted all over his available lands, saying these
were the unappropriated domain of the United States, to which
they had as good a right as any one. They stole and drove off his
horses and mules, and exchanged or sold them in other parts of
the country; they butchered his cattle, sheep, and hogs, and sold
the meat. One party of five men, during the flood of 1849–50,
when the cattle were surrounded by water, near the Sacramento
river, killed and sold $60,000 worth of these—as it was estimated—
and left for the States. By the first of January, 1852, the so-called
settlers, under pretense of pre-emption claims, had appropri-
ated all Sutter's lands capable of settlement or appropriation,
and had stolen all of his horses, mules, cattle, sheep, and hogs,
except a small portion used and sold by himself.

"There was no law to prevent this stupendous robbery; but when law was established, then came lawyers with it to advocate the squatters' pretensions, although there were none from any part of Christendom who had not heard of Sutter's grants, the peaceful and just possession of which he had enjoyed for ten years, and his improvements were visible to all.

"Sutter's efforts to maintain his rights, and save even enough of his property to give him an economical, comfortable living, constitute a sad history, one that would of itself fill a volume of painful interest. In these efforts he became involved in continuous and expensive litigation, which was not terminated till the final decision of the Supreme Court in 1858–59, a period of ten years. When the United States Court of Land Commissioners was organized in California, Sutter's grants came up in due course for confirmation. These were the grant of eleven leagues, known as New Helvetia, and the grant of twenty-two leagues, known as the *Sobrante*. The land commissioners found these grants perfect. Not a flaw or defect could be discovered in either of them, and they were confirmed by the board, under the provisions of the treaty of Guadalupe Hidalgo.

"The squatter interest then appealed to the United States District Court for the Northern District of California. This court confirmed the decision of the land commissioners. Extraordinary as it may appear, the squatter interest then appealed both cases to the Supreme Court of the United States at Washington, and still more extraordinary to relate, that court, though it confirmed the eleven-league grant, decided that of the *Sobrante* — twenty-two leagues — in favor of the squatters. The court acknowledged that the grant was a "genuine and meritorious" one, and then decided in favor of the squatter interest on purely technical grounds.

"Sutter's ruin was complete, and its method may be thus stated: He had been subjected to a very great outlay of money in the maintenance of his title, the occupancy and the improvement of the grant of New Helvetia. From a mass of interesting documents which I have been permitted to examine, I obtained the following statement relative to the expenses incurred on that grant:

Expenses in money, and services which formed
  the original consideration of the grant $50,000
Surveys and taxes on the same 50,000
Cost of litigation extending through ten years,
  including fees to eminent counsel, witness
   fees, traveling expenses, etc 125,000
Amount paid out to make good the covenants
  of deeds upon the grant, over and above
  what was received from sales 100,000

$\overline{\qquad\qquad\qquad}$
$ 325,000

"In addition, General Sutter had given titles to much of the *Sobrante* grant, under deeds of general warranty, which, after the decision of the supreme court of the United States in favor of the squatter interest, Sutter was obliged to make good, at an immense sacrifice, out of the New Helvetia grant; so that the confirmation of his title to this grant was comparatively of little advantage to him. Thus Sutter lost all his landed estate.

"But amid the wreck and ruin that came upon him in cumulative degree, from year to year, Sutter managed to save, for a period, what is known as Hock farm, a very extensive and valuable estate on the Feather River. This estate he proposed to secure as a resting-place in his old age, and for the separate benefit of his wife and children, whom he had brought from Switzerland in 1852, having been separated from them eighteen years. Sutter's titles being generally discredited, his vast flocks and herds having dwindled to a few head, and his resources being all gone, he was no longer able to hire labor to work the farm; and as a final catastrophe, the farm mansion was totally destroyed by fire in 1865, and with it all General Sutter's valuable records of his pioneer life." As difficulties augmented, Hock farm became incumbered with mortgages, and ultimately it was swallowed up in the general ruin.

For some years he received a small allowance from the State of California; but after a time this appropriation expired, and was never thereafter renewed. The later years of the pioneer's life were passed at Litiz, Lancaster County, Pennsylvania, and his time was devoted to endeavoring to obtain from Congress an appropriation of $50,000, as compensation for the expenditures he made for the relief of the early settlers of California. His death occurred at Washington, D. C., on the eighteenth day of June, 1880, and his remains were laid at rest in Litiz, Pennsylvania. The termination of this grand, heroic life, under circumstances of abject poverty and destitution, forms as strange and mournful a story as can be found in the annals of the present age.

In concluding this chapter, it may not be inappropriate to quote from a private letter written by Mrs. S. O. Houghton, *née* Eliza P. Donner, immediately after the General's death. It aptly illustrates the feeling entertained toward him by the members of the Donner Party. Writing from San Jose, she says:

"I have been sad, oh! so sad, since tidings flashed across the continent telling the friends of General Sutter to mourn his loss. In tender and loving thought I have followed the remains to his home, have stood by his bier, touched his icy brow, and brushed back his snowy locks, and still it is hard for me to realize that he is dead; that he who in my childhood became my ideal of all that is generous, noble, and good; he who has ever awakened the warmest gratitude of my nature, is to be laid away in a distant land! But I must not yield to this mood longer. God has only harvested the ripe and golden grain. Nor has He left us comfortless, for recollection, memory's faithful messenger, will bring from her treasury records of deeds so noble, that the name of General Sutter will be stamped in the hearts of all people, so long as California has a history. Yes, his name will be written in letters of sunlight on Sierra's snowy mountain sides, will be traced on the clasps of gold which rivet the rocks of our State, and will be arched in transparent characters over the gate which guards our western tide. All who see this land of the sunset will read, and know, and love the name of John A. Sutter, who fed the hungry, clothed the naked, and comforted the sorrowing children of California's pioneer days."

CHAPTER XXII

WITH the arrival of the emigrants at places of safety, this history properly closes. The members of the Donner Party were actively and intimately associated with all the early pioneer history of the State. The life of almost every one would furnish foundation for a most interesting biographical sketch. Ninety names were mentioned in the first chapter. Of these, forty-two perished. Mrs. Sarah Keyes, Halloran, John Snyder, Hardcoop, Wolfinger and William M. Pike did not live to reach the mountain camps. The first victim of starvation, Baylis Williams, died in the Reed cabin. About this time Jacob Donner, Samuel Shoemaker, Joseph Rhinehart and James Smith perished at Alder Creek. The five deaths last mentioned occurred within one week, about the middle of December. During the journey of the "Forlorn Hope," the fifteen were reduced to seven by the deaths of C. T. Stanton, F. W. Graves, Antoine, Patrick Dolan, Lemuel Murphy, Jay Fosdick, Lewis, and Salvador. Meantime, enrolled on the death-list at Donner Lake, were the names of Charles Burger,

Lewis Keseberg, Jr., John Landrum Murphy, Margaret Eddy, Harriet McCutchen, Augustus Spitzer, Mrs. Eleanor Eddy, Milton Elliott, and Catherine Pike.

During the journey of the first relief party, Ada Keseberg, John Denton, and William Hook perished, and with the second relief party died Mrs. Elizabeth Graves, Isaac Donner, and F. W. Graves, Jr. About this time, at the tents, died Lewis Donner, Mrs. Elizabeth Donner, and Samuel Donner, George Foster and James Eddy. No deaths occurred in the party of the third relief, and no names are to be added to the fatal list save Mrs. Lavina Murphy, George Donner, and Mrs. Tamsen Donner.

Out of the Donner Party, forty-eight survived. Walter Herron reached California with James F. Reed, and did not return. Of the "Forlorn Hope," Mary A. Graves, Mrs. Sarah Fosdick, Mrs. Amanda M. McCutchen, Mrs. Harriet F. Pike, Mrs. S. A. C. Foster, William M. Foster, and W. H. Eddy lived. The two last mentioned returned and again braved the dangers which encompassed the emigrants. The first relief party rescued Mrs. Margaret W. Reed, Virginia E. Reed and James F. Reed, Jr., Elitha C. Donner, Leanna C. Donner, George Donner, Jr., Wm. G. Murphy, Mary M. Murphy, Naomi L. Pike, W. C. Graves, Eleanor Graves, Lovina Graves, Mrs. Phillipine Keseberg, Edward J. Breen, Simon P. Breen, Eliza Williams, Noah James, and Mrs. Wolfinger.

The second relief succeeded in reaching the settlements with only Solomon Hook, Patty Reed, and Thomas K. Reed. With this party were its Captain, James F. Reed, and William McCutchen. Those who were brought to Starved Camp by the second relief, and saved by a portion of the third relief, were Patrick Breen, Mrs. Margaret Breen, John Breen, Patrick Breen, Jr., James F. Breen, Peter Breen, Isabella M. Breen, Nancy Graves, Jonathan Graves, Elizabeth Graves, and Mary M. Donner. The remainder of the third relief rescued Simon P. Murphy, Frances E. Donner, Georgia A. Donner, Eliza P. Donner, and John Baptiste. W. H. Eddy remained in the valleys after making this journey. Wm. M. Foster traversed the snow-belt no less than five times—once with the "Forlorn Hope," twice with the third relief, and twice with the fourth. The fourth relief rescued Lewis Keseberg.

General Kearney visited the cabins at Donner Lake on the twenty-second of June, 1847. Edwin Bryant, the author of "What I Saw in California," was with General Kearney, and says: "A halt was ordered for the purpose of collecting and interring the remains. Near the principal cabins I saw two bodies entire, with the exception that the abdomens had been cut open and the entrails extracted. Their flesh bad been either wasted by famine or evaporated by exposure to the dry atmosphere, and they presented the appearance of mummies. Strewn around the cabins were dislocated and broken skulls (in some instances sawed asunder with care, for the purpose of extracting the brains), human skeletons, in short, in every variety of mutilation. A more revolting and appalling spectacle I never witnessed. The remains were, by an order of General Kearney, collected and buried under the superintendence of Major Swords. They were interred in a pit which had been dug in the center of one of the cabins for a cache. These melancholy duties to the dead being performed, the cabins, by order of Major Swords, were fired, and with everything surrounding them connected with this horrid and melancholy tragedy were consumed. The body of George Donner was found at his camp, about eight or ten miles distant, wrapped in a sheet. He was buried by a party of men detailed for that purpose."

To carefully lay out her husband's body, and tenderly enfold it in a winding-sheet, was the last act of devotion to her husband which was performed by Tamsen Donner.

With varying incidents and episodes, the immigrants all reached Sutter's Fort. One very attractive young lady received a proposal of marriage while doing her best to manage the rebellious mule on which she was riding. The would-be lover pleaded his case well, considering the adverse circumstances, but the young lady gave not her consent.

Twenty-six, and possibly twenty-eight, out of the forty-eight survivors, are living to-day. Noah James is believed to be alive, and John Baptiste was living only a short time since, at Ukiah,

Mendocino County, California. Besides these two, there are twenty-six whose residences are known. William McCutchen, who came from Jackson County, Missouri, is hale and strong, and is a highly-respected resident of San Jose, California. Mr. McCutchen is a native of Nashville, Tennessee, was about thirty years old at the time of the disaster, and has a clear, correct recollection of all that transpired. Lewis Keseberg's history has been pretty fully outlined in his statement. He resides in Brighton, Sacramento County, California.

In May, 1847, Mary A. Graves married Edward Pile. He was murdered by a Spaniard in 1848, and this Spaniard was the first person hanged in California under the laws of the United States. In 1851 or 1852 Mrs. Pile married J. T. Clarke. Their children are: Robert F., born in 1852, who is married and living at White River, Tulare County Cal.; Mattie, born in 1854, and now the wife of P. Bequette, Jr., of Visalia; James Thomas, born in 1857; an infant, who died soon after birth; Belle, born in 1860, and died in 1871; Alexander R., born in 1865, and Daniel M., born in 1872. Mrs. M. A. Clarke's address is White River, Tulare County, California.

Eleanor Graves married William McDonnell about the first of September, 1849. Their children are: Ann, born September, 1850; Charles, born in 1852; Mary, born in 1855, married to Lester Green, January 2, 1878, and now living on the Sacramento River, about seventeen miles below the city; Lillie, born April 14, 1857, died in February, 1873; Franklin, born in 1860, died in March, 1873; Henry, born July, 1864; Eleanor, born July, 1868; Leslie, born October, 1872, died March, 1873; Louisa, born in 1878. Mrs. Eleanor McDonnell and family reside in Knights Valley, Sonoma County. Their address is Calistoga, California.

Lovina Graves married John Cyrus June 5, 1856. Their children are: Henry E., born April 12, 1859; James W., born February 16, 1861; Mary A., born April 26, 1863; Sarah Grace, born December 11, 1866; and Rachel E., born January 27, 1873. Their address is Calistoga.

Nancy Graves married Rev. R. W. Williamson in 1855. Their eldest, George, is an artist in Virginia City; Emily is teaching school in Knights Valley; Kate, Frederick, and Lydia Pearl are residing with their parents at Los Gatos, Santa Clara County, Cal.

William C. Graves is a blacksmith, living at Calistoga. He visited Truckee this spring, examined the sites of the different cabins, and has rendered most valuable assistance in the preparation of this history.

The Murphys have always been well and favorably known in the best society of California. Mrs. Harriet F. Pike was married at Sutter's Fort, in 1847, by Alcalde Sinclair, to M. C. Nye. Prior to the discovery of gold, they lived about three miles above Marysville, which, at this time, bore the name of Nye's Ranch. Mrs. Nye died in 1872, at Dalles, Oregon, and her remains were brought to Marysville and laid in the city cemetery. Naomi L. Pike was married, in 1865, to Dr. Mitchell, of Marysville, moved to Oregon, became a widow, and is now the wife of John L. Schenck. Her address is, The Dalles, Wasco County, Oregon.

Mary M. Murphy was married, in 1848, to C. Covillaud, then of Nye's Ranch, Cal. In 1850 the city of Marysville was laid out, and was named in honor of Mrs. Mary Covillaud. After lives of distinguished honor, Mr. and Mrs. Covillaud died, but there are now living five of their children. Mary Ellen is married to a prominent stock dealer, of Dalles, Oregon; Charles J., a very bright and promising young man, is in the law office of his uncle, William G. Murphy; William P., Frank M., and Naomi S., are all living at Dalles, Oregon. William G. Murphy resided at Marysville until 1849, when he went east to receive an education. He graduated with high honors at the State University of Missouri. He was married in Tennessee, returned to the Pacific Coast in 1858, and in 1863 was duly admitted a member of the bar of the Supreme Court of Nevada. He resided and practiced his profession at Virginia City until in the fall of 1866, when he returned to Marysville, Cal. He now holds the position of City

Attorney, and has an excellent and remunerative practice. He has a beautiful and charming home, and his family consists of himself, his wife, and seven children. His eldest, Lulie T., was born in the Territory of Nevada, and his second child, Kate Nye, was born in Nevada subsequent to its admission as a State. William G., Jr., Charles Mitchell, Ernest, Harriet F., and Leander B. were born in Marysville.

Simon P. Murphy went back to Tennessee, and married at his old home. He served in the Union army. He died in 1873, leaving a wife and five children.

William M. Foster gave his name to Foster's Bar, on the Yuba River. He died in 1874, of cancer. Of the children of Mr. and Mrs. Foster, there are now living, Alice, born in 1848; Georgia, born in 1850; Will, born in 1852; Minnie, born in 1855; and Hattie, born in 1858. Mrs. S. A. C. Foster has been residing in San Francisco, but her present address is, care of her brother, Wm. G. Murphy, Marysville.

Mr. and Mrs. Reed settled with their family in San Jose, California. Mrs. Margaret Reed died on the twenty-fifth of November, 1861, and her husband, James F. Reed, on the twenty-fourth of July, 1874. They are buried side by side, their coffins touching. Mrs. Reed died with her entire family gathered about her bedside, and few death-bed scenes ever recorded were more peaceful. As she entered the dark waters, all about her seemed suddenly bright. She spoke of the light, and asked that the windows be darkened. The curtains were arranged by those about her, but a moment afterward she said, "Never mind; I see you can not shut out the bright light which I see." Looking up at the faces of her husband and children, she said very slowly, "I expect, when I die, I will die this way, just as if I was going to sleep. Wouldn't it be a blessing if I did?" The last words were uttered just as the soul took its flight. Thomas K. Reed and James F. Reed, Jr., reside in San Jose, Cal. The latter was married March 16, 1879, to Sarah Adams. Virginia E. Reed was married on the twenty-sixth of

January, 1850, to J. M. Murphy. Their children's names are, Mary M., Lloyd M., Mattie H., John M., Virginia B., J. Ada, Dan James, Annie Mabel, and T. Stanley. Lloyd, Mattie, and Mabel are sleeping in Oak Hill Cemetery, at San Jose, Cal. Mary was married to P. McAran, June 28, 1869. Mr. McAran is one of the directors of the Hibernia Bank, and resides in San Francisco. John M. Murphy, Jr., was married April I, 1880, to Miss Hattie E. Watkins. Martha J. (Patty) Reed was married at Santa Cruz, Cal., December 25, 1856, to Mr. Frank Lewis. They had eight children: Kate, born October 6, 1857; Margaret B., born June 6, 1860; Frank, born March 22, 1862; Mattie J., born April 6, 1864; James Frazier, born August 31, 1866; a babe, born May 30, 1868, who died in infancy; Carrie E., born September 15, 1870; and Susan A., born December 31, 1873. Mr. Lewis died June 18, 1876. Mrs. Lewis and her children reside at San Jose.

Wm. H. Eddy married Mrs. F. Alfred, at Gilroy, California, in July, 1848. They had three children: Eleanor P., James P., and Alonzo H. Eleanor married S. B. Anderson, in 1871, and resides in San Jose. James married in 1875, and with his wife and two children resides in San Jose. Alonzo is a physician in Monument, Colorado. In 1854, Mr. and Mrs. Eddy separated, and in 1856 he married Miss A. M. Pardee, of St. Louis. Mr. Eddy died December 24, 1859, at Petaluma, California.

Patrick Breen removed with his family from Sutter's Fort early in 1848, and permanently settled at the Mission of San Juan Bautista, in San Benito County, California. Mr. Breen lived to see all his children grow to maturity and become happily established in life. On the twenty-first of December, 1868, he peacefully closed his eyes to this world, surrounded by every member of his family, all of whom he preceded to the tomb.

All the surviving members of the Breen family are still residing at or near San Juan. John Breen married in 1852. His family, consisting of his wife and ten children, are all living. His children's names are: Lillie M., Edward P., John J., Thomas F., Adelaide A., Kate, Isabelle, Gertrude, Charlotte, and Ellen A. Breen. Edward J.

Breen married in 1858. His wife died in 1862, leaving the following children: Eugene T., Edward J., and John Roger. Patrick Breen, Jr., married in 1865; his wife is living, and their children are Mary, William, Peter, Eugene. Simon P. Breen married in 1867; his wife is living; their children are Geneva and Mary. James F. Breen, the present Superior Judge of San Benito County, married in 1870; his wife is living; their only surviving children are Margaret and Grace. Peter Breen died, unmarried, on July 3, 1870, by accidental death. Isabella M. Breen was married in 1869, to Thomas McMahon, and with her husband resides at Hollister, San Benito County. William M. Breen, whose portrait appears in the group of the Breen family, was born in San Juan in 1848, and was not of the Donner Party. He married in 1874, leaving a widow, and one child, Mary.

Margaret Breen, the heroic woman, devoted wife, and faithful mother, had the satisfaction of living to see her infant family, for whose preservation she had struggled so hard and wrought so ceaselessly, grow to manhood and womanhood. In prosperity, as in adversity, she was ever good, kind, courageous, and "affable to the congregation of the Lord." She was always self-reliant, and equal to the most trying emergencies; and yet, at all times, she had a deep and abiding faith in God, and firmly relied on the mercy and goodness of Him to whom she prayed so ardently and confidently in the heavy hours of her tribulation. The hope of her later years was that she might not be required to witness the death of any of her children; but it was willed differently, as two of them preceded her to the grave. April 13, 1874, ripe in years, loved by the poor, honored and respected by all for her virtues and her well-spent life, she quietly and peacefully passed from the midst of her sorrowing family to the other and better shore.

The following lines from the pen of Miss Marcella A. Fitzgerald, the gifted poetess of Notre Dame Convent, San Jose, were published in the San Francisco Monitor, at the time of Mrs. Breen's death:

IN MEMORIAM.

MRS. MARGARET BREEN.

The spring's soft light, its tender, dreamy beauty
    Veils all the land around us, and the dome
Of the blue skies is ringing with the music
Of birds that come to seek their summer home.

But one whose heart this beauty often gladdened
    No more shall see the fragrant flowers expand;
For her no more of earth—but fairer portion
    Is hers, the beauty of the Better Land;

The beauty of that land to which with yearning
    Her true heart turned in faith and trust each day;
The land whose hope a glorious bow of promise
    Illumed her path across life's desert way.

A loving wife; a fond, devoted mother;
    A friend who reckoned friendship not a name;
A woman who with gentle influence brightened
    The hearts of all who to her presence came.

A halo of good deeds her life surrounded;
    Her crown of years was bright with deeds of love;
Hers was a gift of charity whose merits
    A golden treasure waiteth her above.

Out of the wealth the Master gave unto her
    She clothed the needy and the hungry fed;
The poor will mourn a true friend taken from them—
    Above her will the orphan's tear be shed.

The orphan's prayer, a prayer of power unbounded,
    In grateful accents shall for her ascend,
And strength and consolation for her children
    Down from the Savior's pitying heart descend;

For over death the Christian's faith doth triumph—
    The crown of victory shines above the Cross;
Hers is the fadeless joy and ours the sorrow—
    Hers is the gain and ours the bitter loss.

And while the hearts of kindred ache in sadness,
    And gloom rests on her once fair home to-day,
As a true friend who mourns a loved one taken,
    This simple wreath upon her grave I lay.

CHAPTER XXIII

THE ORPHAN CHILDREN OF GEORGE AND TAMSEN DONNER —
SUTTER, THE PHILANTHROPIST — "IF MOTHER WOULD ONLY
COME!" — CHRISTIAN AND MARY BRUNNER — AN ENCHANTING
HOME — "CAN'T YOU KEEP BOTH OF US?" — ELIZA DONNER
CROSSING THE TORRENT — EARNING A SILVER DOLLAR —
THE GOLD EXCITEMENT — GETTING AN EDUCATION —
ELITHA C. DONNER, LEANNA C. DONNER, FRANCES E. DONNER,
GEORGIA A. DONNER, ELIZA P. DONNER.

UNUSUAL interest attaches to the three little orphan children
mentioned in a preceding chapter. Frances, Georgia, and Eliza
Donner reached Sutter's Fort in April, 1847. Here they met their
two elder sisters, who, in charge of the first relief party, had arrived
at the Fort a few weeks earlier. The three little girls were pitiable-
looking objects as they gathered around the blazing fire, answering
and asking questions respecting what had taken place since they
parted with their sisters at their mountain cabins.

Among the first to stretch forth a helping hand to clothe the
needy children was that noble philanthropist, Capt. John A. Sutter.
Other newly-found friends gave food from their scanty supplies,
and the children would have been comfortable for a time, had not
some pilfering hand taken all that had been given them. They were
again obliged to ask for food of those whom they thought would
give. As the weather became warmer it had a cheering influence
over them. They forgot their wish for heavier clothing; but oftener
repeated the more heartfelt one — "If mother would only come!"

Those who have suffered bereavement under similar circumstances can understand how fully these little girls realized their situation when they were told that their mother was dead.

Not long after it became known that their parents were dead, Georgia and Eliza enlisted the sympathies of a kind-hearted Swiss couple, Christian and Mary Brunner, who lived a short distance from the Fort. Mrs. Brunner brought them bread, butter, eggs, and cheese, with the kind remark to those in whose hands she placed the articles: "These are for the little girls who called me grandma; but don't give them too much at a time." A few days later, upon inquiring of them how they liked what she brought, grandma was told they had not had anything, and was so surprised that she decided to take Georgia home with her for a week. Georgia was more delicate than her younger sister. Eliza was promised that she should be treated as kindly upon Georgia's return. The week passed, and Georgia returned, looking stronger. She told such wonderful stories about the many cows! lots of chickens! two sheep that would not let her pass unless she carried a big stick in sight! about the kindness grandma, grandpa, and Jacob, his brother, had shown to her, that it seemed to Eliza the time would never come when she and grandma were to start to that enchanting home! Such a week of pleasure! Who but that little girl could describe it! Grandma's bread and milk gave strength to her limbs and color to her cheeks. She chased the chickens, and drove the cows; she brought chips for grandma, rode the horse for Jacob, and sat upon grandpa's knee so cheerfully, that they began to feel as if she belonged to them. But her week had come to an end! Grandma, all dressed for a walk to the Fort, sought the little girl, who was busy at play, and said: "Come, Eliza, I hear that Georgia is sick, and I am going to take you back, and bring her in your place." The sweet little girl looked very grave for a moment, then glancing up with her large black eyes into that dear old face, she took courage, and asked, with the earnestness of an anxious child: "Grandma, can't you keep both of us?"

This simple question provided a home for both until after Hiram Miller was appointed their guardian. He was intrusted with their money, obtained from Keseberg and from other sources. The little sisters were then again separated. Frances had found a home in Mrs. Reed's family. Georgia was to go with grandpa, who was about to remove to Sonoma. Eliza went to her eldest sister, who was now married and living on the Cosumnes River. Here she remained until winter. Then, hearing that Mr. Brunner's family and Georgia desired her return, she became so homesick that her sister consented to her going to them. Fortunately, they heard of two families who were to move to Sonoma in a very short time, and Eliza was placed in their charge. This journey was marked with many incidents which seemed marvelous to her child-mind. The one which impressed itself most forcibly occurred upon their arrival at the bank of the Sonoma River. She was told that Jacob would meet her here and take her to grandma's, and was delighted that her journey was so nearly over. Imagine her disappointment at finding the recent rains had raised the river until a torrent flowed between her and her anxious friends. For days Jacob sought the slowly-decreasing flood and called across the rushing stream to cheer the eager child. Finally, an Indian, who understood Jacob's wish, offered to carry her safely over for a silver dollar. Never did silver look brighter than that which Jacob held between his fingers, above his head, that sunny morning, to satisfy the Indian that his price would be paid when he and his charge reached the other bank.

What a picture this scene presents to the mind! There is the Indian leading his gray pony to the river's side! He examines him carefully, and puts the blanket on more securely! He waits for the approaching child. How small she is—not five years old! How she trembles with dread as the swift current meets her eye! Yet she is anxious to go. One pleading look in the Indian's face, and she is ready. He mounts; she is placed behind him; her little arms are stretched tightly around his dusky form! He presses his elbows to his sides to made her more secure, and, by signs, warns her against loosening her grasp, or she, like the passing branches, will be the water's prey! They enter the stream. Oh! how cold the water is! They reach the middle; her grasp is tighter, and she holds her breath with fear, for they are drifting with the current past where Jacob stands! But joy comes at last. They have crossed the river. There stands the pony shaking the water from his sides. The Indian takes his dollar with a grunt of satisfaction, and Jacob catches up the little girl, mounts his horse, and hurries off to grandpa's, where grandma, Leanna, and Georgia are waiting to give her a warm welcome.

Months passed pleasantly, but gradually changes occurred. The war with Mexico ended, and gold was discovered. All the men who were able to go, hurried off to the mines to make a fortune. The little girls gave up their plays, for grandma was not able to do all the work, and grandpa and Jacob were away. They spent seven years with Mr. and Mrs. Brunner. They were kindly treated, but their education was neglected. In 1854, their eldest sister, Elitha, and her husband, came to Sonoma, and offered them a home and an opportunity of attending school. This kind offer was accepted. For six years Eliza remained in Sacramento, in the family of her sister, Elitha. To her she was indebted for the opportunity she enjoyed of attending, for one year, with her sister Frances and afterwards Georgia, St. Catherine's Academy, at Benicia, and the public schools of Sacramento.

Elitha C. Donner married Perry McCoon, who was subsequently killed by a runaway horse. On the eighth of December, 1853, Mrs. McCoon was married to Benj. W. Wilder. They reside on the Cosumnes River, a few miles from Elk Grove, Sacramento County, Cal., and have six children. Leanna C. Donner was married September 26, 1852, to John App. They now reside in Jamestown, Tuolumne County, Cal., and their family consists of Rebecca E., born February 9, 1854; John Q., born January 19, 1864; and Lucy E., born August 12, 1868, who reside with their parents.

Frances E. Donner was married November 24, 1858, to William R. Wilder, and now resides at Point of Timber, Contra Costa County, Cal. Their children are: Harriet, born August 24, 1859;

James William, born May 30, 1863; Frances Lillian, born July 17, 1867; Asaph, born May 7, 1870; and Susan Tamsen, born September 3, 1878. Georgia A. Donner was married November 4, 1863, to W. A. Babcock. Their family consists of Henry A., born August 23, 1864; Frank B., born June 29, 1866; and Edith M., born August 24, 1868. Their address is Mountain View, Santa Clara County, Cal.

Eliza P. Donner, on the tenth of October, 1861, was married to Sherman O. Houghton. Mr. Houghton was born in New York City, April 10, 1828, served in the Mexican war, was Mayor of San Jose in 1855 and 1856, represented California in the Forty-second and Forty-third Congress, and is at present a prominent member of the San Jose bar. Mr. and Mrs. Houghton have six children. The youngest living was born in Washington, D. C., at which city his family resided during the four years he served as member of Congress. Their children are: Eliza P., Sherman O., Clara H., Charles D., Francis J., and Stanley W. Their youngest born, Herbert S., died March 18, 1878, aged twenty months. Mary M. Donner, daughter of Jacob Donner, was adopted into the family of Mr. James F. Reed, in 1848. She continued a member of this family until her marriage with Hon. S. O. Houghton, of San Jose, August 23, 1859. June 21, 1860, Mrs. Mary M. Houghton died, leaving an infant daughter, Mary M., who is now a young lady, and a member of the family of Mr. and Mrs. Houghton.

George Donner, Jr., son of Jacob Donner, married Miss Margaret J. Watson, June 8, 1862. Their children now living are: Mary E., Cora J., George W., John C., Betty L., and Frank M. Albert, their eldest, died in 1869, and an infant son died in 1875. George Donner, Jr., died at Sebastopol, February 17, 1874. Mrs. Donner now lives with her children on their farm near Sebastopol, Sonoma County, California.

CHAPTER XXIV

YERBA BUENA'S GIFT TO GEORGE AND MARY DONNER —
AN ALCALDE'S NEGLIGENCE — MARY DONNER'S LAND
REGRANTED — SQUATTERS JUMP GEORGE DONNER'S LAND —
A CHARACTERISTIC LAND LAW SUIT — VEXATIOUS LITIGATION —
TWICE APPEALED TO SUPREME COURT, AND ONCE TO UNITED
STATES SUPREME COURT — A WELL-TAKEN LAW POINT —
MUTILATING RECORDS — A PALPABLE ERASURE — RELICS OF
THE DONNER PARTY — FIVE HUNDRED ARTICLES — BURIED
THIRTY-TWO YEARS — KNIVES, FORKS, SPOONS — PRETTY
PORCELAIN — IDENTIFYING CHINAWARE — BEADS AND ARROW-
HEADS — A QUAINT BRIDLE BIT — REMARKABLE ACTION OF
RUST — A FLINTLOCK PISTOL — A BABY'S SHOE — THE RESTING
PLACE OF THE DEAD — VANISHING LANDMARKS.

YERBA Buena's citizens, shortly after the arrival of George and
Mary Donner, contributed a fund for the purpose of purchasing
for each of them a town lot. It happened that these lots were
being then distributed among the residents of the town. Upon
the petition of James F. Reed, a grant was made to George
Donner of one hundred vara lot number thirty-nine, and the
adjoining lot, number thirty-eight, was granted to Mary. The
price of each lot was thirty-two dollars, and both were paid for out
of the fund. The grants were both entered of record by the
Alcalde, George Hyde. The grant made to George was signed by
the Alcalde, but that made to Mary was, through inadvertence,
not signed. A successor of Hyde, as Alcalde, regranted the lot of

Mary Donner to one Ward, who discovered the omission of the Alcalde's name to her grant. This omission caused her to lose the lot. In 1851, a number of persons squatted on the lot of George Donner, and in 1854 brought suit against him in the United States Circuit Court to quiet their title. This suit was subsequently abandoned under the belief that George Donner was dead. In 1856, a suit was instituted by George Donner, through his guardian, to recover possession of the lot. Down to the spring of 1860, but little progress had been made toward recovering the possession of the lot from the squatters. The attorneys who had thus far conducted the litigation on behalf of George Donner, were greatly embarrassed because of their inability to fully prove the delivery of the grant to him, or to some one for him, the courts of the State having, from the first litigation concerning similar grants, laid down and adhered to the rule that such grants did not take effect unless the original grant was delivered to the grantee. Such proof was therefore deemed indispensable.

After such proofs upon this point as were accessible had been made, the proceedings had ceased, and for several months there had been no prospect of any further progress being made. During this time, one Yontz, who had undertaken to recover possession of the lot at his own expense for a share of it, had the management of the case, and had employed an attorney to conduct the litigation. Yontz became unable, pecuniarily, to proceed further with the case, and informed Donner of the fact, whereupon the latter induced his brother-in-law, S. O. Houghton, to attempt to prosecute his claim to some final result. Mr. Houghton applied to the court to be substituted as attorney in the case, but resistance was made by the attorney of Yontz, and the application was denied. Houghton then applied to the Supreme Court for a writ of mandate to compel the judge of the court before which the suit was pending, to order his substitution as attorney of record for Donner. This writ was granted by the Supreme Court, and in January, 1861, Mr. Houghton became the attorney of record. This suit had been brought by Green McMahon, who had been appointed Donner's guardian for that purpose, and after a full examination of the case, Mr. Houghton dismissed it, and immediately commenced another in the name of George Donner, who was then of age. In the following year, February, 1862, it was brought to trial before a jury, and after a contest which lasted ten days, a verdict was rendered in favor of Donner.

The squatters appealed to the Supreme Court of the State where the verdict of the jury was set aside, a new trial ordered, and the case sent back for that purpose. This new trial was procured by means of an amendment of the law regulating trials by jury in civil cases. This amendment was passed by the Legislature, at the instance of the squatters, after the verdict had been rendered. A new trial was had in 1864, before a jury, and resulted in another verdict for Donner. The first trial had attracted much attention, and was frequently mentioned in the newspapers of San Francisco, and thus several persons who were present when the grant was made had their attention called to the controversy, and to the difficulty encountered in proving a delivery of the grant. They communicated to Donner the fact that it was delivered for him to William McDonald, the man with whom he lived at the time. They also narrated the circumstances attending the delivery of the grant. This information, however, came too late for the purposes of the trial. Prior to the second trial, the written testimony of all these witnesses was procured and in readiness for use when required, but it was never required. Mr. Houghton and the attorneys whom he had called upon to aid in the case, determined to rest its decision upon another ground. They concluded to insist that, as it was a grant issuing from the government through its instrument, the Alcalde, who was invested with authority for the purpose, no delivery of the grant was necessary, and that none was possible, as the entry on the record book of the Alcalde was the original, it bearing his official signature and being a public record of his official act. This was a bold attack upon the rule which the courts had long established to the contrary. After a full argument of the question at the second trial, the court sustained the view of the law taken by Mr. Houghton and his associates, and, on appeal, the decision was sustained by the Supreme Court of the State, and subsequently affirmed by the Supreme Court of the United States, before which the question was carried by writ of error.

Donner's attorneys adopted this course because, at the first trial, the squatters had produced the copy of the grant which had actually been issued and delivered. This they had obtained possession of and mutilated, and then had surreptitiously placed it in the office of the County Clerk of San Francisco, who was the custodian of the records of the office of the Alcaldes of San Francisco. Their purpose was to make it appear that it had never been signed or issued by the Alcalde, but had been transferred with the other papers and records of that office to the office of the County Clerk. This document was written on paper having the same watermarks as numerous other grants to other persons, admitted to be genuine, made about the same time as the grant to Donner. The body of this instrument was in the handwriting of the then clerk of the Alcalde, and the certificate that the Alcalde's fees had been paid bore the genuine signature of the clerk. There was, however, no signature or name where the signature of the Alcalde should have been; but there was, instead, a plain, palpable erasure, easily seen by holding the paper to the light.

George Donner lived to see his property become very valuable, but the vexatious litigation above described was not terminated until after his death. Meantime, however, he sold his interest, receiving therefor a considerable sum of money.

In conclusion it may be proper to speak of the many interesting relics which have recently been found under the former sites of the cabins of the Donner Party. When the last relief party left Donner Lake, all articles of minor value were left scattered here and there about the floors and door-yards. Soon afterward the tide of emigrant travel turned principally to other routes, and the Donner Lake road was comparatively deserted. Years passed, and the loose soil, the wind-blown dust, the grass and fallen leaves covered the articles from sight. It was twenty years before men began to search for the sites of the cabins, and to carry away little mementos of the mournful place. Nothing at this time remained in sight save a few charred logs, and a few score of tall, unsightly stumps. Even the old pioneers had great difficulty in pointing out the location of more than one or two of the cabins. After the preparation of this history began, the author induced several of the survivors to visit Donner Lake, and to assist in definitely determining the location and boundaries of the cabins. Digging in the earth which thirty-two years ago formed the cabin floors, the most interesting relics were found. A collection of over five hundred of these articles is in the author's possession. There are spoons which are bent and rust-eaten, some of which are partially without bowls, and some destitute of handles, the missing portions being vaguely shadowed in the rust-stained earth in which they were imbedded. Knives there are whose blades are mere skeleton outlines of what they formerly were, and which in some instances appear to be only thin scales of rust. The tines of the forks are sometimes pretty well preserved, sometimes almost entirely worn away by the action of rust.

Among the relics found at the Breen cabin are numerous pieces of old porcelain, and china-ware. These fragments are readily distinguished by painted flowers, or unique designs enameled in red, blue, or purple colors upon the pure white ground-surface of the china-ware. This ware is celebrated for the durability of its glaze or enamel, which can not be scratched with a knife, and is not acted upon by vegetable acids. The relics unearthed were found at a depth of from one to six inches beneath the ground which formed the floor. A fragment of this ware, together with an old-fashioned gun-flint, was sent to Hon. James F. Breen, who wrote in reply:

"The relics, piece of chinaware and gun-flint, are highly appreciated. The chinaware was at once recognized by my brother. In fact, there is one piece of the china set (a cream pitcher) still in the possession of my brother. The piece sent is recognizable by the decoration figures, which correspond exactly with those on the pitcher."

There is less of the "ghastly" and "horrible" among the relics thus far discovered than would be supposed. There are many, like the beads and arrow-heads, which were evidently treasured by members of the party as relics or curiosities collected while crossing the plains. There are pieces of looking-glass which reflected the sunken, starved features of the emigrants. Among the porcelain are pieces of pretty cups and saucers, and dainty, expensive plates, which in those days were greatly prized. Bits of glassware, such as tumblers, vials, and dishes, are quite numerous. Bolts, nails, screws, nuts, chains, and portions of the wagon irons, are almost unrecognizable on account of the rust. The nails are wrought, and some of them look as if they might have been hammered out by the emigrants. One of these nails is so firmly imbedded in rust alongside a screw, that the two are inseparable. Metallic buttons are found well preserved, a sewing awl is quite plainly distinguishable, and an old-fashioned, quaint-looking bridle-bit retains much of its original form. Some of the more delicate and perishable articles present the somewhat remarkable appearance of having increased in size by the accumulations of rust and earth in which they are encased. This is especially the case with a darning-needle, which has increased its circumference in places nearly one half, while in other places it is eaten away until only a mere filament of steel remains. The sharp point of a curved sewing-awl has grown with rust until it is larger than the body of the awl. Several fish-hooks have been found, all more or less rust-eaten. A brass pistol, single-barreled, apparently a century old, was found under the Graves cabin, and near it was an old flint-lock. In the corner of the fire-place of the Reed cabin were found several bullets and number two shot. Gun-flints, ready for use or in a crude form, were found in each of the cabins.

W. C. Graves visited the site of his father's cabin on the twenty-first of April, 1879, and many articles were dug up in his presence which he readily recognized. A large number of the leading citizens of Truckee were present, and assisted in searching for the relics. Among other things was a cooper's inshave, which belonged to his father, who was a cooper by trade. An iron wagon-hammer was also immediately recognized as having been used in their wagon. A small tin box, whose close-fitting cover was hermetically sealed with rust, was found, and while it was being examined, one of the gentlemen, Mr. Frank Rabel, tapped it lightly with his knife-handle. The side of the box crushed as easily as if it had been an egg-shell. The wonderful fact connected with this relic, however, is that Mr. Graves said, before the box was crushed, that his mother kept oil of hemlock in this box, and that upon examination a distinct odor of oil of hemlock was found remaining in the box.

A whetstone, or what might more properly be called an oil-stone, was discovered at the Breen cabin. On this stone were the initials "J. F. R.," which had evidently been cut into its surface with a knife-blade. Mrs. V. E. Murphy and Mrs. Frank Lewis, the daughters of James F. Reed, at once remembered this whetstone as having belonged to their father, and fully identified it upon examination.

A great many pins have been found, most of which are the old-fashioned round-headed ones. A strange feature it regard to these pins is that although bright and clean, they crumble and break at almost the slightest touch. The metal of which they are made appears to be entirely decomposed. One of the most touching relics, in view of the sad, sad history, is the sole of an infant's shoe. The tiny babe who wore the shoe was probably among the number who perished of starvation.

The big rock against which the Murphy cabin stood is half hidden by willows and by fallen tamaracks, whose branches are interlaced so as to form a perfect net-work above the place where the cabin stood. Under the floor of this cabin the remains of the poor victims are supposed to have been buried. Nature appears to have made every effort to conceal the spot. In addition to the bushes and the fallen trees there is a rank growth of marsh grass, whose rootlets extend far down in the soil, and firmly resist either shovel or spade. Until very late in the summer this mournful spot is still further protected by being inundated by the waters of Donner Creek. It is hardly necessary to remark that no relics have ever been found under the site of the Murphy cabin. The tall stumps which surround this rock, and the site of the Graves and Reed cabin, and which are particularly numerous around the site of the Donner tents at Alder Creek, are of themselves remarkable relics. Many of them were cut by persons who stood on the top of very deep snow. They are frequently ten, fifteen, and twenty feet in height. Time and the action of the elements have caused them to decay until, in some instances, a child's hand might cause them to totter and fall. In a few years more they all will have disappeared.

SUGGESTED READING

BILLINGTON, RAY ALLEN, AND MARTIN RIDGE. *Westward Expansion: A History of the American Frontier.* Albuquerque, NM: University of New Mexico Press, 2001.

HARDESTY, DONALD L. *The Archaeology of the Donner Party.* Reno, NV: University of Nevada Press, 1997.

HINE, ROBERT V., AND JOHN MACK FARAGHER. *The American West: A New Interpretive History.* New Haven, CT: Yale University Press, 1999.

HOUGHTON, ELIZA DONNER. *The Expedition of the Donner and Its Tragic Fate.* Lincoln, NE: University of Nebraska Press, 1997.

JOHNSON, KRISTIN, ED. *Unfortunate Emigrants: Narratives of the Donner Party.* Logan, UT: Utah State University Press, 1996.

KEITHLEY, GEORGE. *Donner Party.* New York: George Braziller, 1990.

MCLYNN, FRANK. *Wagons West: The Epic Story of America's Overland Trails.* New York: Grove, 2003.

MILNER, CLYDE A. ET AL., EDS. *Oxford History of the American West.* New York: Oxford University Press, 1996.

STEGNER, PAGE. *Winning the Wild West: The Epic Saga of the American Frontier 1800-1899.* New York: Free Press, 2002.

STEWART, GEORGE R. *Ordeal by Hunger.* Boston: Houghton Mifflin, 1992.